Bayesian Analysis with Python

Third Edition

A practical guide to probabilistic modeling

Osvaldo Martin

BIRMINGHAM—MUMBAI

Bayesian Analysis with Python

Third Edition

Lead Senior Publishing Product Manager: Tushar Gupta

Acquisition Editor – Peer Reviews: Bethany O'Connell

Project Editor: Namrata Katare

Development Editor: Tanya D'cruz

Copy Editor: Safis Editing

Technical Editor: Aniket Shetty

Indexer: Rekha Nair

Proofreader: Safis Editing

Presentation Designer: Pranit Padwal

Developer Relations Marketing Executive: Monika Sangwan

First published: November 2016
Second edition: December 2018
Third edition: January 2024

Production reference: 1290124

Published by Packt Publishing Ltd.
Grosvenor House
11 St Paul's Square
Birmingham
B3 1RB, UK.

ISBN 978-1-80512-716-1

www.packt.com

In gratitude to my family: Romina, Abril, and Bruno.

Foreword

As we present this new edition of Bayesian Analysis with Python, it's essential to recognize the profound impact this book has had on advancing the growth and education of the probabilistic programming user community. The journey from its first publication to this current edition mirrors the evolution of Bayesian modeling itself – a path marked by significant advancements, growing community involvement, and an increasing presence in both academia and industry.

The field of probabilistic programming is in a different place today than it was when the first edition was devised in the middle of the last decade. As long-term practitioners, we have seen firsthand how Bayesian methods grew from a more fringe methodology to the primary way of solving some of the most advanced problems in science and various industries. This trend is supported by the continued development of advanced, performant, high-level tools such as PyMC. With this is a growing number of new applied users, many of whom have limited experience with either Bayesian methods, PyMC, or the underlying libraries that probabilistic programming packages increasingly rely on to accelerate computation. In this context, this new edition comes at the perfect time to introduce the next generation of data scientists to this increasingly powerful methodology.

Osvaldo Martin, a teacher, applied statistician, and long-time core PyMC developer, is the perfect guide to help readers navigate this complex landscape. He provides a clear concise and comprehensive introduction to Bayesian methods and the PyMC library, and he walks readers through a variety of real-world examples. As the population of data scientists using probabilistic programming grows, it is important to instill them with good habits and a sound workflow; Dr. Martin here provides sound, engaging guidance for doing so.

What makes this book a go-to reference is its coverage of most of the key questions posed by applied users: How do I express my problem as a probabilistic program? How do I know if my model is working? How do I know which model is best? Herein you will find a primer on Bayesian best practices, updated to current standards based on methodological improvements since the release of the last edition. This includes innovations related to the PyMC library itself, which has come a long way since PyMC3, much to the benefit of you, the end-user.

Complementing these improvements is the expansion of the PyMC ecosystem, a reflection of the broadening scope and capabilities of Bayesian modeling. This edition includes discussions on four notable new libraries: Bambi, Kulprit, PreliZ, and PyMC-BART. These additions, along with the continuous refinement of text and code, ensure that readers are equipped with the latest tools and methodologies in Bayesian analysis. This edition is not just an update but a significant step forward in the journey of probabilistic programming, mirroring the dynamic evolution of PyMC and its community.

The previous two editions of this book have been cornerstones for many in understanding and applying Bayesian methods. Each edition, including this latest one, has evolved to incorporate new developments, making it an indispensable resource for both newcomers and experienced practitioners. As PyMC continues to evolve - perhaps even to newer versions by the time this book is read - the content here remains relevant, providing foundational knowledge and insights into the latest advancements. In this edition, readers will find not only a comprehensive introduction to Bayesian analysis but also a window into the cutting-edge techniques that are currently shaping the field. We hope this book serves as both a guide and an inspiration, showcasing the power and flexibility of Bayesian modeling in addressing complex data-driven challenges.

As co-authors of this foreword, we are excited about the journey that lies ahead for readers of this book. You are joining a vibrant, ever-expanding community of enthusiasts and professionals who are pushing the boundaries of what's possible in data analysis. We trust that this book will be a valuable companion in your exploration of Bayesian modeling and a catalyst for your own contributions to this dynamic field.

Christopher Fonnesbeck,
PyMC's original author and Principal Quantitative Analyst for the Philadelphia Phillies

Thomas Wiecki,
CEO & Founder of PyMC Labs

Contributors

About the author

Osvaldo Martin is a researcher at The National Scientific and Technical Research Council (CONICET), in Argentina. He has worked on structural bioinformatics of biomolecules and has used Markov Chain Monte Carlo methods to simulate molecular systems. He is currently working on computational methods for Bayesian statistics and probabilistic programming. He has taught courses about structural bioinformatics, data science, and Bayesian data analysis. He was also the head of the organizing committee of PyData San Luis (Argentina) 2017, the first PyData in LatinAmerica. He contributed to many open-source projects, including ArviZ, Bambi, Kulprit, PreliZ, and PyMC.

I would like to thank Romina for her continuous support. I also want to thank Tomás Capretto, Alejandro Icazatti, Juan Orduz, and Bill Engels for providing invaluable feedback and suggestions on my drafts. A special thanks go to the core developers and all contributors of the Python packages used in this book. Their dedication, love, and hard work have made this book possible.

About the reviewer

Joon (Joonsuk) Park is a former quantitative psychologist and currently a machine learning engineer. He graduated from the Ohio State University with a PhD in Quantitative Psychology in 2019. His research during graduate study was focused on the applications of Bayesian statistics to cognitive modeling and behavioral research methodology. He transitioned into an industry data science and has worked as a data scientist since 2020. He has also published several books on psychology, statistics, and data science in Korean.

Join our community Discord space

Join our Discord community to meet like-minded people and learn alongside more than 5000 members at:

https://packt.link/bayesian

Table of Contents

Preface   **xix**

Who this book is for xx

What this book covers xx

What's new in this edition? xxii

Installation instructions xxiv

Conventions used xxvi

Chapter 1: Thinking Probabilistically   **1**

Statistics, models, and this book's approach 2

Working with data 3

Bayesian modeling 4

A probability primer for Bayesian practitioners 5

    Sample space and events • 5

    Random variables • 9

    Discrete random variables and their distributions • 11

    Continuous random variables and their distributions • 16

    Cumulative distribution function • 18

    Conditional probability • 20

    Expected values • 22

    Bayes' theorem • 23

Interpreting probabilities 26

Probabilities, uncertainty, and logic 28

Single-parameter inference 29

    The coin-flipping problem • 29

    Choosing the likelihood • 30

    Choosing the prior • 31

    Getting the posterior • 33

    The influence of the prior • 37

How to choose priors 38

Communicating a Bayesian analysis 41

    Model notation and visualization • 41

    Summarizing the posterior • 42

Summary 44

Exercises 45

Chapter 2: Programming Probabilistically   49

Probabilistic programming 50

    Flipping coins the PyMC way • 51

Summarizing the posterior 54

Posterior-based decisions 57

    Savage-Dickey density ratio • 58

    Region Of Practical Equivalence • 59

    Loss functions • 61

Gaussians all the way down 64

    Gaussian inferences • 64

Posterior predictive checks 68

Robust inferences 70

    Degrees of normality • 71

    A robust version of the Normal model • 72

InferenceData 76

Groups comparison 78

    The tips dataset • 80

    Cohen's d • 83

    Probability of superiority • 84

    Posterior analysis of mean differences • 85

Summary 87

Exercises 88

Chapter 3: Hierarchical Models   91

Sharing information, sharing priors 92

Hierarchical shifts 93

Water quality 97

Shrinkage 100

Hierarchies all the way up 103

Summary 107

Exercises 108

Chapter 4: Modeling with Lines   111

Simple linear regression 112

Linear bikes 114

    Interpreting the posterior mean • 116

    Interpreting the posterior predictions • 119

Generalizing the linear model 120

Counting bikes 121

Robust regression 123

Logistic regression 126

    The logistic model • 126

    Classification with logistic regression • 129

    Interpreting the coefficients of logistic regression • 131

Variable variance 133

Hierarchical linear regression **136**

    Centered vs. noncentered hierarchical models • 139

Multiple linear regression **141**

Summary **144**

Exercises **145**

Chapter 5: Comparing Models   147

Posterior predictive checks **148**

The balance between simplicity and accuracy **154**

    Many parameters (may) lead to overfitting • 154

    Too few parameters lead to underfitting • 156

Measures of predictive accuracy **157**

    Information criteria • 158

        Akaike Information Criterion • 159

        Widely applicable information criteria • 160

        Other information criteria • 160

    Cross-validation • 161

        Approximating cross-validation • 162

Calculating predictive accuracy with ArviZ **164**

Model averaging **167**

Bayes factors **168**

    Some observations • 170

    Calculation of Bayes factors • 171

        Analytically • 171

        Sequential Monte Carlo • 174

        Savage–Dickey ratio • 175

Bayes factors and inference **178**

Regularizing priors **179**

Summary **181**

Exercises **182**

Chapter 6: Modeling with Bambi — 185

One syntax to rule them all — 186

The bikes model, Bambi's version — 190

Polynomial regression — 193

Splines — 195

Distributional models — 198

Categorical predictors — 200

Categorical penguins • 200

Relation to hierarchical models • 203

Interactions — 204

Interpreting models with Bambi — 207

Variable selection — 209

Projection predictive inference • 211

Projection predictive with Kulprit • 212

Summary — 217

Exercises — 218

Chapter 7: Mixture Models — 221

Understanding mixture models — 222

Finite mixture models — 224

The Categorical distribution • 226

The Dirichlet distribution • 226

Chemical mixture • 227

The non-identifiability of mixture models — 229

How to choose K — 231

Zero-Inflated and hurdle models — 234

Zero-Inflated Poisson regression • 235

Hurdle models • 237

Mixture models and clustering — 240

Non-finite mixture model 241

Dirichlet process • 241

Continuous mixtures 247

Some common distributions are mixtures • 247

Summary 248

Exercises 250

Chapter 8: Gaussian Processes   253

Linear models and non-linear data 254

Modeling functions 255

Multivariate Gaussians and functions 257

Covariance functions and kernels • 258

Gaussian processes 261

Gaussian process regression 262

Gaussian process regression with PyMC 262

Setting priors for the length scale • 266

Gaussian process classification 267

GPs for space flu • 270

Cox processes 271

Coal mining disasters • 272

Red wood • 274

Regression with spatial autocorrelation 277

Hilbert space GPs 282

HSGP with Bambi • 285

Summary 286

Exercises 287

Chapter 9: Bayesian Additive Regression Trees   289

Decision trees 290

BART models 292

    Bartian penguins • 293

    Partial dependence plots • 295

    Individual conditional plots • 296

    Variable selection with BART • 297

Distributional BART models 300

Constant and linear response 302

Choosing the number of trees 304

Summary 305

Exercises 305

Chapter 10: Inference Engines   307

Inference engines 308

The grid method 309

Quadratic method 312

Markovian methods 314

    Monte Carlo • 314

    Markov chain • 316

    Metropolis-Hastings • 317

    Hamiltonian Monte Carlo • 322

Sequential Monte Carlo 324

Diagnosing the samples 327

Convergence 328

    Trace plot • 328

    Rank plot • 330

    $\hat{R}$ (R hat) • 331

Effective Sample Size (ESS) 333

Monte Carlo standard error 335

Divergences 336

Keep calm and keep trying 338

Summary 339

Exercises 340

Chapter 11: Where to Go Next   343

Other Books You May Enjoy   354

Index   360

Preface

Bayesian statistics has been developing for more than 250 years. During this time, it has enjoyed as much recognition and appreciation as it has faced disdain and contempt. Throughout the last few decades, it has gained more and more attention from people in statistics and almost all the other sciences, engineering, and even outside the boundaries of the academic world. This revival has been possible due to theoretical and computational advancements developed mostly throughout the second half of the 20th century. Indeed, modern Bayesian statistics is mostly computational statistics. The necessity for flexible and transparent models and a more intuitive interpretation of statistical models and analysis has only contributed to the trend.

In this book, our focus will be on a practical approach to Bayesian statistics and we will not delve into discussions about the frequentist approach or its connection to Bayesian statistics. This decision is made to maintain a clear and concise focus on the subject matter. If you are interested in that perspective, *Doing Bayesian Data Analysis* may be the book for you [Kruschke, 2014]. We also avoid philosophical discussions, not because they are not interesting or relevant, but because this book aims to be a practical guide to Bayesian data analysis. One good reading for such discussion is Clayton [2021].

We follow a modeling approach to statistics. We will learn how to think in terms of probabilistic models and apply Bayes' theorem to derive the logical consequences of our models and data. The approach will also be computational; models will be coded using PyMC [Abril-Pla et al., 2023] and Bambi [Capretto et al., 2022]. These are libraries for Bayesian statistics that hide most of the mathematical details and computations from the user. We will then use ArviZ [Kumar et al., 2019], a Python package for exploratory analysis of Bayesian models, to better understand our results. We will also be assisted by other libraries in the Python ecosystem, including PreliZ [Icazatti et al., 2023] for prior elicitation, Kulprit for variable selection, and PyMC-BART [Quiroga et al., 2022] for flexible regression. And of course, we will also use common tools from the standard Python Data stack, like NumPy [Harris et al., 2020], matplotlib [Hunter, 2007], Pandas [Wes McKinney, 2010], etc.

Bayesian methods are theoretically grounded in probability theory, and so it's no wonder that many books about Bayesian statistics is full of mathematical formulas requiring a certain level of mathematical sophistication. Learning the mathematical foundations of statistics will certainly help you build better models and gain intuition about problems, models, and results. Nevertheless, libraries such as PyMC allow us to learn and do Bayesian statistics with only a modest amount of mathematical knowledge, as you will be able to verify yourself throughout this book.

Who this book is for

If you are a student, data scientist, researcher in the natural or social sciences, or developer looking to get started with Bayesian data analysis and probabilistic programming, this book is for you. The book is introductory, so no previous statistical knowledge is required. However, the book assumes you have experience with Python and familiarity with libraries like NumPy and matplotlib.

What this book covers

Chapter 1, *Thinking Probabilistically*, covers the basic concepts of Bayesian statistics and its implications for data analysis. This chapter contains most of the foundational ideas used in the rest of the book.

Chapter 2, *Programming Probabilistically*, revisits the concepts from the previous chapter from a more computational perspective. The PyMC probabilistic programming library and ArviZ, a Python library for exploratory analysis of Bayesian models are introduced.

Chapter 3, *Hierarchical Models*, illustrates the core ideas of hierarchical models through examples.

Chapter 4, *Modeling with Lines*, covers the basic elements of linear regression, a very widely used model and the building block of more complex models, and then moves into generalizing linear models to solve many data analysis problems.

Chapter 5, *Comparing Models*, discusses how to compare and select models using posterior predictive checks, LOO, and Bayes factors. The general caveats of these methods are discussed and model averaging is also illustrated.

Chapter 6, *Modeling with Bambi*, introduces Bambi, a Bayesian library built on top of PyMC that simplifies working with generalized linear models. In this chapter, we will also discuss variable selection and new models like splines.

Chapter 7, *Mixture Models*, discusses how to add flexibility to models by mixing simpler distributions to build more complex ones. The first non-parametric model in the book is also introduced: the Dirichlet process.

Chapter 8, *Gaussian Processes*, covers the basic idea behind Gaussian processes and how to use them to build non-parametric models over functions for a wide array of problems.

Chapter 9, *Bayesian Additive Regression Trees*, introduces readers to a flexible regression model that combines decision trees and Bayesian modeling techniques. The chapter will cover the key features of BART, including its flexibility in capturing non-linear relationships between predictors and outcomes and how it can be used for variable selection.

Chapter 10, *Inference Engines*, provides an introduction to methods for numerically approximating the posterior distribution, as well as a very important topic from the practitioner's perspective: how to diagnose the reliability of the approximated posterior.

Chapter 11, *Where to Go Next?*, provides a list of resources to keep learning from beyond this book, and a concise farewell speech.

What's new in this edition?

We have incorporated feedback from readers of the second edition to refine the text and the code in this third edition, to improve clarity and readability. We have also added new examples and new sections and removed some sections that in retrospect were not that useful.

In the second edition, we extensively use PyMC and ArviZ. In this new edition, we use the last available version of PyMC and ArviZ at the time of writing and we showcase some of its new features. This new edition also reflects how the PyMC ecosystem has bloomed in the last few years. We discuss 4 new libraries:

- Bambi, a library for Bayesian regression models with a very simple interface. We have a dedicated chapter to it.
- Kulprit, a very new library for variable selection built on top of Bambi. We show one example of how to use it and provide the intuition for the theory behind this package.
- PreliZ is a library for prior elicitation. We use it from Chapter 1 and in many chapters after that.
- PyMC-BART, a library that extends PyMC to support Bayesian Additive Regression Trees. We have a dedicated chapter to it.

The following list delineates the changes introduced in the third edition as compared to the second edition.

Chapter 1, Thinking Probabilistically

We have added a new introduction to probability theory. This is something many readers asked for. The introduction is not meant to be a replacement for a proper course in probability theory, but it should be enough to get you started.

Chapter 2, Programming Probabilistically

We discuss the Savage-Dickey density ratio (also discussed in Chapter 5). We explain the InferenceData object from ArviZ and how to use coords and dims with PyMC and ArviZ. We moved the section on hierarchical models to its own chapter, Chapter 3.

Chapter 3, Hierarchical Models

We have promoted the discussion of hierarchical models to its dedicated chapter. We refine the discussion of hierarchical models and add a new example, for which we use a dataset from football European leagues.

Chapter 4, Modeling with Lines

This chapter has been extensively rewritten. We use the Bikes dataset to introduce both simple linear regression and negative binomial regression. Generalized linear models (GLMs) are introduced early in this chapter (in the previous edition they were introduced in another chapter). This helps you to see the connection between linear regression and GLMs and allows us to introduce more advanced concepts in Chapter 6. We discuss the centered vs non-centered parametrization of linear models.

Chapter 5, Comparing Models

We have cleaned the text to make it more clear and removed some bits that were not that useful after all. We now recommend the use of LOO over WAIC. We have added a discussion about the Savage-Dickey density ratio to compute Bayes factors.

Chapter 6, Modeling with Bambi

We show you how to use Bambi, a high-level Bayesian model-building interface written in Python. We take advantage of the simple syntax offered by Bambi to expand what we learned in Chapter 4, including splines, distributional models, categorical models, and interactions. We also show how Bambi can help us to interpret complex linear models that otherwise can become confusing, error-prone, or just time-consuming. We close the chapter by discussing variable selection with Kulprit, a Python package that tightly integrates with Bambi.

Chapter 7, Mixture Models

We have clarified some of the discussions based on feedback from readers. We also discuss Zero-Inflated and hurdle models and show how to use rootograms to evaluate the fit of discrete models.

Chapter 8, Gaussian Processes

We have cleaned the text to make explanations clear and removed some of the boilerplate code and text for a more fluid reading. We also discuss how to define a kernel with a custom distance instead of the default Euclidean distance. We discuss the practical application of Hilbert Space Gaussian processes, a fast approximation to Gaussian processes.

Chapter 9, Bayesian Additive Regression Trees

This is an entirely new chapter discussing BART models, a flexible and easy-to-use non-parametric Bayesian method.

Chapter 10, Inference Engines

We have removed the discussion on variational inference as it is not used in the book. We have updated and expanded the discussion of trace plots, $\hat{R}$, ESS, and MCSE. We also included a discussion on rank plots and a better example of divergences and centered vs non-centered parameterizations.

Installation instructions

The code in the book was written using Python version 3.11.6. To install Python and Python libraries, I recommend using Anaconda, a scientific computing distribution. You can read more about Anaconda and download it at `https://www.anaconda.com/products/distribution`. This will install many useful Python packages on your system.

Additionally, you will need to install some packages. To do that, please use:

```
conda install -c conda-forge pymc==5.8.0 arviz==0.16.1 bambi==0.13.0
pymc-bart==0.5.2 kulprit==0.0.1 preliz==0.3.6 nutpie==0.9.1
```

You can also use pip if you prefer:

```
pip install pymc==5.8.0 arviz==0.16.1 bambi==0.13.0 pymc-bart==0.5.2
kulprit==0.0.1 preliz==0.3.6 nutpie==0.9.1
```

An alternative way to install the necessary packages once Anaconda is installed in your system is to go to `https://github.com/aloctavodia/BAP3` and download the environment file named `bap3.yml`. With it, you can install all the necessary packages using the following command:

```
conda env create -f bap3.yml
```

The Python packages used to write this book are listed here:

- ArviZ 0.16.1
- Bambi 0.13.0
- Kulprit 0.0.1
- PreliZ 0.3.6
- PyMC 5.8.0
- PyMC-BART 0.5.2
- Python 3.11.6
- Notebook 7.0.6
- Matplotlib 3.8.0
- NumPy 1.24.4
- Numba 0.58.1
- Nutpie 0.9.1
- SciPy 1.11.3
- Pandas 2.1.2
- Xarray 2023.10.1

> **How to run the code while reading**
>
> The code presented in each chapter assumes that you have imported at least some of these packages. Instead of copying and pasting the code from the book, I recommend downloading the code from `https://github.com/aloctavodia/B AP3` and running it using Jupyter Notebook (or Jupyter Lab). Additionally, most figures in this book are generated using code that is present in the notebooks but not always shown in the book.

If you find a technical problem while running the code in this book, a typo in the text, or any other errors, please fill in the issue at `https://github.com/aloctavodia/BAP3` and I will try to resolve it as soon as possible.

Conventions used

There are several text conventions used throughout this book.

`code_in_text`: Indicates code words in the text, filenames, or names of functions. Here is an example: "Most of the preceding code is for plotting; the probabilistic part is performed by the `y = stats.norm(mu, sd).pdf(x)` line."

A block of code is set as follows:

Code 1:

```
1  μ = 0.
2  σ = 1.
3  X = pz.Normal(μ, σ)
4  x = X.rvs(3)
```

Bold: Indicates a new term, or an important word.

Italics: Suggests a less rigorous or colloquial utilization of a term.

Get in touch

Feedback from our readers is always welcome.

General feedback: If you have questions about any aspect of this book, mention the book title in the subject of your message and email us at customercare@packtpub.com.

Errata: Although we have taken every care to ensure the accuracy of our content, mistakes do happen. If you have found a mistake in this book, we would be grateful if you open an issue ticket at `https://github.com/aloctavodia/BAP3`

Becoming an author: If there is a topic that you have expertise in and you are interested in either writing or contributing to a book, please visit `authors.packtpub.com`.

For more information about Packt, please visit `https://www.packtpub.com/`.

Share your thoughts

Once you've read *Bayesian Analysis with Python, Third Edition*, we'd love to hear your thoughts! Scan the QR code below to go straight to the Amazon review page for this book and share your feedback.

https://packt.link/r/1805127160

Your review is important to us and the tech community and will help us make sure we're delivering excellent quality content.

Download a free PDF copy of this book

Thanks for purchasing this book!

Do you like to read on the go but are unable to carry your print books everywhere? Is your eBook purchase not compatible with the device of your choice?

Don't worry, now with every Packt book you get a DRM-free PDF version of that book at no cost.

Read anywhere, any place, on any device. Search, copy, and paste code from your favorite technical books directly into your application.

The perks don't stop there, you can get exclusive access to discounts, newsletters, and great free content in your inbox daily

Follow these simple steps to get the benefits:

1. Scan the QR code or visit the link below

https://packt.link/free-ebook/9781805127161

2. Submit your proof of purchase

3. That's it! We'll send your free PDF and other benefits to your email directly

1

Thinking Probabilistically

> Probability theory is nothing but common sense reduced to calculation.
>
> – Pierre Simon Laplace

In this chapter, we will learn about the core concepts of Bayesian statistics and some of the instruments in the Bayesian toolbox. We will use some Python code, but this chapter will be mostly theoretical; most of the concepts we will see here will be revisited many times throughout this book. This chapter, being heavy on the theoretical side, is perhaps a little anxiogenic for the coder in you, but I think it will ease the path to effectively applying Bayesian statistics to your problems.

In this chapter, we will cover the following topics:

- Statistical modeling
- Probabilities and uncertainty
- Bayes' theorem and statistical inference
- Single-parameter inference and the classic coin-flip problem
- Choosing priors and why people often don't like them but should

- Communicating a Bayesian analysis

Statistics, models, and this book's approach

Statistics is about collecting, organizing, analyzing, and interpreting data, and hence statistical knowledge is essential for data analysis. Two main statistical methods are used in data analysis:

- **Exploratory Data Analysis (EDA)**: This is about numerical summaries, such as the mean, mode, standard deviation, and interquartile ranges. EDA is also about visually inspecting the data, using tools you may be already familiar with, such as histograms and scatter plots.

- **Inferential statistics**: This is about making statements beyond the current data. We may want to understand some particular phenomenon, maybe we want to make predictions for future (yet unobserved) data points, or we need to choose among several competing explanations for the same set of observations. In summary, inferential statistics allow us to draw meaningful insights from a limited set of data and make informed decisions based on the results of our analysis.

> A Match Made in Heaven
>
> The focus of this book is on how to perform Bayesian inferential statistics, but we will also use ideas from EDA to summarize, interpret, check, and communicate the results of Bayesian inference.

Most introductory statistical courses, at least for non-statisticians, are taught as a collection of recipes that go like this: go to the statistical pantry, pick one tin can and open it, add data to taste, and stir until you obtain a consistent p-value, preferably under 0.05. The main goal of these courses is to teach you how to pick the proper can. I never liked this approach, mainly because the most common result is a bunch of confused people unable to grasp, even at the conceptual level, the unity of the different learned methods. We will take a different approach: we will learn some recipes, but they will be homemade rather than canned food; we will learn how to mix fresh ingredients that will suit different statistical occasions and, more importantly, that will let you apply concepts far beyond the examples in this book.

Taking this approach is possible for two reasons:

- **Ontological**: Statistics is a form of modeling unified under the mathematical framework of probability theory. Using a probabilistic approach provides a unified view of what may seem like very disparate methods; statistical methods and machine learning methods look much more similar under the probabilistic lens.
- **Technical**: Modern software, such as PyMC, allows practitioners, just like you and me, to define and solve models in a relatively easy way. Many of these models were unsolvable just a few years ago or required a high level of mathematical and technical sophistication.

Working with data

Data is an essential ingredient in statistics and data science. Data comes from several sources, such as experiments, computer simulations, surveys, and field observations. If we are the ones in charge of generating or gathering the data, it is always a good idea to first think carefully about the questions we want to answer and which methods we will use, and only then proceed to get the data. There is a whole branch of statistics dealing with data collection, known as experimental design. In the era of the data deluge, we can sometimes forget that gathering data is not always cheap. For example, while it is true that the **Large Hadron Collider** (**LHC**) produces hundreds of terabytes a day, its construction took years of manual and intellectual labor.

As a general rule, we can think of the process of generating the data as stochastic, because there is ontological, technical, and/or epistemic uncertainty, that is, the system is intrinsically stochastic, there are technical issues adding noise or restricting us from measuring with arbitrary precision, and/or there are conceptual limitations veiling details from us. For all these reasons, we always need to interpret data in the context of models, including mental and formal ones. Data does not speak but through models.

In this book, we will assume that we already have collected the data. Our data will also be clean and tidy, something that's rarely true in the real world. We will make these assumptions to focus on the subject of this book. I just want to emphasize, especially for newcomers to data analysis, that even when not covered in this book, there are important skills that you should learn and practice to successfully work with data.

A very useful skill when analyzing data is knowing how to write code in a programming language, such as Python. Manipulating data is usually necessary given that we live in a messy world with even messier data, and coding helps to get things done. Even if you are lucky and your data is very clean and tidy, coding will still be very useful since modern Bayesian statistics is done mostly through programming languages such as Python or R. If you want to learn how to use Python for cleaning and manipulating data, you can find a good introduction in *Python for Data Analysis* by McKinney [2022].

Bayesian modeling

Models are simplified descriptions of a given system or process that, for some reason, we are interested in. Those descriptions are deliberately designed to capture only the most relevant aspects of the system and not to explain every minor detail. This is one reason a more complex model is not always a better one. There are many different kinds of models; in this book, we will restrict ourselves to Bayesian models. We can summarize the Bayesian modeling process using three steps:

1. Given some data and some assumptions on how this data could have been generated, we design a model by combining building blocks known as **probability distributions**. Most of the time these models are crude approximations, but most of the time that's all we need.

2. We use Bayes' theorem to add data to our models and derive the logical consequences of combining the data and our assumptions. We say we are **conditioning** the model on our data.

3. We evaluate the model, and its predictions, under different criteria, including the data, our expertise on the subject, and sometimes by comparing it to other models.

In general, we will find ourselves performing these three steps in an iterative non-linear fashion. We will retrace our steps at any given point: maybe we made a silly coding mistake, or we found a way to change the model and improve it, or we realized that we need to add more data or collect a different kind of data.

Bayesian models are also known as **probabilistic models** because they are built using probabilities. Why probabilities? Because probabilities are a very useful tool to model uncertainty; we even have good arguments to state they are the correct mathematical concept. So let's take a walk through *the garden of forking paths* [Borges, 1944].

A probability primer for Bayesian practitioners

In this section, we are going to discuss a few general and important concepts that are key for better understanding Bayesian methods. Additional probability-related concepts will be introduced or elaborated on in future chapters, as we need them. For a detailed study of probability theory, however, I highly recommend the book *Introduction to Probability* by Blitzstein [2019]. Those already familiar with the basic elements of probability theory can skip this section or skim it.

Sample space and events

Let's say we are surveying to see how people feel about the weather in their area. We asked three individuals whether they enjoy sunny weather, with possible responses being "yes" or "no." The sample space of all possible outcomes can be denoted by S and consists of eight possible combinations:

S = {(yes, yes, yes), (yes, yes, no), (yes, no, yes), (no, yes, yes), (yes, no, no), (no, yes, no), (no, no, yes), (no, no, no)}

Here, each element of the sample space represents the responses of the three individuals in the order they were asked. For example, (yes, no, yes) means the first and third people answered "yes" while the second person answered "no."

We can define events as subsets of the sample space. For example, event A is when all three individuals answered "yes":

$A = \{(\text{yes, yes, yes})\}$

Similarly, we can define event B as when at least one person answered "no," and then we will have:

$B = \{(\text{yes, yes, no}), (\text{yes, no, yes}), (\text{no, yes, yes}), (\text{yes, no, no}), (\text{no, yes, no}), (\text{no, no, yes}), (\text{no, no, no})\}$

We can use probabilities as a measure of how likely these events are. Assuming all events are equally likely, the probability of event A, which is the event that all three individuals answered "yes," is:

$$P(A) = \frac{\text{number of outcomes in } A}{\text{total number of outcomes in } S}$$

In this case, there is only one outcome in A, and there are eight outcomes in S. Therefore, the probability of A is:

$$P(A) = \frac{1}{8} = 0.125$$

Similarly, we can calculate the probability of event B, which is the event that at least one person answered "no." Since there are seven outcomes in B and eight outcomes in S, the probability of B is:

$$P(B) = \frac{7}{8} = 0.875$$

Considering all events equally likely is just a particular case that makes calculating probabilities easier. This is something called the naive definition of probability since it is restrictive and relies on strong assumptions. However, it is still useful if we are cautious when using it. For instance, it is not true that all yes-no questions have a 50-50 chance. Another example. What is the probability of seeing a purple horse? The right answer can vary a lot depending on whether we're talking about the natural color of a real horse, a horse from a cartoon, a horse dressed in a parade, etc. Anyway, no matter if the events are equally likely or not, the probability of the entire sample space is always equal to 1. We can see that this is true by computing:

$$P(S) = \frac{\text{number of outcomes in } S}{\text{total number of outcomes in } S}$$

1 is the highest value a probability can take. Saying that $P(S) = 1$ is saying that S is not only very likely, it is certain. If everything that can happen is defined by S, then S will happen.

If an event is impossible, then its probability is 0. Let's define the event C as the event of three persons saying "banana":

$C = \{(\text{banana, banana, banana})\}$

As C is not part of S, by definition, it cannot happen. Think of this as the questionnaire from our survey only having two boxes, *yes* and *no*. By design, our survey is restricting all other possible options.

We can take advantage of the fact that Python includes sets and define a Python function to compute probabilities following their naive definition:

Code 1.1:

```
1  def P(S, A):
2      if set(A).issubset(set(S)):
3          return len(A)/len(S)
4      else:
5          return 0
```

I left for the reader the joy of playing with this function.

One useful way to conceptualize probabilities is as conserved quantities distributed throughout the sample space. This means that if the probability of one event increases, the probability of some other event or events must decrease so that the total probability remains equal to 1. This can be illustrated with a simple example.

Suppose we ask one person whether it will rain tomorrow, with possible responses of "yes" and "no." The sample space for possible responses is given by S = {yes, no}. An event that will rain tomorrow is represented by A = {yes}. If $P(A)$, is 0.5, then the probability of the complement of event A, denoted by $P(A^c)$, must also be 0.5. If for some reason $P(A)$ increases to 0.8, then $P(A^c)$ must decrease to 0.2. This property holds for disjoint events, which are events that cannot occur simultaneously. For instance, it cannot *rain* and *not rain* at the same time tomorrow. You may object that it can rain during the morning and not rain during the afternoon. That is true, but that's a different sample space!

So far, we have avoided directly defining probabilities, and instead, we have just shown some of their properties and ways to compute them. A general definition of probability that works for non-equally likely events is as follows. Given a sample space S, and the event A, which is a subset of S, a probability is a function P, which takes A as input and returns a real number between 0 and 1, as output. The function P has some restrictions, defined by the following 3 axioms. Keep in mind that an axiom is a statement that is taken to be true and that we use as the starting point in our reasoning:

1. The probability of an event is a non-negative real number
2. $P(S) = 1$
3. If $A1, A2, \ldots$ are disjoint events, meaning they cannot occur simultaneously then
   $P(A1, A2, \ldots) = P(A1) + P(A2) + \ldots$

If this were a book on probability theory, we would likely dedicate a few pages to demonstrating the consequences of these axioms and provide exercises for manipulating probabilities. That would help us to become proficient in manipulating probabilities. However, our main focus is not on those topics. My motivation to present these axioms is just to show that probabilities are well-defined mathematical concepts with rules that govern their operations. They are a particular type of function, and there is no mystery surrounding them.

Random variables

A random variable is a function that maps the sample space into the real numbers $\mathbb{R}$ (see Figure 1.1). Let's assume the events of interest are the number of a die, the mapping is very simple, we associate ⊡ with the number 1, ⊡ with 2, etc. Another simple example is the answer to the question, will it rain tomorrow? We can map "yes" to 1 and "no" to 0. It is common, but not always the case, to use a capital letter for random variables like X and a lowercase letter for their outcomes x. For example, if X represents a single roll of a die, then x represents some specific integer $\{1, 2, 3, 4, 5, 6\}$. Thus, we can write $P(X = 3)$ to indicate the probability of getting the value 3, when rolling a die. We can also leave x unspecified, for instance, we can write $P(X = x)$ to indicate the probability of getting some value x, or $P(X \leq x)$, to indicate the probability of getting a value less than or equal to x.

Being able to map symbols like ⊡ or strings like "yes" to numbers makes analysis simpler as we already know how to do math with numbers. Random variables are also useful because we can operate with them without directly thinking in terms of the sample space. This feature becomes more and more relevant as the sample space becomes more complex. For example, when simulating molecular systems, we need to specify the position and velocity of each atom; for complex molecules like proteins this means that we will need to track thousands, millions, or even larger numbers. Instead, we can use random variables to summarize certain properties of the system, such as the total energy or the relative angles between certain atoms of the system.

If you are still confused, that's fine. The concept of a random variable may sound too abstract at the beginning, but we will see plenty of examples throughout the book that will help you cement these ideas. Before moving on, let me try one analogy that I hope you find useful. Random variables are useful in a similar way to how Python functions are useful. We often encapsulate code within functions, so we can store, reuse, and *hide* complex manipulations of data into a single call. Even more, once we have a few functions, we can sometimes combine them in many ways, like adding the output of two functions or using the output of one function as the input of the other. We can do all this without functions, but abstracting away the inner workings not only makes the code cleaner, it also helps with understanding and fostering new ideas. Random variables play a similar role in statistics.

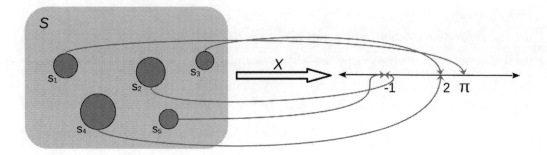

Figure 1.1: A random variable X defined on a sample space with 5 elements $\{S_1, \cdots S_5\}$, and possible values -1, 2, and π

The mapping between the sample space and $\mathbb{R}$ is deterministic. There is no randomness involved. So why do we call it a *random* variable? Because we can *ask* the variable for values, and every time we ask, we will get a different number. The randomness comes from the probability associated with the events. In Figure 1.1, we have represented P as the size of the circles.

The two most common types of random variables are discrete and continuous ones. Without going into a proper definition, we are going to say that discrete variables take only discrete values and we usually use integers to represent them, like 1, 5, 42. And continuous variables take real values, so we use floats to work with them, like 3.1415, 1.01, 23.4214, and so on. When we use one or the other is problem-dependent. If we ask people about their favorite color, we will get answers like "red," "blue," and "green." This is an example of a discrete random variable. The answers are categories – there are no intermediate values between "red" and "green." But if we are studying the properties of light absorption, then discrete values like "red" and "green" may not be adequate and instead working with wavelength could be more appropriate. In that case, we will expect to get values like 650 nm and 510 nm and any number in between, including 579.1.

Discrete random variables and their distributions

Instead of calculating the probability that all three individuals answered "yes," or the probability of getting a 3 when rolling a die, we may be more interested in finding out the *list of probabilities* for all possible answers or all possible numbers from a die. Once this list is computed, we can inspect it visually or use it to compute other quantities like the probability of getting at least one "no," the probability of getting an odd number, or the probability of getting a number equal to or larger than 5. The formal name of this *list* is **probability distribution**.

We can get the empirical probability distribution of a die, by rolling it a few times and tabulating how many times we got each number. To turn each value into a probability and the entire list into a valid probability distribution, we need to *normalize* the counts. We can do this by dividing the value we got for each number by the number of times we roll the die.

Empirical distributions are very useful, and we are going to extensively use them. But instead of rolling dice by hand, we are going to use advanced computational methods to do the hard work for us; this will not only save us time and boredom but it will allow us to get samples from really complicated distributions effortlessly. But we are getting ahead of ourselves. Our priority is to concentrate on theoretical distributions, which are central in statistics because, among other reasons, they allow the construction of probabilistic models.

As we saw, there is nothing random or mysterious about random variables; they are just a type of mathematical function. The same goes for theoretical probability distributions. I like to compare probability distributions with circles. Because we are all familiar with circles even before we get into school, we are not afraid of them and they don't look mysterious to us. We can define a circle as the geometric space of points on a plane that is equidistant from another point called the center. We can go further and provide a mathematical expression for this definition. If we assume the location of the center is irrelevant, then the circle of radius r can simply be described as the set of all points (x, y) such that:

$$x^2 + y^2 = r^2$$

From this expression, we can see that given the **parameter** r, the circle is completely defined. This is all we need to plot it and all we need to compute properties such as the perimeter, which is $2\pi r$.

Now notice that all circles look very similar to each other and that any two circles with the same value of r are essentially the same objects. Thus we can think of the family of circles, where each member is set apart from the rest precisely by the value of r.

So far, so good, but why are we talking about circles? Because all this can be directly applied to probability distributions. Both circles and probability distributions have mathematical expressions that define them, and these expressions have parameters that we can change to define all members of a family of probability distributions. Figure 1.2 shows four members of one probability distribution known as BetaBinomial. In Figure 1.2, the height of the bars represents the probability of each x value. The values of x below 1 or above 6 have a probability of 0 as they are out of the support of the distribution.

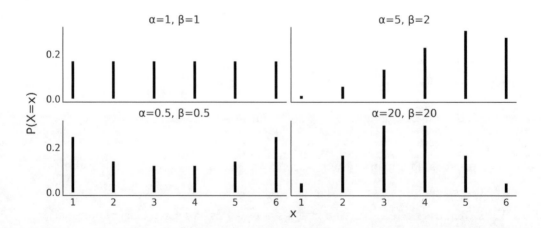

Figure 1.2: Four members of the BetaBinomial distribution with parameters α and β

This is the mathematical expression for the BetaBinomial distribution:

$$\text{pmf}(x) = \binom{n}{x} \frac{B(x + \alpha, n - x + \beta)}{B(\alpha, \beta)}$$

pmf stands for **probability mass function**. For discrete random variables, the pmf is the function that returns probabilities. In mathematical notation, if we have a random variable X, then $\text{pmf}(x) = P(X = x)$.

Understanding or remembering the pmf of the BetaBinomial has zero importance for us. I'm just showing it here so you can see that this is just another function; you put in one number and you get out another number. Nothing weird, at least not in principle. I must concede that to fully understand the details of the BetaBinomial distribution, we need to know what $\binom{n}{x}$ is, known as the binomial coefficient, and what B is, the Beta function. But that's not fundamentally different from showing $x^2 + y^2 = r^2$.

Mathematical expressions can be super useful, as they are concise and we can use them to derive properties from them. But sometimes that can be too much work, even if we are good at math. Visualization can be a good alternative (or complement) to help us understand probability distributions. I cannot fully show this on paper, but if you run the following, you will get an interactive plot that will update every time you move the sliders for the parameters alpha, beta, and n:

Code 1.2:

```
pz.BetaBinomial(alpha=10, beta=10, n=6).plot_interactive()
```

Figure 1.3 shows a static version of this interactive plot. The black dots represent the probabilities for each value of the random variable, while the dotted black line is just a visual aid.

On the x-axis, we have the support of the BetaBinomial distribution, i.e., the values it can take, $x \in \{0, 1, 2, 3, 4, 5\}$. On the y-axis, the probabilities associated with each of those values. The full list is shown in Table 1.1.

Notice that for a BetaBinomial(alpha=10, beta=10, n=6) distribution, the probability of

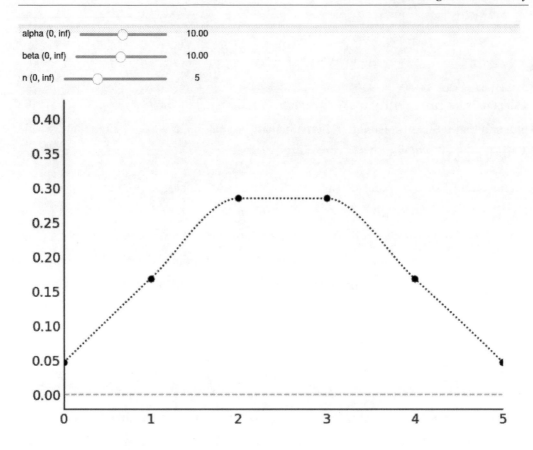

Figure 1.3: The output of `pz.BetaBinomial(alpha=10, beta=10,`
`n=6).plot_interactive()`

x value	probability
0	0.047
1	0.168
2	0.285
3	0.285
4	0.168
5	0.047

Table 1.1: Probabilities for `pz.BetaBinomial(alpha=10, beta=10, n=6)`

values not in $\{0, 1, 2, 3, 4, 5\}$, including values such as $-1, 0.5, \pi, 42$, is 0.

We previously mentioned that we can *ask* a random variable for values and every time we ask, we will get a different number. We can simulate this with PreliZ [Icazatti et al., 2023], a Python library for prior elicitation. Take the following code snippet for instance:

Code 1.3:

```
pz.BetaBinomial(alpha=10, beta=10, n=6).rvs()
```

This will give us an integer between 0 and 5. Which one? We don't know! But let's run the following code:

Code 1.4:

```
1 plt.hist(pz.BetaBinomial(alpha=2, beta=5, n=5).rvs(1000))
2 pz.BetaBinomial(alpha=2, beta=5, n=5).plot_pdf();
```

We will get something similar to Figure 1.4. Even when we cannot predict the next value from a random variable, we can predict the probability of getting any particular value and by the same token, if we get many values, we can predict their overall distribution.

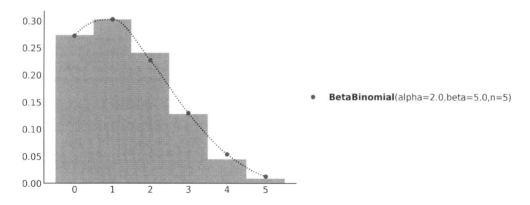

Figure 1.4: The gray dots represent the pmf of the BetaBinomial sample. In light gray, a histogram of 1,000 draws from that distribution

In this book, we will sometimes know the parameters of a given distribution and we will want to get random samples from it. Other times, we are going to be in the opposite scenario: we will have a set of samples and we will want to estimate the parameters of a distribution. Playing back and forth between these two scenarios will become second nature as we move forward through the pages.

Continuous random variables and their distributions

Probably the most widely known continuous probability distribution is the **Normal distribution**, also known as the **Gaussian distribution**. Its **probability density function** is:

$$\text{pdf}(x) = \frac{1}{\sigma\sqrt{2\pi}} \exp\left\{-\frac{1}{2}\left(\frac{x-\mu}{\sigma}\right)^2\right\}$$

Again, we only show this expression to remove the mystery veil. No need to pay too much attention to its details, other than to the fact that this distribution has two parameters μ, which controls the location of the peak of the curve, and σ, which controls the spread of the curve. Figure 1.5 shows 3 examples from the Gaussian family. If you want to learn more about this distribution, I recommend you watch this video: `https://www.youtube.com/watch?v=cy8r7WSuT1I`.

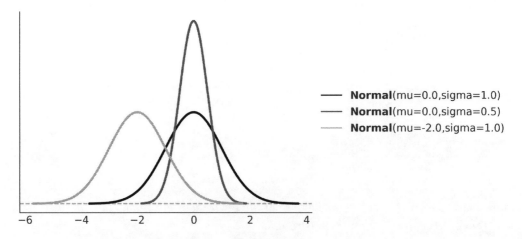

Figure 1.5: Three members of the Gaussian family

If you have been paying attention, you may have noticed that we said **probability density function (pdf)** instead of **probability mass function (pmf)**. This was no typo – they are actually two different objects. Let's take one step back and think about this; the output of a discrete probability distribution is a probability. The height of the bars in Figure 1.2 or the height of the dots in Figure 1.3 are probabilities. Each bar or dot will never be higher than 1 and if you sum all the bars or dots, you will always get 1. Let's do the same but with the curve in Figure 1.5. The first thing to notice is that we don't have bars or dots; we have a continuous, smooth curve. So maybe we can think that the curve is made up of super thin bars, so thin that we assign one bar for every real value in the support of the distributions, we measure the height of each bar, and we perform an infinite sum. This is a sensible thing to do, right?

Well yes, but it is not immediately obvious what are we going to get from this. Will this sum give us exactly 1? Or are we going to get a large number instead? Is the sum finite? Or does the result depend on the parameters of the distribution?

A proper answer to these questions requires measure theory, and this is a very informal introduction to probability, so we are not going into that rabbit hole. But the answer essentially is that for a continuous random variable, we can only assign a probability of 0 to every individual value it may take; instead, we can assign densities to them and then we can calculate probabilities for a range of values. Thus, for a Gaussian, the probability of getting exactly the number -2, i.e. the number -2 followed by an infinite number of zeros after the decimal point, is 0. But the probability of getting a number between -2 and 0 is some number larger than 0 and smaller than 1. To find out the exact answer, we need to compute the following:

$$P(a < X < b) = \int_a^b \text{pdf}(x)dx$$

And to compute that, we need to replace the symbols for a concrete quantity. If we replace the pdf by Normal(0, 1), and $a = -2, b = 0$, we will get that $P(-2 < X < 0) \approx 0.477$, which is the shaded area in Figure 1.6.

You may remember that we can approximate an integral by summing areas of rectangles

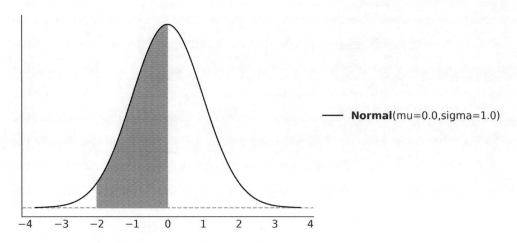

Figure 1.6: The black line represents the pdf of a Gaussian with parameters mu=0 and sigma=1, the gray area is the probability of a value being larger than -2 and smaller than 0

and the approximation becomes more and more accurate as we reduce the length of the base of the rectangles (see the Wikipedia entry for Riemann integral). Based on this idea and using PreliZ, we can estimate $P(-2 < X < 0)$ as:

Code 1.5:

```
1  dist = pz.Normal(0, 1)
2  a = -2
3  b = 0
4  num = 10
5  x_s = np.linspace(a, b, num)
6  base = (b-a)/num
7  np.sum(dist.pdf(x_s) * base)
```

If we increase the value of num, we will get a better approximation.

Cumulative distribution function

We have seen the pmf and the pdf, but these are not the only ways to characterize distributions. An alternative is the **cumulative distribution function (cdf)**. The cdf of a random variable X is the function F_X given by $F_X(x) = P(X \leq x)$. In words, the cdf is the answer to the question: what is the probability of getting a number lower than or equal to x? On the first column of Figure 1.7, we can see the pmf and cdf of a BetaBinomial, and in the second column, the pdf and cdf of a Gaussian. Notice how the cdf *jumps* for the discrete variable but it is smooth for the continuous variable. The height of each jump represents a probability – just compare them with the height of the dots. We can use the plot of the cdf of a continuous variable as visual proof that probabilities are zero for any value of the continuous variable. Just notice how there are no *jumps* for continuous variables, which is equivalent to saying that the height of the jumps is exactly zero.

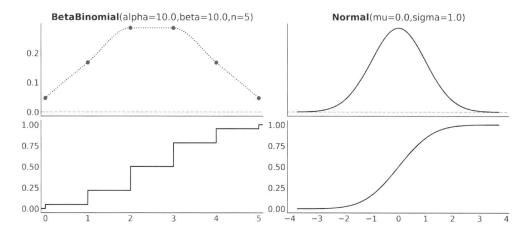

Figure 1.7: The pmf of the BetaBinomial distribution with its corresponding cdf and the pdf of the Normal distribution with its corresponding cdf

Just by looking at a cdf, it is easier to find what is the probability of getting a number smaller than, let's say, 1. We just need to go to the value 1 on the x-axis, move up until we cross the black line, and then check the value of the y-axis. For instance, in Figure 1.7 and for the Normal distribution, we can see that the value lies between 0.75 and 1. Let's say it is ≈ 0.85. This is way harder to do with the pdf because we would need to compare the entire area below 1 to the total area to get the answer. Humans are worse at judging areas than judging heights or lengths.

Conditional probability

Given two events A and B with $P(B) > 0$, the probability of A given B, which we write as $P(A \mid B)$ is defined as:

$$P(A \mid B) = \frac{P(A,B)}{P(B)}$$

$P(A,B)$ is the probability that both the event A and event B occur. $P(A \mid B)$ is known as conditional probability, and it is the probability that event A occurs, **conditioned** by the fact that we know (or assume, imagine, hypothesize, etc.) that B has occurred. For example, the probability that the pavement is wet is different from the probability that the pavement is wet if we know it's raining.

A conditional probability can be larger than, smaller than, or equal to the unconditional probability. If knowing B does not provide us with information about A, then $P(A \mid B) = P(A)$. This will be true only if A and B are independent of each other. On the contrary, if knowing B gives us useful information about A, then the conditional probability could be larger or smaller than the unconditional probability, depending on whether knowing B makes A less or more likely. Let's see a simple example using a fair six-sided die. What is the probability of getting the number 3 if we roll the die? $P\,(\text{die} = 3) = \frac{1}{6}$ since each of the six numbers has the same chance for a fair six-sided die. And what is the probability of getting the number 3 given that we have obtained an odd number? $P\,(\text{die} = 3 \mid \text{die} = \{1,3,5\}) = \frac{1}{3}$, because if we know we have an odd number, the only possible numbers are $\{1,3,5\}$ and each of them has the same chance. Finally, what is the probability of getting 3 if we have obtained an even number? This is $P\,(\text{die} = 3 \mid \text{die} = \{2,4,6\}) = 0$, because if we know the number is even, then the only possible ones are $\{2,4,6\}$ and thus getting a 3 is not possible.

As we can see from these simple examples, by conditioning on observed data, we are changing the sample space. When asking about $P\,(\text{die} = 3)$, we need to evaluate the sample space $S = \{1,2,3,4,5,6\}$, but when we **condition on** having got an even number, then the new sample space becomes $T = \{2,4,6\}$.

Conditional probabilities are at the heart of statistics, irrespective of whether your problem is rolling dice or building self-driving cars.

The central panel of Figure 1.8 represents $p(A, B)$ using a grayscale with darker colors for higher probability densities. We see the joint distribution is elongated, indicating that the higher the value of A, the higher the one of B, and vice versa. Knowing the value of A tells us something about the values of B and the other way around. On the top and right *margins* of Figure 1.8 we have the **marginal distributions** $p(A)$ and $p(B)$ respectively. To compute the marginal of A, we take $p(A, B)$ and we average overall values of B, intuitively this is like taking a 2D object, the joint distribution, and projecting it into one dimension. The marginal distribution of B is computed similarly. The dashed lines represent the **conditional probability** $p(A \mid B)$ for 3 different values of B. We get them by slicing the joint $p(A, B)$ at a given value of B. We can think of this as the distribution of A given that we have observed a particular value of B.

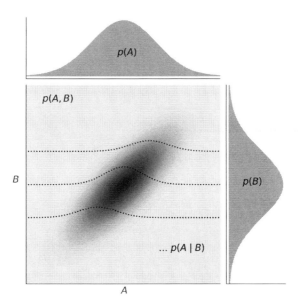

Figure 1.8: *Representation of the relationship between the joint* $p(A, B)$, *the marginals* $p(A)$ *and* $p(B)$, *and the conditional* $p(A \mid B)$ *probabilities*

Expected values

If X is a discrete random variable, we can compute its expected value as:

$$\mathbb{E}(X) = \sum_x xP(X = x)$$

This is just the mean or average value.

You are probably used to computing means or averages of samples or collections of numbers, either by hand, on a calculator, or using Python. But notice that here we are not talking about the mean of a bunch of numbers; we are talking about the mean of a distribution. Once we have defined the parameters of a distribution, we can, in principle, compute its expected values. Those are properties of the distribution in the same way that the perimeter is a property of a circle that gets defined once we set the value of the radius.

Another expected value is the variance, which we can use to describe the spread of a distribution. The variance appears *naturally* in many computations in statistics, but in practice, it is often more useful to use the standard deviation, which is the square root of the variance. The reason is that the standard deviation is in the same units as the random variable.

The mean and variance are often called the **moments** of a distribution. Other moments are skewness, which tells us about the asymmetry of a distribution, and the kurtosis, which tells us about the behavior of the tails or the *extreme values* [Westfall, 2014]. Figure 1.9 shows examples of different distributions and their mean μ, standard deviation σ, skew γ, and kurtosis κ. Notice that for some distributions, some moments may not be defined or they may be inf.

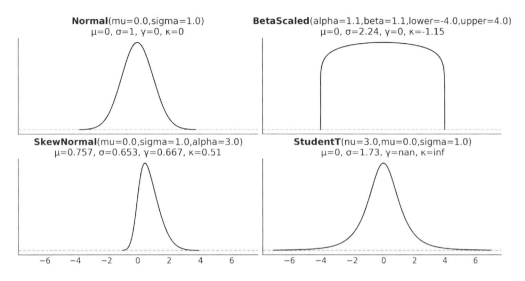

Figure 1.9: Four distributions with their first four moments

Now that we have learned about some of the basic concepts and jargon from probability theory, we can move on to the moment everyone was waiting for.

Bayes' theorem

Without further ado, let's contemplate, in all its majesty, Bayes' theorem:

$$p(\theta \mid Y) = \frac{p(Y \mid \theta)p(\theta)}{p(Y)}$$

Well, it's not that impressive, is it? It looks like an elementary school formula, and yet, paraphrasing Richard Feynman, this is all you need to know about Bayesian statistics. Learning where Bayes' theorem comes from will help us understand its meaning. According to the product rule, we have:

$$p(\theta, Y) = p(\theta \mid Y)\ p(Y)$$

This can also be written as:

$$p(\theta, Y) = p(Y \mid \theta) \; p(\theta)$$

Given that the terms on the left are equal for both equations, we can combine them and write:

$$p(\theta \mid Y) \; p(Y) = p(Y \mid \theta) \; p(\theta)$$

On reordering, we get Bayes' theorem:

$$p(\theta \mid Y) = \frac{p(Y \mid \theta) p(\theta)}{p(Y)}$$

Why is Bayes' theorem that important? Let's see.

First, it says that $p(\theta \mid Y)$ is not necessarily the same as $p(Y \mid \theta)$. This is a very important fact – one that is easy to miss in daily situations, even for people trained in statistics and probability. Let's use a simple example to clarify why these quantities are not necessarily the same. The probability of a person being the Pope given that this person is Argentinian is not the same as the probability of being Argentinian given that this person is the Pope. As there are around 47,000,000 Argentinians alive and a single one of them is the current Pope, we have $p\,(\text{Pope} \mid \text{Argentinian}) \approx \frac{1}{47000000}$ and we also have $p\,(\text{Argentinian} \mid \text{Pope}) = 1$.

If we replace θ with "hypothesis" and Y with "data," Bayes' theorem tells us how to compute the probability of a hypothesis, θ, given the data, Y, and that's the way you will find Bayes' theorem is explained in a lot of places. But, how do we turn a hypothesis into something that we can put inside Bayes' theorem? Well, we do it by using probability distributions. So, in general, our hypothesis is a hypothesis in a very, very, very narrow sense; we will be more precise if we talk about finding a suitable value for parameters in our models, that is, parameters of probability distributions. By the way, don't try to set θ to statements such as "unicorns are real," unless you are willing to build a realistic probabilistic model of unicorn existence!

Bayes' theorem is central to Bayesian statistics. As we will see in Chapter 2, using tools such as PyMC frees us of the need to explicitly write Bayes' theorem every time we build a Bayesian model. Nevertheless, it is important to know the name of its parts because we will constantly refer to them and it is important to understand what each part means because this will help us to conceptualize models. So, let me rewrite Bayes' theorem now with labels:

$$\overbrace{p(\theta \mid Y)}^{\text{posterior}} = \frac{\overbrace{p(Y \mid \theta)}^{\text{likelihood}} \overbrace{p(\theta)}^{\text{prior}}}{\underbrace{p(Y)}_{\text{marginal likelihood}}}$$

The **prior distribution** should reflect what we know about the value of the parameter θ before seeing the data, Y. If we know nothing, like Jon Snow, we could use flat priors that do not convey too much information. In general, we can do better than flat priors, as we will learn in this book. The use of priors is why some people still talk about Bayesian statistics as subjective, even when priors are just another assumption that we made when modeling and hence are just as subjective (or objective) as any other assumption, such as likelihoods.

The **likelihood** is how we will introduce data in our analysis. It is an expression of the plausibility of the data given the parameters. In some texts, you will find people call this term sampling model, statistical model, or just model. We will stick to the name likelihood and we will model the combination of priors and likelihood.

The **posterior distribution** is the result of the Bayesian analysis and reflects all that we know about a problem (given our data and model). The posterior is a probability distribution for the parameters in our model and not a single value. This distribution is a balance between the prior and the likelihood. There is a well-known joke: a Bayesian is one who, vaguely expecting a horse, and catching a glimpse of a donkey, strongly believes they have seen a mule. One excellent way to kill the mood after hearing this joke is to explain that if the likelihood and priors are both vague, you will get a posterior reflecting vague beliefs about seeing a mule rather than strong ones. Anyway, I like the joke, and I like how it captures the idea of a posterior being somehow a compromise between prior and likelihood. Conceptually, we can think of the posterior as the updated prior in light of (new) data. In theory, the posterior from one analysis can be used as the prior for a new analysis (in practice, life can be harder). This makes Bayesian analysis particularly suitable for analyzing data that becomes available in sequential order. One example could be an early warning system for natural disasters that processes online data coming from meteorological stations and satellites. For more details, read about online machine-learning methods.

The last term is the **marginal likelihood**, sometimes referred to as the **evidence**. Formally, the marginal likelihood is the probability of observing the data averaged over all the possible values the parameters can take (as prescribed by the prior). We can write this as $\int_\Theta p(Y \mid \theta)p(\theta)d\theta$. We will not really care about the marginal likelihood until Chapter 5. But for the moment, we can think of it as a normalization factor that ensures the posterior is a proper pmf or pdf. If we ignore the marginal likelihood, we can write Bayes' theorem as a proportionality, which is also a common way to write Bayes' theorem:

$$p(\theta \mid Y) \propto p(Y \mid \theta)p(\theta)$$

Understanding the exact role of each term in Bayes' theorem will take some time and practice, and it will require a few examples, but that's what the rest of this book is for.

Interpreting probabilities

Probabilities can be interpreted in various useful ways. For instance, we can think that $P(A) = 0.125$ means that if we repeat the survey many times, we would expect all three individuals to answer "yes" about 12.5% of the time. We are interpreting probabilities as the outcome of long-run experiments. This is a very common and useful interpretation. It not only can help us think about probabilities but can also provide an empirical method to estimate probabilities. Do we want to know the probability of a car tire exploding if filled with air beyond the manufacturer's recommendation? Just inflate 120 tires or so, and you may get a good approximation. This is usually called the frequentist interpretation.

Another interpretation of probability, usually called subjective or Bayesian interpretation, states that probabilities can be interpreted as measures of an individual's uncertainty about events. In this interpretation, probabilities are about our state of knowledge of the world and are not necessarily based on repeated trials. Under this definition of probability, it is valid and natural to ask about the probability of life on Mars, the probability of the mass of an electron being 9.1×10^{-31} kg, or the probability that the 9th of July of 1816 was a sunny day in Buenos Aires. All these are one-time events. We cannot re-create 1 million universes, each with one Mars, and check how many of them develop life. Of course, we can do this as a mental experiment, so long-term frequencies can still be a valid mental scaffold.

Sometimes the Bayesian interpretation of probabilities is described in terms of personal beliefs; I don't like that. I think it can lead to unnecessary confusion as beliefs are generally associated with the notion of faith or unsupported claims. This association can easily lead people to think that Bayesian probabilities, and by extension Bayesian statistics, is less objective or less scientific than alternatives. I think it also helps to generate confusion about the role of prior knowledge in statistics and makes people think that being objective or rational means not using prior information.

Bayesian methods are as subjective (or objective) as any other well-established scientific method we have. Let me explain myself with an example: life on Mars exists or does not exist; the outcome is binary, a yes-no question. But given that we are not sure about that fact, a sensible course of action is trying to find out how likely life on Mars is. To answer this question any honest and scientific-minded person will use all the relevant geophysical data about Mars, all the relevant biochemical knowledge about necessary conditions for life, and so on. The response will be necessarily about our epistemic state of knowledge, and others could disagree and even get different probabilities. But at least, in principle, they all will be able to provide arguments in favor of their data, their methods, their modeling decisions, and so on. A scientific and rational debate about life on Mars does not admit *arguments* such as "an angel told me about tiny green creatures." Bayesian statistics, however, is just a procedure to make scientific statements using probabilities as building blocks.

Probabilities, uncertainty, and logic

Probabilities can help us to quantify uncertainty. If we do not have information about a problem, it is reasonable to state that every possible event is equally likely. This is equivalent to assigning the same probability to every possible event. In the absence of information, our uncertainty is maximum, and I am not saying this colloquially; this is something we can compute using probabilities. If we know instead that some events are more likely, then this can be formally represented by assigning a higher probability to those events and less to the others. Notice that when we talk about events in stats-speak, we are not restricting ourselves to things that can happen, such as an asteroid crashing into Earth or my auntie's 60th birthday party. An event is just any of the possible values (or a subset of values) a variable can take, such as the event that you are older than 30, the price of a Sachertorte, or the number of bikes that will be sold next year around the world.

The concept of probability is also related to the subject of logic. Under classical logic, we can only have statements that take the values of true or false. Under the Bayesian definition of probability, certainty is just a special case: a true statement has a probability of 1, and a false statement has a probability of 0. We would assign a probability of 1 to the statement that there is Martian life only after having conclusive data indicating something is growing, reproducing, and doing other activities we associate with living organisms.

Notice, however, that assigning a probability of 0 is harder because we could always think that there is some Martian spot that is unexplored, or that we have made mistakes with some experiments, or there are several other reasons that could lead us to falsely believe life is absent on Mars even if it is not. This is related to Cromwell's rule, which states that we should reserve the probabilities of 0 or 1 to logically true or false statements. Interestingly enough, it can be shown that if we want to extend the logic to include uncertainty, we must use probabilities and probability theory.

As we will soon see, Bayes' theorem is just a logical consequence of the rules of probability. Thus, we can think of Bayesian statistics as an extension of logic that is useful whenever we are dealing with uncertainty. Thus, one way to justify using the Bayesian method is to recognize that uncertainty is commonplace. We generally have to deal with incomplete and or noisy data, we are intrinsically limited by our evolution-sculpted primate brain, and so on.

> **The Bayesian Ethos**
>
> Probabilities are used to measure the uncertainty we have about parameters, and Bayes' theorem is a mechanism to correctly update those probabilities in light of new data, hopefully reducing our uncertainty.

Single-parameter inference

Now that we know what Bayesian statistics is, let's learn how to do Bayesian statistics with a simple example. We are going to begin inferring a single, unknown parameter.

The coin-flipping problem

The coin-flipping problem, or the BetaBinomial model if you want to sound fancy at parties, is a classical problem in statistics and goes like this: we toss a coin several times and record how many heads and tails we get. Based on this data, we try to answer questions such as, is the coin fair? Or, more generally, how biased is the coin? While this problem may sound dull, we should not underestimate it.

The coin-flipping problem is a great example to learn the basics of Bayesian statistics because it is a simple model that we can solve and compute with ease. Besides, many real problems consist of binary, mutually exclusive outcomes such as 0 or 1, positive or negative, odds or evens, spam or ham, hotdog or not a hotdog, cat or dog, safe or unsafe, and healthy or unhealthy. Thus, even when we are talking about coins, this model applies to any of those problems. To estimate the bias of a coin, and in general, to answer any questions in a Bayesian setting, we will need data and a probabilistic model. For this example, we will assume that we have already tossed a coin several times and we have a record of the number of observed heads, so the data-gathering part is already done. Getting the model will take a little bit more effort. Since this is our first model, we will explicitly write Bayes' theorem and do all the necessary math (don't be afraid, I promise it will be painless) and we will proceed very slowly. From 2 onward, we will use PyMC and our computer to do the math for us.

The first thing we will do is generalize the concept of bias. We will say that a coin with a bias of 1 will always land heads, one with a bias of 0 will always land tails, and one with a bias of 0.5 will land heads half of the time and tails half of the time. To represent the bias, we will use the parameter θ, and to represent the total number of heads for several tosses, we will use the variable Y. According to Bayes' theorem, we have to specify the prior, $p(\theta)$, and likelihood, $p(Y \mid \theta)$, we will use. Let's start with the likelihood.

Choosing the likelihood

Let's assume that only two outcomes are possible—heads or tails—and let's also assume that a coin toss does not affect other tosses, that is, we are assuming coin tosses are independent of each other. We will further assume all coin tosses come from the same distribution. Thus the random variable coin toss is an example of an **independent and identically distributed (iid)** variable. I hope you agree that these are very reasonable assumptions to make for our problem. Given these assumptions, a good candidate for the likelihood is the Binomial distribution:

$$p(Y \mid \theta) = \underbrace{\frac{N!}{y!(N-y)!}}_{\text{normalizing constant}} \theta^y (1-\theta)^{N-y}$$

This is a discrete distribution returning the probability of getting y heads (or, in general, successes) out of N coin tosses (or, in general, trials or experiments) given a fixed value of θ.

Figure 1.10 shows nine distributions from the Binomial family; each subplot has its legend indicating the values of the parameters. Notice that for this plot, I did not omit the values on the y-axis. I did this so you can check for yourself that if you sum the height of all bars, you will get 1, that is, for discrete distributions, the height of the bars represents actual probabilities.

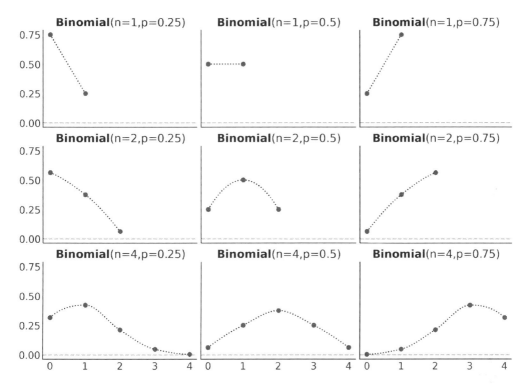

Figure 1.10: Nine members of the Binomial family

The Binomial distribution is a reasonable choice for the likelihood. We can see that θ indicates how likely it is to obtain a head when tossing a coin. This is easier to see when $N = 1$ but is valid for any value of N, just compare the value of θ with the height of the bar for $y = 1$ (heads).

Choosing the prior

As a prior, we will use a Beta distribution, which is a very common distribution in Bayesian statistics and looks as follows:

$$p(\theta) = \underbrace{\frac{\Gamma(\alpha + \beta)}{\Gamma(\alpha) + \Gamma(\beta)}}_{\text{normalizing constant}} \theta^{\alpha-1}(1-\theta)^{\beta-1}$$

If we look carefully, we will see that the Beta distribution looks similar to the Binomial except for the first term. Γ is the Greek uppercase gamma letter, which represents the gamma function, but that's not really important. What is relevant for us is that the first term is a normalizing constant that ensures the distribution integrates to 1. We can see from the preceding formula that the Beta distribution has two parameters, α and β. Figure 1.11 shows nine members of the Beta family.

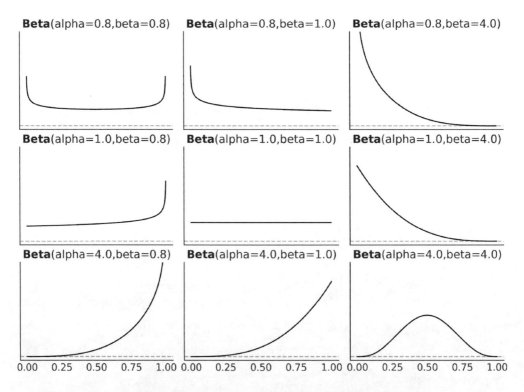

Figure 1.11: Nine members of the Beta family

I like the Beta distribution and all the shapes we can get from it, but why are we using it for our model? There are many reasons to use a Beta distribution for this and other problems.

One of them is that the Beta distribution is restricted to be between 0 and 1, in the same way our θ parameter is. In general, we use the Beta distribution when we want to model the proportions of a Binomial variable. Another reason is its versatility. As we can see in Figure 1.11, the distribution adopts several shapes (all restricted to the [0, 1] interval), including a Uniform distribution, Gaussian-like distributions, and U-like distributions.

As a third reason, the Beta distribution is the conjugate prior to the Binomial distribution (which we are using as the likelihood). A conjugate prior of a likelihood is a prior that, when used in combination with a given likelihood, returns a posterior with the same functional form as the prior. Untwisting the tongue, every time we use a Beta distribution as the prior and a Binomial distribution as the likelihood, we will get a Beta as the posterior distribution. There are other pairs of conjugate priors; for example, the Normal distribution is the conjugate prior to itself. For many years, Bayesian analysis was restricted to the use of conjugate priors. Conjugacy ensures mathematical tractability of the posterior, which is important given that a common problem in Bayesian statistics ends up with a posterior we cannot solve analytically. This was a deal breaker before the development of suitable computational methods to solve probabilistic methods. From Chapter 2 onwards, we will learn how to use modern computational methods to solve Bayesian problems, whether we choose conjugate priors or not.

Getting the posterior

Let's remember that Bayes' theorem says the posterior is proportional to the likelihood times the prior. So, for our problem, we have to multiply the Binomial and the Beta distributions:

$$p(\theta \mid Y) = \overbrace{\frac{N!}{y!(N-y)!}\theta^y(1-\theta)^{N-y}}^{\text{likelihood}} \; \overbrace{\frac{\Gamma(\alpha+\beta)}{\Gamma(\alpha)+\Gamma(\beta)}\theta^{\alpha-1}(1-\theta)^{\beta-1}}^{\text{prior}}$$

We can simplify this expression by dropping all the terms that do not depend on θ and our results will still be valid. Accordingly, we can write:

$$p(\theta \mid Y) \propto \overbrace{\theta^y(1-\theta)^{N-y}}^{\text{likelihood}} \overbrace{\theta^{\alpha-1}(1-\theta)^{\beta-1}}^{\text{prior}}$$

Reordering it, and noticing this has the form of a Beta distribution, we get:

$$p(\theta \mid Y) = \text{Beta}\left(\alpha_{\text{prior}} + y, \beta_{\text{prior}+N-y}\right)$$

Based on this analytical expression, we can compute the posterior. Figure 1.12 shows the results for 3 priors and different numbers of trials. The following block of code shows the gist to generate Figure 1.12 (omitting the code necessary for plotting).

Code 1.6:

```
1  n_trials = [0, 1, 2, 3, 4, 8, 16, 32, 50, 150]
2  n_heads = [0, 1, 1, 1, 1, 4, 6, 9, 13, 48]
3  beta_params = [(1, 1), (20, 20), (1, 4)]
4
5  x = np.linspace(0, 1, 2000)
6  for idx, N in enumerate(n_trials):
7      y = n_heads[idx]
8      for (α_prior, β_prior) in beta_params:
9          posterior = pz.Beta(α_prior + y, β_prior + N - y).pdf(x)
```

On the first subplot of Figure 1.12, we have zero trials, thus the three curves represent our priors:

- The Uniform prior (black): This represents all the possible values for the bias being equally probable a priori.
- The Gaussian-like prior (dark gray): This is centered and concentrated around 0.5, so this prior is compatible with information indicating that the coin has more or less about the same chance of landing heads or tails. We could also say this prior is compatible with the knowledge that coins are fair.

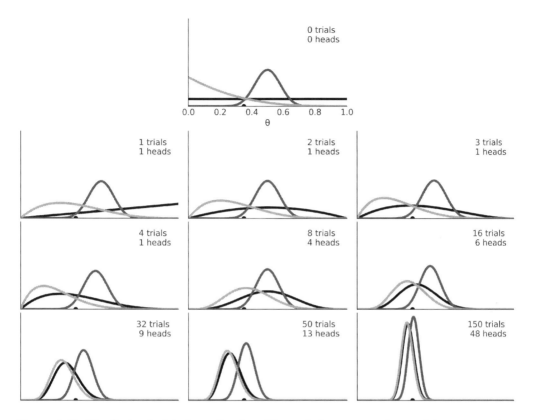

Figure 1.12: The first subplot shows 3 priors. The rest show successive updates as we get new data

- The skewed prior (light gray): This puts most of the weight on a tail-biased outcome.

The rest of the subplots show posterior distributions for successive trials. The number of trials (or coin tosses) and the number of heads are indicated in each subplot's legend. There is also a black dot at 0.35 representing the true value for θ. Of course, in real problems, we do not know this value, and it is here just for pedagogical reasons. Figure 1.12, can teach us a lot about Bayesian analysis, so grab your coffee, tea, or favorite drink, and let's take a moment to understand it:

- The result of a Bayesian analysis is a posterior distribution – not a single value but a distribution of plausible values given the data and our model.
- The most probable value is given by the mode of the posterior (the peak of the

distribution).

- The spread of the posterior is proportional to the uncertainty about the value of a parameter; the more spread out the distribution, the less certain we are.

- Intuitively, we are more confident in a result when we have observed more data supporting that result. Thus, even when numerically $\frac{1}{2} = \frac{4}{8} = 0.5$, seeing four heads out of eight trials gives us more confidence that the bias is 0.5 than observing one head out of two trials. This intuition is reflected in the posterior, as you can check for yourself if you pay attention to the (black) posterior in the third and sixth subplots; while the mode is the same, the spread (uncertainty) is larger in the third subplot than in the sixth subplot.

- Given a sufficiently large amount of data, two or more Bayesian models with different priors will tend to converge to the same result. In the limit of infinite data, no matter which prior we use, all of them will provide the same posterior.

- Remember that infinite is a limit and not a number, so from a practical point of view, we could get practically equivalent posteriors for a finite and relatively small number of data points.

- How fast posteriors converge to the same distribution depends on the data and the model. We can see that the posteriors arising from the black prior (Uniform) and gray prior (biased towards tails) converge faster to almost the same distribution, while it takes longer for the dark gray posterior (the one arising from the concentrated prior). Even after 150 trials, it is somehow easy to recognize the dark gray posterior as a different distribution from the two others.

- Something not obvious from the figure is that we will get the same result if we update the posterior sequentially as if we do it all at once. We can compute the posterior 150 times, each time adding one more observation and using the obtained posterior as the new prior, or we can just compute one posterior for the 150 tosses at once. The result will be exactly the same. This feature not only makes perfect sense, but it also leads to a natural way of updating our estimations when we get new data, a situation common in many data-analysis problems.

The influence of the prior

From the preceding example, it is clear that priors can influence inferences. That's fine – priors are supposed to do that. Maybe it would be better to not have priors at all. That would make modeling easier, right? Well, not necessarily. If you are not setting the prior, someone else will be doing it for you. Sometimes this is fine – *default priors* can be useful and have their place – but sometimes it is better to have more control. Let me explain.

We can think that every (statistical) model, Bayesian or not, has some kind of prior, even if the prior is not set explicitly. For instance, many procedures typically used in frequentist statistics can be seen as special cases of a Bayesian model under certain conditions, such as flat priors. One common way to estimate parameters is known as maximum likelihood; this method avoids setting a prior and works just by finding the single value maximizing the likelihood. This value is usually notated by adding a little hat on top of the name of the parameter we are estimating, such as $\hat{\theta}$. Contrary to the posterior estimate, which is a distribution, $\hat{\theta}$ is a point estimate, a number. For the coin-flipping problem, we can compute it analytically:

$$\hat{\theta} = \frac{y}{N}$$

If you go back to Figure 1.12, you will be able to check for yourself that the mode of the black posterior (the one corresponding to the uniform/flat prior) agrees with the values of $\hat{\theta}$, computed for each subplot. This is not a coincidence; it is a consequence of the fact that setting a Uniform prior and then taking the mode of the posterior is equivalent to maximum likelihood.

We cannot avoid priors, but if we include them in our analysis, we can get some potential benefits. The most direct benefit is that we get a posterior distribution, which is a distribution of plausible values and not only the most probable ones. Having a distribution can be more informative than a single-point estimate, as we saw the width of the distribution is related to the uncertainty we have for the estimate. Another benefit is that computing the posteriors means to average over the prior. This can lead to models that are more difficult to overfit and more robust predictions [Wilson and Izmailov, 2022].

Priors can bring us other benefits. Starting in the next chapter, we are going to use numerical methods to get posteriors. These methods feel like magic, until they don't. The folk theorem of statistical computing states, "When you have computational problems, often there's a problem with your model" [Gelman, 2008]. Sometimes a wise choice of prior can make inference easier or faster. It is important to remark that we are not advocating for setting priors specifically to make inference faster, but it is often the case that by thinking about priors, we can get faster models.

One advantage of priors, one that is sometimes overlooked, is that having to think about priors can *force us* to think a little bit deeper about the problem we are trying to solve and the data we have. Sometimes the modeling process leads to a better understanding by itself irrespective of how well we end and fit the data or make predictions. By being explicit about priors, we get more transparent models, meaning they're easier to criticize, debug (in a broad sense of the word), explain to others, and hopefully improve.

How to choose priors

Newcomers to Bayesian analysis (as well as detractors of this paradigm) are generally a little nervous about how to choose priors. Usually, they are afraid that the prior distribution will not let the data speak for itself! That's OK, but we have to remember that data does not speak; at best, data murmurs. We can only make sense of data in the context of our models, including mathematical and mental models. There are plenty of examples in the history of science where the same data led people to think differently about the same topics, and this can happen even if you base your opinions on formal models.

Some people like the idea of using non-informative priors (also known as flat, vague, or diffuse priors). These priors have the least possible amount of impact on the analysis. While it is possible to use them for some problems deriving truly non-informative priors can be hard or just impossible. Additionally, we generally can do better as we usually have some prior information.

Throughout this book, we will follow the recommendations of Gelman, McElreath, Kruschke, and many others, and we will prefer weakly informative priors. For many problems, we often know something about the values a parameter can take. We may know that a parameter is restricted to being positive, or we may know the approximate range it can take, or whether we expect the value to be close to zero or below/above some value. In such cases, we can use priors to put some weak information in our models without being afraid of being too pushy. Because these priors work to keep the posterior distribution within certain reasonable bounds, they are also known as regularizing priors.

Informative priors are very strong priors that convey a lot of information. Using them is also a valid option. Depending on your problem, it could be easy or not to find good-quality information from your domain knowledge and turn it into priors. I used to work on structural bioinformatics. In this field, people have been using, in Bayesian and non-Bayesian ways, all the prior information they could get to study and predict the structure of proteins. This is reasonable because we have been collecting data from thousands of carefully designed experiments for decades and hence we have a great amount of trustworthy prior information at our disposal. Not using it would be absurd! There is nothing "objective" or "scientific" about throwing away valuable information. If you have reliable prior information, you should use it. Imagine if every time an automotive engineer had to design a new car, they had to start from scratch and reinvent the combustion engine, the wheel, and for that matter, the whole concept of a car.

PreliZ is a very new Python library for prior elicitation [Mikkola et al., 2023, Icazatti et al., 2023]. Its mission is to help you to elicit, represent, and visualize your prior knowledge. For instance, we can ask PreliZ to compute the parameters of a distribution satisfying a set of constraints. Let's say we want to find the Beta distribution with 90% of the mass between 0.1 and 0.7, then we can write:

Code 1.7:

```
1 dist = pz.Beta()
2 pz.maxent(dist, 0.1, 0.7, 0.9)
```

The result is a Beta distribution with parameters $\alpha = 2.5$ and $\beta = 3.6$ (rounded to the first decimal point). The pz.maxent function computes the **maximum entropy** distribution given the constraints we specified. Why maximum entropy distribution? Because that is equivalent to computing the least informative distribution under those constraints. By default, PreliZ will plot the distribution as shown here:

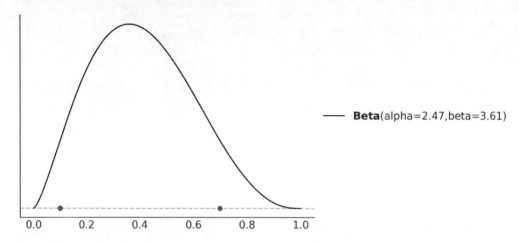

Figure 1.13: Maximum entropy Beta distribution with 90% of the mass between 0.1 and 0.7

As eliciting prior has many facets, PreliZ offers many other ways to elicit priors. If you are interested in learning more about PreliZ, you can check the documentation at `https://preliz.readthedocs.io`.

Building models is an iterative process; sometimes the iteration takes a few minutes, and sometimes it could take years. Reproducibility matters and transparent assumptions in a model contribute to it. We are free to use more than one prior (or likelihood) for a given analysis if we are not sure about any special one; exploring the effect of different priors can also bring valuable information to the table. Part of the modeling process is about questioning assumptions, and priors (and likelihoods) are just that. Different assumptions will lead to different models and probably different results. By using data and our domain knowledge of the problem, we will be able to compare models and, if necessary, decide on a winner. Chapter 5 will be devoted to this issue. Since priors have a central role in

Bayesian statistics, we will keep discussing them as we face new problems. So if you have doubts and feel a little bit confused about this discussion, just keep calm and don't worry, people have been confused for decades and the discussion is still going on.

Communicating a Bayesian analysis

Creating reports and communicating results is central to the practice of statistics and data science. In this section, we will briefly discuss some of the peculiarities of this task when working with Bayesian models. In future chapters, we will keep looking at examples of this important matter.

Model notation and visualization

If you want to communicate the results of an analysis, you should also communicate the model you used. A common notation to succinctly represent probabilistic models is:

$$\theta \sim \text{Beta}(\alpha, \beta)$$
$$y \sim \text{Bin}(n = 1, p = \theta)$$

This is just the model we use for the coin-flip example. As you may remember, the $\sim$ symbol indicates that the variable on the left of it is a random variable distributed according to the distribution on the right. In many contexts, this symbol is used to indicate that a variable takes *approximately* some value, but when talking about probabilistic models, we will read this symbol out loud, saying *is distributed as*. Thus, we can say θ is distributed as a Beta with parameters α and β, and y is distributed as a Binomial with parameters $n = 1$ and $p = \theta$. The very same model can be represented graphically using Kruschke diagrams as in Figure 1.14.

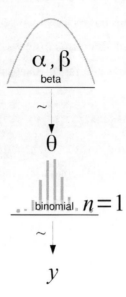

Figure 1.14: A Kruschke diagram of a BetaBinomial model

On the first level, we have the prior that generates the values for θ, then the likelihood, and on the last line, the data, y. Arrows indicate the relationship between variables and the symbol ~ indicates the stochastic nature of the variables. All Kruschke diagrams in the book were made using the templates provided by Rasmus Bååth (`http://www.sumsar.net/blog/2013/10/diy-kruschke-style-diagrams/`).

Summarizing the posterior

The result of a Bayesian analysis is a posterior distribution, and all the information about the parameters (given a model and dataset) is contained in the posterior distribution. Thus, by summarizing the posterior, we are summarizing the logical consequences of a model and data. A common practice is to report, for each parameter, the mean (or mode or median) to have an idea of the location of the distribution and some measure of dispersion, such as the standard deviation, to have an idea of uncertainty in our estimates. The standard deviation works well for Normal-like distributions but can be misleading for other types of distributions, such as skewed ones.

A commonly used device to summarize the spread of a posterior distribution is to use a **Highest-Density Interval (HDI)**. An HDI is the shortest interval containing a given portion of the probability density. If we say that the 95% HDI for some analysis is [2, 5], we mean that according to our data and model, the parameter in question is between 2 and 5 with a probability of 0.95. There is nothing special about choosing 95%, 50%, or any other value. We are free to choose the 82% HDI interval if we like. Ideally, justifications should be context-dependent and not automatic, but it is okay to settle on some common value like 95%. As a friendly reminder of the arbitrary nature of this choice, the ArviZ default is 94%.

ArviZ is a Python package for exploratory analysis of Bayesian models, and it has many functions to help us summarize the posterior. One of those functions is `az.plot_posterior`, which we can use to generate a plot with the mean and HDI of θ. The distribution does not need to be a posterior distribution; any distribution will work. Figure 1.15 shows the result for a random sample from a Beta distribution:

Code 1.8:

```
1  np.random.seed(1)
2  az.plot_posterior({'θ':pz.Beta(4, 12).rvs(1000)})
```

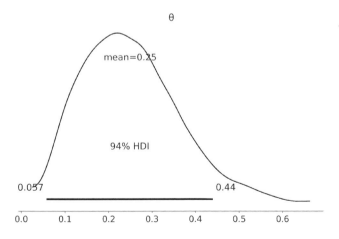

Figure 1.15: A KDE of a sample from a Beta distribution with its mean and 94% HDI

> **Not Confidence Intervals**
>
> If you are familiar with the frequentist paradigm, please note that HDIs are not the same as confidence intervals. In the frequentist framework, parameters are fixed by design; a frequentist confidence interval either contains or does not contain the true value of a parameter. In the Bayesian framework, parameters are random variables, and thus we can talk about the probability of a parameter having specific values or being inside some interval. The unintuitive nature of confident intervals makes them easily misinterpreted and people often talk about frequentist confidence intervals as if they were Bayesian credible intervals.

Summary

We began our Bayesian journey with a very brief discussion of statistical modeling, probabilities, conditional probabilities, random variables, probability distributions and Bayes' theorem. We then used the coin-flipping problem as an excuse to introduce basic aspects of Bayesian modeling and data analysis. We used this classic toy example to convey some of the most important ideas of Bayesian statistics, such as using probability distributions to build models and represent uncertainties. We tried to demystify the use of priors and put them on an equal footing with other elements that are part of the modeling process, such as the likelihood, or even more meta-questions, such as why we are trying to solve a particular problem in the first place.

We ended the chapter by discussing the interpretation and communication of the results of a Bayesian analysis. We assume there is a true distribution that in general is unknown (and in principle also unknowable), from which we get a finite sample, either by doing an experiment, a survey, an observation, or a simulation. To learn something from the true distribution, given that we have only observed a sample, we build a probabilistic model. A probabilistic model has two basic ingredients: a prior and a likelihood. Using the model and the sample, we perform Bayesian inference and obtain a posterior distribution; this distribution encapsulates all the information about a problem, given our model and data.

From a Bayesian perspective, the posterior distribution is the main object of interest and everything else is derived from it, including predictions in the form of a posterior predictive distribution. As the posterior distribution (and any other derived quantity from it) is a consequence of the model and data, the usefulness of Bayesian inferences is restricted by the quality of models and data. Finally, we briefly summarized the main aspects of doing Bayesian data analysis. Throughout the rest of this book, we will revisit these ideas to absorb them and use them as the scaffold of more advanced concepts.

In the next chapter, we will introduce PyMC, which is a Python library for Bayesian modeling and probabilistic machine learning and will use more features from ArviZ, a Python library for the exploratory analysis of Bayesian models, and PreliZ a Python library for prior elicitation.

Exercises

We do not know whether the brain works in a Bayesian way, in an approximately Bayesian fashion, or maybe some evolutionary (more or less) optimized heuristics. Nevertheless, we know that we learn by exposing ourselves to data, examples, and exercises... Well you may say that humans never learn, given our record as a species on subjects such as wars or economic systems that prioritize profit and not people's well-being... Anyway, I recommend you do the proposed exercises at the end of each chapter:

1. Suppose you have a jar with 4 jelly beans: 2 are strawberry-flavored, 1 is blueberry-flavored, and 1 is cinnamon-flavored. You draw one jelly bean at random from the jar.

   (a) What is the sample space for this experiment?

   (b) We define event *A* as *the jelly bean drawn is strawberry-flavored* and event *B* as *The jelly bean drawn is not cinnamon-flavored.* What are the probabilities of events *A* and *B*?

   (c) Are events *A* and *B* mutually exclusive? Why or why not?

2. Previously, we defined a Python function P to compute the probability of an event

using the naive definition of probability. Generalize that function to compute the probability of events when they are not all equally likely. Use this new function to compute the probability of events *A* and *B* from the previous exercise. Hint: you can pass a third argument with the probability of each event.

3. Use PreliZ to explore different parameters for the BetaBinomial and Gaussian distributions. Use the methods `plot_pdf`, `plot_cdf`, and `plot_interactive`.

4. We discussed the probability mass/density functions and the cumulative density function. But there are other ways to represent functions like the percentile point function ppf. Using the `plot_ppf` method of PreliZ, plot the percentile point function for the BetaBinomial and Gaussian distributions. Can you explain how the ppf is related to the cdf and pmf/pdf?

5. From the following expressions, which one corresponds to: the probability of being sunny given that it is 9th of July of 1816?

   (a) $p(\text{sunny})$

   (b) $p(\text{sunny}|\text{July})$

   (c) $p(\text{sunny}|9 \text{ of July of } 1816)$

   (d) $p(9^{\text{th}} \text{ of July of } 1816|\text{sunny})$

   (e) $\dfrac{p(\text{sunny}, 9^{\text{th}} \text{ of July of } 1816)}{p(9^{\text{th}} \text{ of July of } 1816)}$

6. We showed that the probability of choosing a human at random and picking the Pope is not the same as the probability of the Pope being human. In the animated series Futurama, the (Space) Pope is a reptile. How does this change your previous calculations?

7. Following the example in Figure 1.9, use PreliZ to compute the moments for the SkewNormal distribution for a different combination of parameters. Generate random samples of different sizes, like 10, 100, and 1,000, and see if you can recover the values of the first two moments (mean and variance) from the samples. What do you observe?

8. Repeat the previous exercise for the Student's t-distribution. Try values of v like 2, 3, 500. What do you observe?

9. In the following definition of a probabilistic model, identify the prior and the likelihood:

$$Y \sim \text{Normal}(\mu, \sigma)$$

$$\mu \sim \text{Normal}(0, 2)$$

$$\sigma \sim \text{HalfNormal}(0.75)$$

10. In the previous model, how many parameters will the posterior have? Compare it with the model for the coin-flipping problem.

11. Write Bayes' theorem for the model in exercise 9.

12. Let's suppose that we have two coins; when we toss the first coin, half of the time it lands on tails and half of the time on heads. The other coin is a loaded coin that always lands on heads. If we take one of the coins at random and get a head, what is the probability that this coin is the unfair one?

13. Try re-plotting Figure 1.12 using other priors (beta_params) and other data (trials and data).

14. Read about the Cromwell rule on Wikipedia: https://en.wikipedia.org/wiki/Cromwell%27s_rule.

15. Read about probabilities and the Dutch book on Wikipedia: https://en.wikipedia.org/wiki/Dutch_book.

Join our community Discord space

Join our Discord community to meet like-minded people and learn alongside more than 5000 members at:

https://packt.link/bayesian

2

Programming Probabilistically

> Our golems rarely have a physical form, but they too are often made of clay
> living in silicon as computer code.
> – Richard McElreath

Now that we have a very basic understanding of probability theory and Bayesian statistics, we are going to learn how to build probabilistic models using computational tools. Specifically, we are going to learn about probabilistic programming with PyMC [Abril-Pla et al., 2023]. The basic idea is that we use code to specify statistical models and then PyMC will solve those models for us. We will not need to write Bayes' theorem in explicit form. This is a good strategy for two reasons. First, many models do not lead to an analytic closed form, and thus we can only solve those models using numerical techniques. Second, modern Bayesian statistics is mainly done by writing code. We will be able to see that probabilistic programming offers an effective way to build and solve complex models and allows us to focus more on model design, evaluation, and interpretation, and less on mathematical or computational details.

This chapter will cover the following topics:

- Probabilistic programming
- A PyMC primer
- The coin-flipping problem revisited
- Summarizing the posterior
- The Gaussian and Student t models
- Comparing groups and the effect size

Probabilistic programming

Bayesian statistics is conceptually very simple. We have the *knowns* and the *unknowns*, and we use Bayes' theorem to condition the latter on the former. If we are lucky, this process will reduce the uncertainty about the *unknowns*. Generally, we refer to the *knowns* as **data** and treat it like constants, and the *unknowns* as **parameters** and treat them as *random variables*.

Although conceptually simple, fully probabilistic models often lead to analytically intractable expressions. For many years, this was a real problem and one of the main issues that hindered the adoption of Bayesian methods beyond some niche applications. The arrival of the computational era and the development of numerical methods that, at least in principle, can be used to solve any inference problem, have dramatically transformed the Bayesian data analysis practice. We can think of these numerical methods as *universal inference engines*. The possibility of automating the inference process has led to the development of **probabilistic programming languages** (**PPLs**), which allows a clear separation between model creation and inference. In the PPL framework, users specify a full probabilistic model by writing a few lines of code, and then inference follows automatically.

It is expected that probabilistic programming will have a major impact on data science and other disciplines by enabling practitioners to build complex probabilistic models in a less time-consuming and less error-prone way. I think one good analogy for the impact that programming languages can have on scientific computing is the introduction of the Fortran programming language more than six decades ago. While nowadays Fortran has lost its shine, at one time, it was considered revolutionary. For the first time, scientists moved away from computational details and began focusing on building numerical methods, models, and simulations more naturally. It is interesting to see that some folks are working on making Fortran cool again, if you are interested you can check their work at `https://fortran-lang.org/en`.

Flipping coins the PyMC way

Let's revisit the coin-flipping problem from Chapter 1, but this time using PyMC. We will use the same synthetic data we used in that chapter. Since we are generating the data, we know the true value of θ, called `theta_real`, in the following block of code. Of course, for a real dataset, we will not have this knowledge:

Code 2.1:

```
1  np.random.seed(123)
2
3  trials = 4
4  theta_real = 0.35 # unknown value in a real experiment
5  data = pz.Binomial(n=1, p=theta_real).rvs(trials)
```

Now that we have the data, we need to specify the model. Remember that this is done by specifying the likelihood and the prior. For the likelihood, we will use the Binomial distribution with parameters $n = 1$, $p = \theta$, and for the prior, a Beta distribution with the parameters $\alpha = \beta = 1$. A Beta distribution with such parameters is equivalent to a Uniform distribution on the interval $[0, 1]$. Using mathematical notation we can write the model as:

$$\theta \sim \text{Beta}(\alpha = 1, \beta = 1)$$

$$Y \sim \text{Binomial}(n = 1, p = \theta)$$

This statistical model has an almost one-to-one translation to PyMC:

Code 2.2:

```
1  with pm.Model() as our_first_model:
2      θ = pm.Beta('θ', alpha=1., beta=1.)
3      y = pm.Bernoulli('y', p=θ, observed=data)
4      idata = pm.sample(1000)
```

The first line of the code creates a container for our model. Everything inside the `with` block will be automatically added to `our_first_model`. You can think of this as syntactic sugar to ease model specification as we do not need to manually assign variables to the model. The second line specifies the prior. As you can see, the syntax follows the mathematical notation closely. The third line specifies the likelihood; the syntax is almost the same as for the prior, except that we pass the data using the `observed` argument. The observed values can be passed as a Python list, a tuple, a NumPy array, or a pandas DataFrame. With that, we are finished with the model specification! Pretty neat, right?

We still have one more line of code to explain. The last line is where the magic happens. Behind this innocent line, PyMC has hundreds of *oompa loompas* singing and baking a delicious Bayesian inference just for you! Well, not exactly, but PyMC is automating a lot of tasks. For the time being, we are going to treat that line as a black box that will give us the correct result. What is important to understand is that under the hood we will be using numerical methods to compute the posterior distribution. In principle, these numerical methods are capable of solving any model we can write. The cost we pay for this generality is that the solution is going to take the form of samples from the posterior. Later, we will be able to corroborate that these samples come from a Beta distribution, as we learned from the previous chapter. Because the numerical methods are stochastic, the samples will vary every time we run them. However, if the inference process works as expected, the samples will be representative of the posterior distribution and thus we will obtain the same conclusion from any of those samples. The details of what happens under the hood and how to check if the samples are indeed trustworthy will be explained in Chapter 10.

One more thing: the `idata` variable is an `InferenceData` object, which is a container for all the data generated by PyMC. We will learn more about this later in this chapter.

OK, so on the last line, we are asking for 1,000 samples from the posterior. If you run the code, you will get a message like this:

```
Auto-assigning NUTS sampler...
Initializing NUTS using jitter+adapt_diag...
Multiprocess sampling (4 chains in 4 jobs)
NUTS: [θ]
Sampling 4 chains for 1_000 tune and 1_000 draw iterations
(4_000 + 4_000 draws total) took 1 second.
```

The first and second lines tell us that PyMC has automatically assigned the NUTS sampler (one inference engine that works very well for continuous variables), and has used a method to initialize that sampler (these methods need some initial guess of where to start sampling). The third line says that PyMC will run four chains in parallel, thus we will get four independent samples from the posterior. As PyMC attempts to parallelize these chains across the available processors in your machine, we will get the four for the price of one. The exact number of chains is computed taking into account the number of processors in your machine; you can change it using the chains argument for the sample function. The next line tells us which variables are being sampled by which sampler. For this particular case, this line is not adding new information because NUTS is used to sample the only variable we have, θ. However, this is not always the case because PyMC can assign different samplers to different variables. PyMC has rules to ensure that each variable is associated with the best possible sampler. Users can manually assign samplers using the step argument of the sample function, but you will hardly need to do that.

Finally, the last line is a progress bar, with several related metrics indicating how fast the sampler is working, including the number of iterations per second. If you run the code, you will see the progress bar get updated really fast. Here, we are seeing the last stage when the sampler has finished its work. You will notice that we have asked for 1,000 samples, but PyMC is computing 8,000 samples. We have 1,000 draws per chain to tune the sampling algorithm (NUTS, in this example). These draws will be discarded by default; PyMC uses them to increase the efficiency and reliability of the sampling method, which are both important to obtain a useful approximation to the posterior. We also have 1,000 productive draws per chain for a total of 4,000. These are the ones we are going to use as our posterior. We can change the number of tuning steps with the `tune` argument of the sample function and the number of draws with the `draw` argument.

> **Faster Sampling**
>
> Under the hood, PyMC uses PyTensor, a library that allows one to define, optimize, and efficiently evaluate mathematical expressions involving multi-dimensional arrays. PyTensor significantly enhances the speed and performance of PyMC. Despite the advantages, it's worth noting that the samplers in PyMC are implemented in Python, which may result in slower execution at times. To address this limitation, PyMC allows external samplers. I recommend using nutpie, a sampler written in Rust. For more information on how to install and call nutpie from PyMC, please check Chapter 10.

Summarizing the posterior

Generally, the first task we will perform after sampling from the posterior is to check what the results look like. The `plot_trace` function from ArviZ is ideally suited to this task:

Code 2.3:

```
az.plot_trace(idata)
```

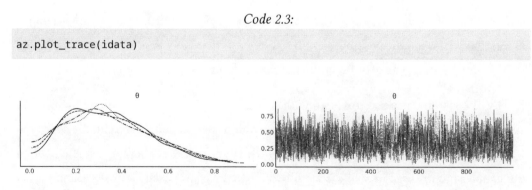

Figure 2.1: A trace plot for the posterior of `our_first_model`

Figure 2.1 shows the default result when calling `az.plot_trace`; we get two subplots for each unobserved variable. The only unobserved variable in our model is θ. Notice that y is an observed variable representing the data; we do not need to sample that because we already know those values. Thus we only get two subplots. On the left, we have a **Kernel Density Estimation (KDE)** plot; this is like the smooth version of the histogram. Ideally, we want all chains to have a very similar KDE, like in Figure 2.1. On the right, we get the individual values at each sampling step; we get as many lines as chains. Ideally, we want it to be something that looks noisy, with no clear pattern, and we should have a hard time identifying one chain from the others. In Chapter 10, we give more details on how to interpret these plots. The gist is that if we ran many chains, we would expect them to be practically indistinguishable from each other. The sampler did a good job and we can trust the samples.

As with other ArviZ functions, `az.plot_trace` has many options. For instance, we can run this function with the `combined` argument set to `True` to get a single KDE plot for all chains and with `kind=rank_bars` to get a **rank plot**.

Code 2.4:

```
az.plot_trace(idata, kind="rank_bars", combined=True)
```

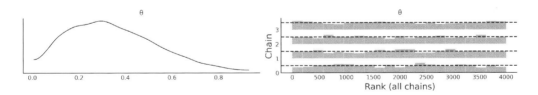

Figure 2.2: A trace plot for the posterior of `our_first_model`, *using the options* `kind="rank_bars"`, `combined=True`

A rank plot is another way to check if we can trust the samples; for this plot, we get one histogram per chain and we want all of them to be as uniform as possible, like in Figure 2.2. Some small deviations for uniformity are expected due to random sampling, but large deviations from uniformity are a signal that chains are exploring different regions of the posteriors. Ideally, we want all chains to explore the entire posterior. In Chapter 10, we provide further details on how to interpret rank plots and how they are constructed.

ArviZ provides several other plots to help interpret the posterior, and we will see them in the following pages. We may also want to have a numerical summary of the posterior. We can get that using az.summary, which will return a pandas DataFrame as shown in Table 2.1.

Code 2.5:

```
az.summary(idata, kind="stats").round(2)
```

	mean	sd	hdi_3%	hdi_97%
θ	0.34	0.18	0.03	0.66

Table 2.1: Summary statistics

On the first column we have the name of the variable, the second column is the mean of the posterior, the third column is the standard deviation of the posterior, and the last two columns are the lower and upper boundaries of the 94% highest density interval. Thus, according to our model and data, we think the value of θ is likely to be 0.34 with a 94% probability that it is actually between 0.03 and 0.66. We can report a similar summary using the standard deviation. The advantage of the standard deviation over the HDI is that it is a more popular statistic. As a disadvantage, we have to be more careful interpreting it; otherwise, it can lead to meaningless results. For example, if we compute the mean ± 2 standard deviations, we will get the intervals (-0.02, 0.7); the upper value is not that far from 0.66, which we got from the HDI, but the lower bound is actually outside the possible values of θ, which is between 0 and 1.

Another way to visually summarize the posterior is to use the az.plot_posterior function that comes with ArviZ (see Figure 2.3). We used this function in the previous chapter for a fake posterior. We are going to use it now for a real posterior.

Code 2.6:

```
az.plot_posterior(idata)
```

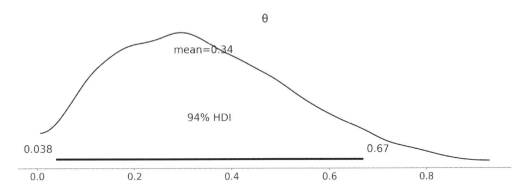

Figure 2.3: The plot shows the posterior distribution of θ and the 94% HDI

By default, `plot_posterior` shows a histogram for discrete variables and KDEs for continuous variables. We also get the mean of the distribution (we can ask for the median or mode using the `point_estimate` argument) and the 94% HDI as a black line at the bottom of the plot. Different interval values can be set for the HDI with the `hdi_prob` argument. This type of plot was introduced by John K. Kruschke in his great book Doing Bayesian Data Analysis [Kruschke, 2014].

Posterior-based decisions

Sometimes, describing the posterior is not enough. We may need to make decisions based on our inferences and reduce a continuous estimation to a dichotomous one: yes-no, healthy-sick, contaminated-safe, and so on. For instance, is the coin fair? A fair coin is one with a θ value of exactly 0.5. We can compare the value of 0.5 against the HDI interval. From Figure 2.3, we can see that the HDI goes from 0.03 to 0.7 and hence 0.5 is included in the HDI. We can interpret this as an indication that the coin may be tail-biased, but we cannot completely rule out the possibility that the coin is actually fair. If we want a sharper decision, we will need to collect more data to reduce the spread of the posterior, or maybe we need to find out how to define a more informative prior.

Savage-Dickey density ratio

One way to evaluate how much support the posterior provides for a given value is to compare the ratio of the posterior and prior densities at that value. This is called the Savage-Dickey density ratio and we can compute it with ArviZ using the `az.plot_bf` function:

Code 2.7:

```
1  az.plot_bf(idata, var_name="θ",
2             prior=np.random.uniform(0, 1, 10000), ref_val=0.5);
```

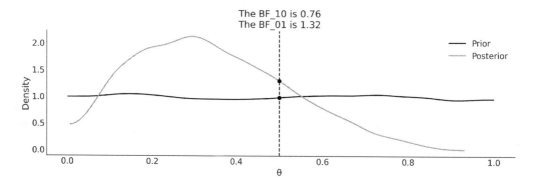

Figure 2.4: The plot shows the prior and posterior for `our_first_model`*; the black dots represent their values evaluated at the reference value 0.5*

From Figure 2.4, we can see that the value of `BF_01` is 1.3, which means that the value of $\theta = 0.5$ is 1.3 times more likely under the posterior distribution than under the prior distribution. To compute this value we just divided the height of the posterior at $\theta = 0.5$ by the height of the prior at $\theta = 0.5$. The value of `BF_10` is just the inverse $\frac{1}{1.3} \approx 0.8$. We can think of this as the value of $\theta \neq 0.5$ being 0.76 times more likely under the posterior than under the prior. How do we interpret these numbers? With a pinch of salt...the following table shows one possible interpretation originally proposed by Kass and Raftery [1995]:

The Savage-Dickey density ratio is a particular way to compute what is called the Bayes Factor. We will learn more about Bayes Factors, and their caveats, in Chapter 5.

BF_01	Interpretation
1 to 3.2	Not worth more than a bare mention
3.2 to 10	Substantial
10 to 100	Strong
> 100	Decisive

Table 2.2: Interpretation of Bayes Factors (BF_01)

Region Of Practical Equivalence

Strictly speaking, the chance of observing exactly 0.5 (that is, with infinite trailing zeros) is zero. Also, in practice, we generally do not care about exact results but results within a certain margin. Accordingly, in practice, we can relax the definition of fairness and we can say that a fair coin is one with a value of *around* 0.5. For example, we could say that any value in the interval [0.45, 0.55] will be, for our purposes, practically equivalent to 0.5. We call this interval a Region Of Practical Equivalence (ROPE). Once the ROPE is defined, we compare it with the HDI. We can get at least three scenarios:

- The ROPE does not overlap the HDI; we can say the coin is not fair
- The ROPE contains the entire HDI; we can say the coin is fair
- The ROPE partially overlaps HDI; we cannot say the coin is fair or unfair

If we choose the ROPE to match the support of a parameter, like [0, 1] for the coin-flipping example, we will always say we have a fair coin. Notice that we do not need to collect data to perform any type of inference.

The choice of ROPE is completely arbitrary: we can choose any value we want. Some choices are not very useful. If, for the coin-flipping example, we choose the ROPE to be [0, 1], then we will always say the coin is fair. Even more, we don't need to collect data or perform any analysis to reach this conclusion, this is a trivial example. More worrisome is to pick the ROPE after performing the analysis. This is problematic because we can accommodate the results to say whatever we want them to say. But why do we even bother to do an analysis, if we are going to accommodate the result to our expectations? The ROPE should be informed from domain knowledge.

We can use the `plot_posterior` function to plot the posterior with the HDI interval and the ROPE. The ROPE appears as a semi-transparent thick (gray) line:

Code 2.8:

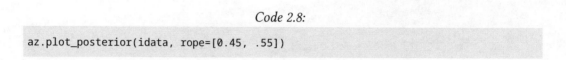

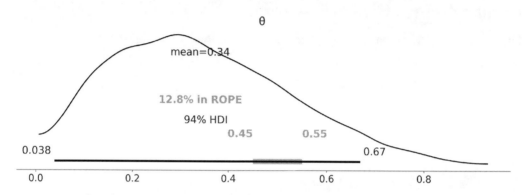

Figure 2.5: The plot shows the posterior distribution of θ and the 94% HDI. The ROPE is shown as a thick light-gray line

Another tool we can use to help us make a decision is to compare the posterior against a reference value. We can do this using `plot_posterior`. As you can see in Figure 2.6, we get a vertical (gray) line and the proportion of the posterior above and below our reference value:

Code 2.9:

```
az.plot_posterior(idata, ref_val=0.5)
```

For a more detailed discussion on the use of the ROPE, you could read Chapter 12 of Doing Bayesian Data Analysis by Kruschke [2014]. That chapter also discusses how to perform hypothesis testing in a Bayesian framework and the caveats of hypothesis testing, whether in a Bayesian or non-Bayesian setting.

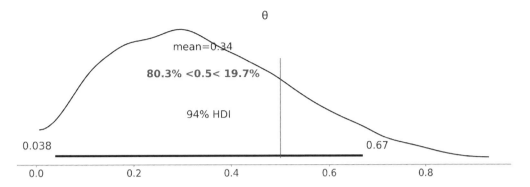

Figure 2.6: The plot shows the posterior distribution of θ and the 94% HDI. The reference value is shown as a gray vertical line

Loss functions

If you think these ROPE rules sound a little bit clunky and you want something more formal, loss functions are what you are looking for! To make a good decision, it is important to have the highest possible level of precision for the estimated value of the relevant parameters, but it is also important to take into account the cost of making a mistake. The cost/benefit trade-off can be mathematically formalized using loss functions. The names for loss functions or their inverses vary across different fields, and we could find names such as cost functions, objective functions, fitness functions, utility functions, and so on. No matter the name, the key idea is to use a function that captures how different the true value and the estimated value of a parameter are. The larger the value of the loss function, the worse the estimation is (according to the loss function). Some common examples of loss functions are:

- The absolute loss function, $|\theta - \hat{\theta}|$
- The quadratic loss function, $(\theta - \hat{\theta})^2$
- The 0-1 loss function, $\mathbb{1}(\theta \neq \hat{\theta})$, where $\mathbb{1}$ is the indicator function

In practice, we don't know the value of the true parameter. Instead, we have an estimation in the form of a posterior distribution. Thus, what we can do is find out the value of θ that minimizes the expected loss function. By expected loss function, we mean the loss function averaged over the whole posterior distribution.

In the following block of code, we have two loss functions: the absolute loss (lossf_a) and the quadratic loss (lossf_b). We will explore the value of over a grid of 200 points. We will then plot those curves and we will also include the value of θ that minimizes each loss function. The following block shows the Python code without the plotting part:

Code 2.10:

```
1  grid = np.linspace(0, 1, 200)
2  θ_pos = idata.posterior['θ']
3  lossf_a = [np.mean(abs(i - θ_pos)) for i in grid]
4  lossf_b = [np.mean((i - θ_pos)**2) for i in grid]
5  for lossf, c in zip([lossf_a, lossf_b], ['C0', 'C1']):
6      ...
```

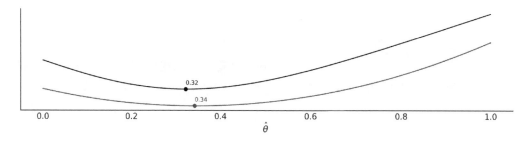

Figure 2.7: The absolute (black) and quadratic (gray) loss functions applied to the posterior from our_first_model

What is more interesting from Figure 2.7 is that the value we got from the absolute loss is equal to the median of the posterior and the one we got from the quadratic loss is equal to the mean of the posterior. You can check this for yourself by computing np.mean(θ_pos), np.median(θ_pos). This is no coincidence: different loss functions are related to different point estimates. The mean is the point estimate that minimizes the quadratic loss, the median, the absolute loss, and the mode, the 1-0 loss.

If we want to be formal and we want to compute a single-point estimate, we must decide which loss function we want. Conversely, if we choose a point estimate, we are implicitly (and maybe unconsciously) choosing a loss function. The advantage of explicitly choosing a loss function is that we can tailor the function to our problem instead of using a predefined rule. It is very common to observe that the cost of making a decision is asymmetric; for example, vaccines can produce an overreaction of the immune system, but the benefit to the vaccinated persons and even non-vaccinated persons overcomes the risk, usually by many orders of magnitude. Thus, if our problem demands it, we can construct an asymmetric loss function. It is also important to notice that, as the posterior is in the form of numerical samples, we can compute complex loss functions that don't need to be restricted by mathematical convenience or mere simplicity. The following code, and Figure 2.8 generated from it, is just a silly example of this:

Code 2.11:

```
1  lossf = []
2  for i in grid:
3      if i < 0.5:
4          f = 1/np.median(θ_pos / np.abs(i**2 - θ_pos))
5      else:
6          f = np.mean((i - θ_pos)**2 + np.exp(-i)) - 0.25
7      lossf.append(f)
```

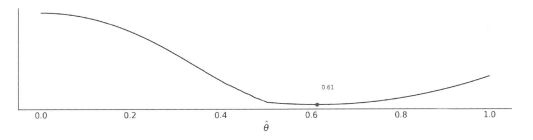

Figure 2.8: A weird loss function applied to the posterior from our_first_model

Up until now, we have been discussing the main notions of Bayesian statistics and probabilistic programming using the BetaBinomial model mainly because of its simplicity. In our path to build more complex models, we now shift our focus to delve into the realm of Gaussian inference.

Gaussians all the way down

Gaussians are very appealing from a mathematical point of view. Working with them is relatively easy, and many operations applied to Guassians return another Gaussian. Additionally, many natural phenomena can be nicely approximated using Gaussians; essentially, almost every time that we measure the average of something, using a *big enough* sample size, that average will be distributed as a Gaussian. The details of when this is true, when this is not true, and when this is more or less true, are elaborated in the **central limit theorem** (CLT); you may want to stop reading now and search about this really *central* statistical concept (terrible pun intended).

Well, we were saying that many phenomena are indeed averages. Just to follow a cliché, the height (and almost any other trait of a person, for that matter) is the result of many environmental factors and many genetic factors, and hence we get a nice Gaussian distribution for the height of adult people. Indeed, we get a mixture of two Gaussians, which is the result of overlapping the distribution of heights of women and men, but you get the idea. In summary, Gaussians are easy to work with and abundant in natural phenomena; hence, many of the statistical methods you may already know assume normality. Thus, it is important to learn how to build these models, and then it is equally important to learn how to relax the normality assumptions, something that is surprisingly easy in a Bayesian framework and with modern computational tools such as PyMC.

Gaussian inferences

Nuclear magnetic resonance (NMR) is a powerful technique used to study molecules and also living things such as humans, sunflowers, and yeast (because, after all, *we are just a bunch of molecules*). NMR allows you to measure different kinds of observable quantities related to interesting unobservable molecular properties Arroyuelo et al. [2021]. One of these observables is known as chemical shift, which we can only get for the nuclei of certain types of atoms. The details belong to quantum chemistry and they are irrelevant to this discussion. For all we care at the moment, we could have been measuring the height of a group of people, the average time to travel back home, or the weights of bags of oranges.

In these examples the variables are continuous, and it makes sense to think of them as an average value plus a dispersion. Sometimes we can use a Gaussian model for discrete variables if the number of possible values is large enough; for example, bonobos are very promiscuous, so maybe we can model the number of sexual partners of our cousins with a Gaussian.

Going back to our example, we have 48 chemical shift values represented in a boxplot in Figure 2.9. We can see that the median (the line inside the box) is around 53 and the interquartile range (the box) is around 52 and 55. We can see that there are two values far away from the rest of the data (empty circles).

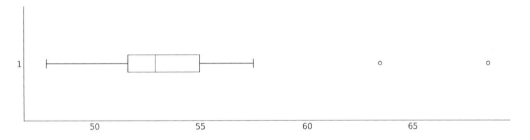

Figure 2.9: Boxplot of the 48 chemical shift values. We observed two values above 60, far away from the rest of the data

Let's forget about those two points for a moment and assume that a Gaussian distribution is a good description of the data. Since we do not know the mean or the standard deviation, we must set priors for both of them. Therefore, a reasonable model could be:

$$\mu \sim \mathcal{U}(l, h)$$
$$\sigma \sim \mathcal{HN}(\sigma_\sigma)$$
$$Y \sim \mathcal{N}(\mu, \sigma)$$

$\mathcal{U}(l, h)$ is the Uniform distribution between l, and h, $\mathcal{HN}(\sigma_\sigma)$ is the HalfNormal distribution with scale σ_σ, and $\mathcal{N}(\mu, \sigma)$ is the Gaussian distribution with mean μ and standard deviation σ. A HalfNormal distribution considers the absolute values of Normal distribution centered around zero. Figure 2.10 shows the graphical representation of this model.

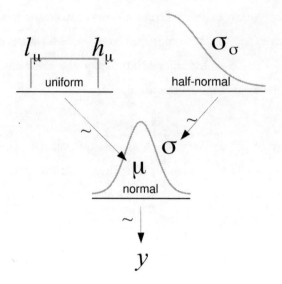

Figure 2.10: Graphical representation of `model_g`

If we do not know the possible values of μ and σ, we can set priors reflecting our ignorance. One option is to set the boundaries of the Uniform distribution to be $l = 40, h = 75$, which is a range that is larger than the range of the data. Alternatively, we can choose a range based on our previous knowledge. For instance, we may know that this is not physically possible to have values below 0 or above 100 for this type of measurement and thus use those values as the boundaries of the Uniform distribution. For the HalfNormal, and in the absence of more information, we can choose a large value compared to the scale of the data. The PyMC code for the model represented in Figure 2.10 is:

Code 2.12:

```
1  with pm.Model() as model_g:
2      μ = pm.Uniform('μ', lower=40, upper=70)
3      σ = pm.HalfNormal('σ', sigma=5)
4      Y = pm.Normal('Y', mu=μ, sigma=σ, observed=data)
5      idata_g = pm.sample()
```

Let's see what the posterior looks like. Figure 2.11 was generated with the ArviZ function `plot_trace`. It has one row for each parameter. For this model, the posterior is bidimensional, so each row shows one marginal distribution.

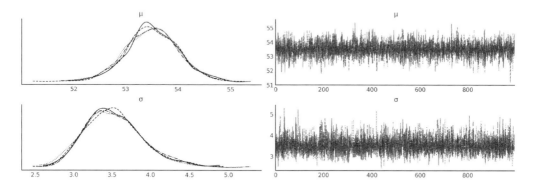

Figure 2.11: Posterior from `model_g` *ploted using* `az.plot_trace(idata_g)`

We can use the `plot_pair` function from ArviZ to see what the bi-dimensional posterior looks like, together with the marginal distributions for μ and σ. See Figure 2.12:

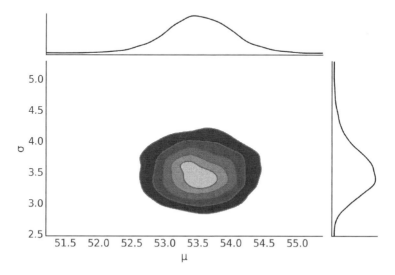

Figure 2.12: Posterior from `model_g` *ploted using* `az.plot_pair(idata_g, kind='kde',`
`marginals=True)`

We are going to print the summary for later use (see Table 2.3). We use the following code:

Code 2.13:

```
az.summary(idata_g, kind="stats").round(2)
```

	mean	sd	hdi_3%	hdi_97%
μ	53.50	0.52	52.51	54.44
σ	3.52	0.38	2.86	4.25

Table 2.3: Summary statistics for μ and σ

Posterior predictive checks

One of the nice elements of the Bayesian toolkit is that once we have a posterior $p(\theta \mid Y)$, it is possible to use it to generate predictions $p(\tilde{Y})$. Mathematically, this can be done by computing:

$$p(\tilde{Y} \mid Y) = \int p(\tilde{Y} \mid \theta) \, p(\theta \mid Y) d\theta$$

This distribution is known as the **posterior predictive distribution**. It is *predictive* because it is used to make predictions, and *posterior* because it is computed using the posterior distribution. So we can think of this as the distribution of future data given the model, and observed data.

Using PyMC is easy to get posterior predictive samples; we don't need to compute any integral. We just need to call the `sample_posterior_predictive` function and pass the `InferenceData` object as the first argument. We also need to pass the `model` object, and we can use the `extend_inferencedata` argument to add the posterior predictive samples to the `InferenceData` object. The code is:

Code 2.14:

```
1  pm.sample_posterior_predictive(idata_g, model=model_g,
2                          extend_inferencedata=True)
```

One common use of the posterior predictive distribution is to perform posterior predictive checks. These are a set of tests that can be used to check if the model is a good fit for the data. We can use the `plot_ppc` function from ArviZ to visualize the posterior predictive distribution and the observed data. The code is:

Code 2.15:

```
az.plot_ppc(idata_g, num_pp_samples=100)
```

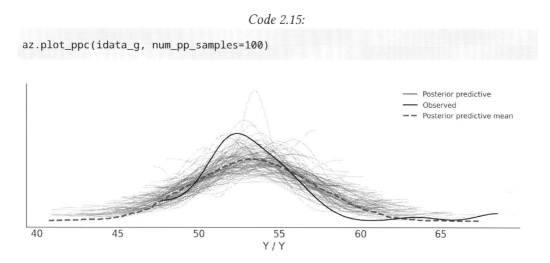

Figure 2.13: Posterior predictive check for `model_g` *ploted using* `az.plot_ppc`

In Figure 2.13, the black line is a KDE of the data and the gray lines are KDEs computed from each one of the 100 posterior predictive samples. The gray lines reflect the uncertainty we have about the distribution of the predicted data. The plots look *hairy* or *wonky*; this will happen when you have very few data points. By default, the KDEs in ArviZ are estimated within the actual range of the data and assumed to be zero outside. While some might consider this a bug, I think it's a feature, since it's reflecting a property of the data instead of over-smoothing it.

From Figure 2.13, we can see that the mean of the simulated data is slightly displaced to the right and that the variance seems to be larger for the simulated data than for the actual data. The source of this discrepancy can be attributed to the combination of our choice of likelihood and the two observations away from the bulk of the data (the empty dots in Figure 2.9). How can we interpret this plot? Is the model wrong or right? Can we use it or do we need a different model? Well, it depends. The interpretation of a model and its evaluation and criticism are always context-dependent. Based on my experience with this kind of measurement, I would say this model is a reasonable enough representation of the data and a useful one for most of my analysis. Nevertheless, it is important to keep in mind that we could find other models that better accommodate the whole dataset, including the two observations that are far from the bulk of the data. Let's see how we can do that.

Robust inferences

One objection we may have with `model_g` is that we are assuming a Normal distribution, but we have two data points away from the bulk of the data. By using a Normal distribution for the likelihood, we are indirectly assuming that we are not expecting to see a lot of data points far away from the bulk. Figure 2.13 shows the result of combining these assumptions with the data. Since the tails of the Normal distribution fall quickly as we move away from the mean, the Normal distribution (at least an anthropomorphized one) is *surprised by seeing* those two points and *reacts* in two ways, moving its mean towards those points and increasing its standard deviation. Another intuitive way of interpreting this is by saying that those points have an excessive weight in determining the parameters of the Normal distribution.

So, what can we do? One option is to check for errors in the data. If we retrace our steps we may find an error in the code while cleaning or preprocessing the data, or we can relate the putative anomalous values to the malfunction of the measuring equipment. Unfortunately, this is not always an option. Many times, the data was collected by others and we don't have a good register of how it was collected, measured or processed. Anyway, inspecting the data before modeling is always a good idea, that's a good practice in general.

Another option is to declare those points outliers and remove them from the data. Two common rules of thumb for identifying outliers in a dataset are:

- Using the interquartile range (IQR): Any data point that falls below 1.5 times the IQR from the lower quartile, or above 1.5 times the IQR from the upper quartile, is considered an outlier.
- Using the standard deviation: Any data point that falls below or above N times the

standard deviation of the data is considered an outlier. With N usually being 2 or 3.

However, it's important to note that, like any automatic method, these rules of thumb are not perfect and may result in discarding valid data points.

From a modeling perspective, instead of blaming the data we can blame the model and change it, as explained in the next section. As a general rule, Bayesians prefer to encode assumptions directly into the model by using different priors and likelihoods rather than through ad hoc heuristics such as outlier removal rules.

Degrees of normality

There is one distribution that looks very similar to a Normal distribution. It has three parameters: a location parameter μ, a scale parameter σ, and a normality parameter v. This distribution's name is Student's t-distribution. Figure 2.14 shows members of this family. When $v = \infty$ the distribution is the Normal distribution, μ is the mean and σ is the standard deviation. When $v = 1$, we get the Cauchy or Lorentz distribution. v can go from 0 to ∞. The lower this number, the heavier their tails. We can also say that the lower the value of v, the higher the kurtosis. The kurtosis is the fourth moment, as you may remember from the previous chapter. By heavy tails, we mean that it is more probable to find values away from the mean compared to a Normal, or in other words, values are not as concentrated around the mean as in a lighter tail distribution like the Normal. For example, 95% of the values from a Student's t ($\mu = 0, \sigma = 1, v = 1$) are found between -12.7 and 12.7. Instead, for a Normal ($\mu = 0, \sigma = 1, v = \infty$), this occurs between -1.96 and 1.96.

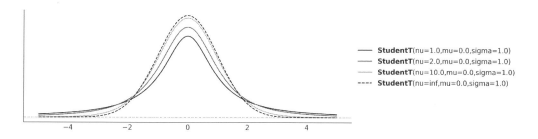

Figure 2.14: The Student's t-distribution

A very curious feature of the Student's t-distribution is that it has no defined mean value when $v \leq 1$. While any finite sample from a Student's t-distribution is just a bunch of numbers from which it is always possible to compute an empirical mean, the theoretical distribution itself is the one without a defined value for the mean. Intuitively, this can be understood as follows: the tails of the distribution are so heavy that at any moment we might get a sampled value from almost anywhere from the real line, so if we keep getting numbers, we will never approach a fixed value. Instead, the estimate will keep wandering around.

> ### Degrees of what?
>
> In most textbooks, the parameter v from the Student's t-distribution is referred to as the degrees of freedom parameter. However, I prefer to follow Kruschke's suggestion and call it the normality parameter. This name is more descriptive of the parameter's role in the distribution, especially as used for robust regression.

Similarly, the variance of this distribution is only defined for values of $v > 2$. So, it's important to note that the scale of the Student's t-distribution isn't the same as its standard deviation. The scale and the standard deviation become closer and closer as v approaches infinity.

A robust version of the Normal model

We are going to rewrite the previous model (`model_g`) by replacing the Gaussian distribution with the Student's t-distribution. Because the Student's t-distribution has one more parameter, v, than the Gaussian, we need to specify one more prior, for this model we decided to use the exponential distribution, but other distributions restricted to the positive interval could also work.

$$\mu \sim \mathcal{U}(l, h)$$

$$\sigma \sim \mathcal{HN}(\sigma_\sigma)$$

$$\nu \sim \text{Exp}(\lambda)$$

$$Y \sim \mathcal{T}(\nu, \mu, \sigma)$$

Figure 2.15 shows the graphical representation of this model

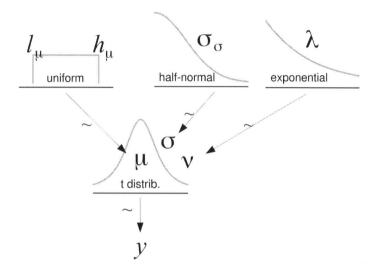

Figure 2.15: Graphical representation of `model_t`

Let's write this model in PyMC; as usual, we can (re)write models by specifying a few lines. The only cautionary word here is that by default the Exponential distribution in PyMC is parameterized with the inverse of the mean. We are going to set ν as an Exponential distribution with a mean of 30. From Figure 2.14, we can see that a Student's t-distribution with $\nu = 30$ looks pretty similar to a Gaussian (even when it is not). In fact, from the same diagram, we can see that *most of the action* happens for relatively small values of ν. Hence, we can say that the Exponential prior with a mean of 30 is a weakly informative prior telling the model we more or less think should be around 30 but can move to smaller and larger values with ease. In many problems, estimating ν is of no direct interest.

Code 2.16:

```
1  with pm.Model() as model_t:
2      μ = pm.Uniform('μ', 40, 75)
3      σ = pm.HalfNormal('σ', sigma=10)
4      ν = pm.Exponential('ν', 1/30)
5      y = pm.StudentT('y', nu=ν, mu=μ, sigma=σ, observed=data)
6      idata_t = pm.sample()
```

Compare the trace from `model_g` (Figure 2.11) with the trace of `model_t` (Figure 2.16):

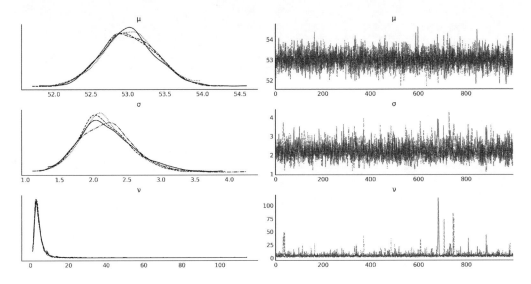

Figure 2.16: Posterior from `model_t` plotted using `az.plot_trace(idata_t)`

Now, print the summary of `model_t`. You should get something like Table 2.4. Compare the results with those from `model_g`.

	mean	sd	hdi_3%	hdi_97%
μ	53.02	0.39	52.27	53.71
σ	2.21	0.42	1.46	3.01
ν	4.94	5.45	1.07	10.10

Table 2.4: Summary statistics for μ, σ, and ν

Before you keep reading, take a moment to compare the preceding results with those from `model_g` and spot the difference between both results. Did you notice something interesting?

The estimation of μ between both models is similar, with a difference of $\approx$ 0.5. The estimation of σ is $\approx$ 3.5 for `model_g` and $\approx$ 2.2 for `model_t`. This is a consequence of the Student's t-distribution allocating less weight to values away from the mean. Loosely speaking, the Student's t-distribution is *less surprised* by values away from the mean. We can also see that the mean of ν is $\approx$ 5, meaning that we have a heavy-tailed distribution and not a Gaussian-like distribution.

Figure 2.17 shows a posterior predictive check for `model_t`. Let's compare it with the one from `model_g` (Figure 2.13). Using the Student's t-distribution in our model leads to predictive samples that seem to better fit the data in terms of the location of the peak of the distribution and also its spread. Notice how the samples extend far away from the bulk of the data, and how a few of the predictive samples look very flat. This is a direct consequence of the Student's t-distribution expecting to see data points far away from the mean or bulk of the data. If you check the code used to generate Figure 2.17 you will see that we have used `ax.set_xlim(40, 70)`.

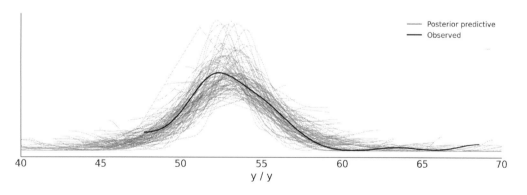

Figure 2.17: Posterior predictive check for `model_t`

The Student's t-distribution allows us to have a more **robust estimation** of the mean and standard deviation because the outliers have the effect of decreasing ν instead of pulling the mean or increasing the standard deviation. Thus, the mean and the scale are estimated by weighting the data points close to the bulk more than those apart from it. As a rule of thumb, for values of $v > 2$ and *not too small*, we can consider the scale of a Student's t-distribution as a reasonable practical proxy for the standard deviation of the data after removing outliers. This is a rule of thumb because we know that the scale is not the standard deviation.

InferenceData

InferenceData is a rich container for the results of Bayesian inference. A modern Bayesian analysis potentially generates many sets of data including posterior samples and posterior predictive samples. But we also have observed data, samples from the prior, and even statistics generated by the sampler. All this data, and more, can be stored in an InferenceData object. To help keep all this information organized, each one of these sets of data has its own group. For instance, the posterior samples are stored in the `posterior` group. The observed data is stored in the `observed_data` group.

Figure 2.18 shows an HTML representation of the InferenceData for `model_g`. We can see 4 groups: `posterior`, `posterior_predictive`, `sample_stats`, and `observed_data`. All of them are collapsed except for the `posterior` group. We can see we have two coordinates `chain` and `draw` of dimensions 4 and 1000 respectively. We also have 2 variables μ and σ.

So far, PyMC has generated an InferenceData object and ArviZ has used that to generate plots or numerical summaries. But we can also manipulate an InferenceData object. Some common operations are to access specific groups. For instance, to access the posterior group we can write:

Code 2.17:

```
posterior = idata_g.posterior
```

This will return an xarray dataset. If you are not familiar with xarray [Hoyer and Hamman, 2017] (https://docs.xarray.dev/en/stable/), imagine NumPy multidimensional arrays but with labels! This makes many operations easier as you don't have to remember the

Figure 2.18: InferenceData object for model_g

order of the dimensions. For example, the following code will return the first draw from chain 0 and chain 2:

Code 2.18:

```
posterior.sel(draw=0, chain=[0, 2])
```

We use the sel method to select a range of values, like the first 100 draws from all chains:

Code 2.19:

```
posterior.sel(draw=slice(0, 100))
```

Additionally, the following returns the mean for μ and σ computed over all draws and chains:

Code 2.20:

```
posterior.mean()
```

Meanwhile, the following code returns the mean over the draws, i.e., this returns four values for μ and four values for σ, one per chain:

Code 2.21:

```
posterior.mean("draw")
```

More often than not, we don't care about chains and draws, we just want to get the posterior samples. In those cases, we can use the `az.extract` function:

Code 2.22:

```
stacked = az.extract(idata_g)
```

This combines the `chain` and `draw` into a `sample` coordinate which can make further operations easier. By default, `az.extract` works on the posterior, but you can specify other groups with the `group` argument. You can also use `az.extract` to get a random sample of the posterior:

Code 2.23:

```
az.extract(idata_g, num_samples=100)
```

We are going to use the InferenceData object all the time in this book, so you will have the time to get familiar with it and learn more about it in the coming pages.

Groups comparison

One pretty common statistical analysis is group comparison. We may be interested in how well patients respond to a certain drug, the reduction of car accidents by the introduction of new traffic regulations, student performance under different teaching approaches, and so on. Sometimes, this type of question is framed under the hypothesis testing scenario and the goal is to declare a result *statistically significant*. Relying only on statistical significance can be problematic for many reasons: on the one hand, statistical significance is not equivalent to practical significance; on the other hand, a really small effect can be declared significant just by collecting enough data.

The idea of hypothesis testing is connected to the concept of p-values. This is not a fundamental connection but a cultural one; people are used to thinking that way mostly because that's what they learn in most introductory statistical courses. There is a long record of studies and essays showing that, more often than not, p-values are used and interpreted the wrong way, even by people who are using them daily. Instead of doing hypothesis testing, we are going to take a different route and we are going to focus on estimating the effect size, that is, quantifying the difference between two groups. One advantage of thinking in terms of effect size is that we move away from yes-no questions like "Does it work?" or "Is there any effect?" and into the more nuanced type of questions like "How well does it work?" or "How large is the effect?".

Sometimes, when comparing groups, people talk about a control group and a treatment group. For example, when we want to test a new drug, we want to compare the new drug (the treatment) against a placebo (the control group). The placebo effect is a psychological phenomenon where a patient experiences perceived improvements in their symptoms or condition after receiving an inactive substance or treatment. By comparing the effects of the drug with a placebo group in clinical trials, researchers can discern whether the drug is genuinely effective. The placebo effect is an example of the broader challenge in experimental design and statistical analysis of the difficulty of accounting for all factors in an experiment.

One interesting alternative to this design is to compare the new drug with the commercially available most popular or efficient drug to treat that illness. In such a case, the control group cannot be a placebo; it should be the other drug. Bogus control groups are a splendid way to lie using statistics.

For example, imagine you work for a dairy product company that wants to sell overly sugared yogurts to kids by telling their dads and moms that this particular yogurt boosts the immune system or helps their kids grow stronger. One way to cheat with data is by using milk or even water as a control group, instead of another cheaper, less sugary, less marketed yogurt. It may sound silly when I put it this way, but I am describing actual experiments published in actual scientific journals. When someone says something is harder, better, faster, or stronger, remember to ask what the baseline used for the comparison was.

The tips dataset

To explore the subject matter of this section, we are going to use the tips dataset [Bryant and Smith, 1995]. We want to study the effect of the day of the week on the tips earned at a restaurant. For this example, the different groups are the days. Notice there is no control group or treatment group. If we wish, we can arbitrarily establish one day (for example, Thursday) as the reference or control. For now, let's start the analysis by loading the dataset as a pandas DataFrame using just one line of code. If you are not familiar with pandas, the `tail` command is used to show the last rows of a DataFrame (see Table 2.5), you may want to try using `head`:

Code 2.24:

```
1  tips = pd.read_csv("data/tips.csv")
2  tips.tail()
```

	total_bill	tip	sex	smoker	day	time	size
239	29.03	5.92	Male	No	Sat	Dinner	3
240	27.18	2.00	Female	Yes	Sat	Dinner	2
241	22.67	2.00	Male	Yes	Sat	Dinner	2
242	17.82	1.75	Male	No	Sat	Dinner	2
243	18.78	3.00	Female	No	Thurs	Dinner	2

Table 2.5: Sample data from a restaurant

From this DataFrame, we are only going to use the day and tip columns. Figure 2.19 shows the distributions of this data using ridge plots. This figure was done with ArviZ. Even though ArviZ is designed for Bayesian model analysis, some of its functions can be useful for data analysis.

We are going to do some small preprocessing of the data. First, we are going to create the `tip` variable representing the tips in dollars. Then we create the `idx` variable, a categorical dummy variable encoding the days with numbers, that is, `[0, 1, 2, 3]` instead of `['Thur', 'Fri', 'Sat', 'Sun']`.

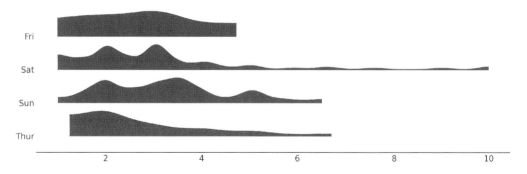

Figure 2.19: Distribution of tips by day

Code 2.25:

```
1 categories = np.array(["Thur", "Fri", "Sat", "Sun"])
2 tip = tips["tip"].values
3 idx = pd.Categorical(tips["day"], categories=categories).codes
```

The model for this problem is almost the same as model_g; the only difference is that now μ and σ are going to be vectors instead of scalars. PyMC syntax is extremely helpful for this situation: instead of writing for loops, we can write our model in a vectorized way.

Code 2.26:

```
1 with pm.Model() as comparing_groups:
2     μ = pm.Normal("μ", mu=0, sigma=10, shape=4)
3     σ = pm.HalfNormal("σ", sigma=10, shape=4)
4
5     y = pm.Normal("y", mu=μ[idx], sigma=σ[idx], observed=tip)
```

Notice how we passed a shape argument for the prior distribution. For μ, this means that we are specifying four independent $\mathcal{N}(0, 10)$ and for σ four independent $\mathcal{HN}(10)$. Also, notice how we use the idx variable to properly index the values of μ and σ we pass to the likelihood.

PyMC provides an alternative syntax, which consists of specifying coordinates and dimensions. The advantage of this alternative is that it allows better integration with ArviZ.

In this example, we have 4 values for the means and 4 for the standard deviations, and that's why we use `shape=4`. The InferenceData will have 4 indices 0, 1, 2, 3 mapping to each of the 4 days. However, it is the user's job to associate those numerical indices with the days. By using coordinates and dimensions we, and ArviZ, can use the labels "Thur", "Fri", "Sat", "Sun" to easily map parameters to their associated days.

We are going to specify two coordinates; "days", with the dimensions "Thur", "Fri", "Sat", "Sun"; and "days_flat", which will contain the same labels but repeated according to the order and length that corresponds to each observation. "days_flat" will be useful later for posterior predictive tests.

Code 2.27:

```
1  coords = {"days": categories, "days_flat":categories[idx]}
2
3  with pm.Model(coords=coords) as comparing_groups:
4      μ = pm.HalfNormal("μ", sigma=5, dims="days")
5      σ = pm.HalfNormal("σ", sigma=1, dims="days")
6
7      y = pm.Gamma("y", mu=μ[idx], sigma=σ[idx], observed=tip, dims="days_flat")
8
9      idata_cg = pm.sample()
10     idata_cg.extend(pm.sample_posterior_predictive(idata_cg))
```

Once the posterior distribution is computed, we can do all the analyses that we believe are pertinent. For instance, we can do a posterior predictive test. With the help of ArviZ, we can do it by calling `az.plot_ppc`. We use the `coords` and `flatten` parameters to get one subplot per day.

Code 2.28:

```
1  _, axes = plt.subplots(2, 2)
2  az.plot_ppc(idata_cg, num_pp_samples=100,
```

3
```
        coords={"days_flat":[categories]}, flatten=[], ax=axes)
```

From the following figure, we can see that the model can capture the general shape of the distributions, but still, some details are elusive. This may be due to the relatively small sample size, factors other than day influencing the tips, or a combination of both.

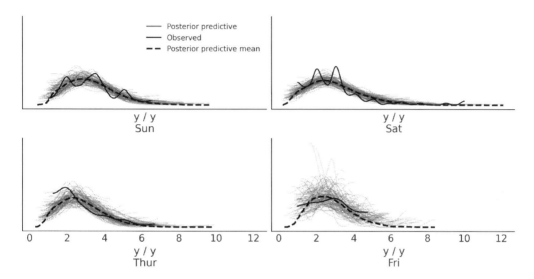

Figure 2.20: Posterior predictive checks for the tips dataset

For now, we are going to consider that the model is good enough for us and move to explore the posterior. We can explain the results in terms of their average values and then find for which days that average is higher. But there are other alternatives; for instance, we may want to express the results in terms of differences in posterior means. In addition, we might want to use some measure of effect size that is popular with our audiences, such as the probability of superiority or Cohen's d. In the next sections, we explain these alternatives.

Cohen's d

A common way to measure the effect size is Cohen's d, which is defined as follows:

$$\frac{\mu_2 - \mu_1}{\sqrt{\frac{\sigma_1^2 + \sigma_2^2}{2}}}$$

Because we have a posterior distribution we can compute a distribution of Cohen's d, and if we want a single value we can compute the mean or median of that distribution.

This expression tells us that the effect size is the difference between the means scaled by the pooled standard deviation of both groups. By taking the pooled standard deviation, we are standardizing the differences of means. This is important because when you have a difference of 1 and a standard deviation of 0.1, the effect size is larger than the same difference when the standard deviation is 10. A Cohen's d can be interpreted as a Z-score (a standard score). A Z-score is the signed number of standard deviations by which a value differs from the mean value of what is being observed or measured. Thus, a value of 0.5 Cohen's d could be interpreted as a difference of 0.5 standard deviations from one group to the other.

Even when the differences of means are standardized, we may still need to calibrate ourselves based on the context of a given problem to be able to say if a given value is big, small, medium, and so on. For instance, if we are used to performing several analyses for the same or similar problems, we can get used to a Cohen's d of say 1. So when we get a Cohen's d of say 2, we know that we have something important (or someone made a mistake somewhere!). If you do not have this practice yet, you can ask a domain expert for their valuable input.

A very nice web page to explore what different values of Cohen's d look like is `http://rpsychologist.com/d3/cohend`. On that page, you will also find other ways to express an effect size; some of them could be more intuitive, such as the probability of superiority, which we will discuss next.

Probability of superiority

This is another way to report the effect size, and this is defined as the probability that a data point taken at random from one group has a larger value than one also taken at random from the other group. If we assume that the data we are using is normally distributed, we can compute the probability of superiority from Cohen's d using the following expression:

$$ps = \Phi \left(\frac{\delta}{\sqrt{2}} \right)$$

Φ is the cumulative Normal distribution and δ is the Cohen's d.

If we are OK with the normality assumption, we can use this formula to get the probability of superiority from the value of Cohen's d. Otherwise, we can compute the probability of superiority directly from the posterior samples just by taking random samples from two groups and counting how many times one value is larger than the other. To do that we don't need Cohen's d or assume normality (see the Exercises section). This is an example of an advantage of using **Markov Chain Monte Carlo** (**MCMC**) methods; once we get samples from the posterior, we can compute many quantities from it often in ways that are easier than with other methods.

Posterior analysis of mean differences

To conclude our previous discussions, let's compute the posterior distributions for differences in means, Cohen's d, and the probability of superiority, and integrate them into a single plot. Figure 2.21 has a lot of information. Depending on the audience, the plot may be overloaded, or too crowded. Perhaps it is useful for a discussion within your team, but for the general public, it may be convenient to remove elements or distribute the information between a figure and a table or two figures. Anyway, here we show it precisely so you can compare different ways of presenting the same information, so take some time to ponder this figure.

One way to read Figure 2.21 is to compare the reference value, of zero difference, with the HDI interval. We have only one case when the 94% HDI excludes the reference value, that is, the difference in tips between Thursday and Sunday. For all the other comparisons, we cannot rule out a difference of zero, at least according to the HDI-reference-value-overlap criteria. But even for that case, the average difference is ≈ 0.5 dollars. Is that difference large enough? Is that difference enough to accept working on Sunday and missing the opportunity to spend time with family or friends? Is that difference enough to justify

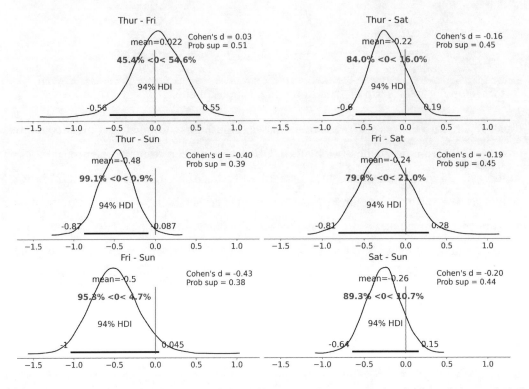

Figure 2.21: Posterior distributions of the differences of means, Cohen's d, and the probability of superiority for the tips dataset

averaging the tips over the four days and giving every waitress and waiter the same amount of tip money?

The short answer is that those kinds of questions cannot be answered by statistics; they can only be informed by statistics. I hope you don't feel cheated by that answer, but we cannot get automatic answers unless we include in the analysis all the values that are important to the stakeholders. Formally, that requires the definition of a loss function or at least the definition of some threshold value for the effect size, which should be informed by those values.

Summary

Although Bayesian statistics is conceptually simple, fully probabilistic models often lead to analytically intractable expressions. For many years, this was a huge barrier, hindering the wide adoption of Bayesian methods. Fortunately, maths, statistics, physics, and computer science came to the rescue in the form of numerical methods that are capable—at least in principle—of solving any inference problem. The possibility of automating the inference process has led to the development of probabilistic programming languages, allowing a clear separation between model definition and inference. PyMC is a Python library for probabilistic programming with a very simple, intuitive, and easy-to-read syntax that is also very close to the statistical syntax used to describe probabilistic models.

We introduced the PyMC library by revisiting the coin-flip model from Chapter 1, this time without analytically deriving the posterior. PyMC models are defined inside a context manager. To add a probability distribution to a model, we just need to write a single line of code. Distributions can be combined and can be used as priors (unobserved variables) or likelihoods (observed variables). If we pass data to a distribution, it becomes a likelihood. Sampling can be achieved with a single line as well. PyMC allows us to get samples from the posterior distribution. If everything goes right, these samples will be representative of the correct posterior distribution and thus they will be a representation of the logical consequences of our model and data. We can explore the posterior generated by PyMC using ArviZ, a Python library that works hand-in-hand with PyMC and can be used, among other tasks, to help us interpret and visualize posterior distributions. One way of using a posterior to help us make inference-driven decisions is by comparing the ROPE against the HDI interval. We also briefly mentioned the notion of loss functions, a formal way to quantify the trade-offs and costs associated with making decisions in the presence of uncertainty. We learned that loss functions and point estimates are intimately associated.

Up to this point, the discussion was restricted to a simple one-parameter model. Generalizing to an arbitrary number of parameters is trivial with PyMC; we exemplify how to do this with the Gaussian and Student's t models. The Gaussian distribution is a special case of the Student's t-distribution and we showed you how to use the latter to perform robust inferences in the presence of outliers. In the next chapters, we will look at how these models can be used as part of linear regression models. We used a Gaussian model to compare groups. While this is sometimes framed in the context of hypothesis testing, we take another route and frame this task as a problem of inferring the effect size, an approach we generally consider to be richer and more productive. We also explored different ways to interpret and report effect sizes.

With all that we have learned in this and the previous chapter, we are ready to study one of the most important concepts in this book, hierarchical models. That will be the topic of the next chapter.

Exercises

1. Using PyMC, change the parameters of the prior Beta distribution in `our_first_model` to match those of the previous chapter. Compare the results to the previous chapter.

2. Compare the model `our_first_model` with prior $\theta \sim \text{Beta}(1, 1)$ with a model with prior $\theta \sim \mathcal{U}(0, 1)$. Are the posteriors similar or different? Is the sampling slower, faster, or the same? What about using a Uniform over a different interval such as [-1, 2]? Does the model run? What errors do you get?

3. PyMC has a function `pm.model_to_graphviz` that can be used to visualize the model. Use it to visualize the model `our_first_model`. Compare the result with the Kruschke diagram. Use `pm.model_to_graphviz` to visualize model `comparing_groups`.

4. Read about the coal mining disaster model that is part of the PyMC documentation (`https://shorturl.at/hyCX2`). Try to implement and run this model by yourself.

5. Modify `model_g`, change the prior for the mean to a Gaussian distribution centered at the empirical mean, and play with a couple of reasonable values for the standard deviation of this prior. How robust/sensitive are the inferences to these changes? What do you think of using a Gaussian, which is an unbounded distribution (goes from $-$ inf to inf), to model bounded data such as this? Remember that we said it is

not possible to observe values below 0 or above 100.

6. Using the data from the `chemical_shifts.csv` file, compute the empirical mean and the standard deviation with and without outliers. Compare those results to the Bayesian estimation using the Gaussian and Student's t-distribution. What do you observe?

7. Repeat the previous exercise by adding more outliers to `chemical_shifts.csv`, and compute new posteriors for `model_g` and `model_t` using this new data. What do you observe?

8. Explore the InferenceData object `idata_cg`.

   - How many groups does it contain?
   - Inspect the posterior distribution of the parameter μ for a specific day using the `sel` method.
   - Compute the distributions of mean differences between Thursday and Sunday. What are the coordinates and dimensions of the resulting DataArray?

9. For the tips example compute the probability of superiority directly from the posterior (without computing Cohen's d first). You can use the `pm.sample_posterior_predictive()` function to take a sample from each group. Is it different from the calculation assuming normality? Can you explain the result?

Join our community Discord space

Join our Discord community to meet like-minded people and learn alongside more than 5000 members at:

`https://packt.link/bayesian`

3

Hierarchical Models

Hierarchical models are one honking great idea – let's do more of those!

- The zen of Bayesian modeling

In Chapter 2, we saw a tips example where we had multiple groups in our data, one for each of Thursday, Friday, Saturday, and Sunday. We decided to model each group separately. That's sometimes fine, but we should be aware of our assumptions. By modeling each group independently, we are assuming the groups are unrelated. In other words, we are assuming that knowing the tip for one day does not give us any information about the tip for another day. That could be too strong an assumption. Would it be possible to build a model that allows us to share information between groups? That's not only possible, but is also the main topic of this chapter. Lucky you!

In this chapter, we will cover the following topics:

- Hierarchical models
- Partial pooling
- Shrinkage

Sharing information, sharing priors

Hierarchical models are also known as multilevel models, mixed-effects models, random-effects models, or nested models. They are particularly useful when dealing with data that can be described as grouped or having different levels, such as data nested within geographic regions (for example, cities belonging to a province and provinces belonging to a country), or with a hierarchical structure (such as students nested within schools, or patients nested within hospitals) or repeated measurements on the same individuals.

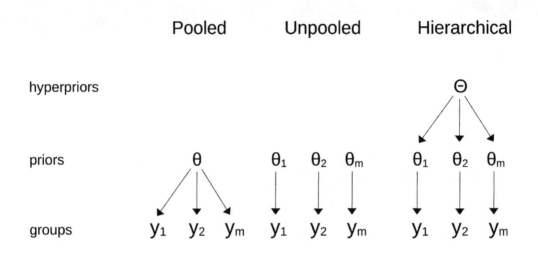

Figure 3.1: The differences between a pooled model, an unpooled model, and a hierarchical model

Hierarchical models are a natural way to share information between groups. In a hierarchical model, the parameters of the prior distributions are themselves given a prior distribution. These higher-level priors are often called hyperpriors; "hyper" means "over" in Greek. Having hyperpriors allows the model to share information between groups, while still allowing differences between groups. In other words, we can think of the parameters of the prior distributions as belonging to a common population of parameters. Figure 3.1 shows a diagram with the high-level differences between a pooled model (a single group), an unpooled model (all separated groups), and a hierarchical model, also known as a partially pooled model.

The concept of a hierarchical model may seem confusingly simple, almost trivial, but it has subtle implications. That is why in the rest of this chapter we will use different examples to understand their implications. I am sure that these examples will not only help you better understand this concept but will also convince you that it is a very useful tool to apply to your own problems.

Hierarchical shifts

Proteins are molecules formed by 20 units called amino acids. Each amino acid can appear in a protein 0 or more times. Just as a melody is defined by a sequence of musical notes, a protein is defined by a sequence of amino acids. Some musical note variations can result in small variations of the melody and other variations in completely different melodies. Something similar happens with proteins. One way to study proteins is by using nuclear magnetic resonance (the same technique used for medical imaging). This technique allows us to measure various quantities, one of which is called a chemical shift. You may remember that we saw an example using chemical shifts in Chapter 2.

Suppose we want to compare a theoretical method of computing chemical shift against the experimental observations to evaluate the ability of the theoretical method to reproduce the experimental values. Luckily for us, someone has already run the experiments and carried out the theoretical calculations, and we just need to compare them. The following dataset contains chemical shift values for a set of proteins. If you inspect the `cs_data` DataFrame, you will see that it has four columns:

1. The first is a code that identifies the protein (you can get a lot of information about that protein by entering that code at `https://www.rcsb.org/`)
2. The second column has the name of the amino acid (you might notice that there are only 19 unique names; one of the amino acids is missing from this dataset)
3. The third contains theoretical values of chemical shift (calculated using quantum methods)
4. The fourth has experimental values

Now that we have the data, how should we proceed? One option is to take the empirical differences and fit a Gaussian or maybe Student's t model. Because amino acids are a family of chemical compounds, it would make sense to assume they are all the same and estimate a single Gaussian for all the differences. But you may argue that there are 20 different kinds of amino acids, each one with different chemical properties, and hence a better choice is to fit 20 separated Gaussians. What should we do?

Let's take a moment to think about which option is the best. If we combine all the data, our estimates are going to be more accurate, but we will not be able to get information from individual groups (amino acids). On the contrary, if we treat them as separate groups, we will get a much more detailed analysis but with less accuracy. What should we do?

When in doubt, everything! (Not sure this is good general advice for your life, but I like the song `https://www.youtube.com/watch?v=1di09XZUlIw`). We can build a hierarchical model; that way, we allow estimates at the group level but with the restriction that they all belong to a larger group or population. To better understand this, let's build a hierarchical model for the chemical shift data.

To see the difference between a non-hierarchical (unpooled) model and a hierarchical one, we are going to build two models. The first one is essentially the same as the `comparing_groups` model from Chapter 2:

Code 3.1:

```
1  with pm.Model(coords=coords) as cs_nh:
2      μ = pm.Normal('μ', mu=0, sigma=10, dims="aa")
3      σ = pm.HalfNormal('σ', sigma=10, dims="aa")
4      y = pm.Normal('y', mu=μ[idx], sigma=σ[idx], observed=diff)
5      idata_cs_nh = pm.sample()
```

Now, we will build the hierarchical version of the model. We are adding two hyperpriors, one for the mean of μ and one for the standard deviation of μ. We are leaving σ without hyperpriors; in other words, we are assuming that the variance between observed and theoretical values should be the same for all groups. This is a modeling choice, and you may face a problem where this seems unacceptable and consider it necessary to add a hyperprior for σ; feel free to do that:

Code 3.2:

```
1  with pm.Model(coords=coords) as cs_h:
2      # hyper_priors
3      μ_mu = pm.Normal('μ_mu', mu=0, sigma=10)
4      μ_sd = pm.HalfNormal('μ_sd', 10)
5      # priors
6      μ = pm.Normal('μ', mu=μ_mu, sigma=μ_sd, dims="aa")
7      σ = pm.HalfNormal('σ', sigma=10, dims="aa")
8      # likelihood
9      y = pm.Normal('y', mu=μ[idx], sigma=σ[idx], observed=diff)
10     idata_cs_h = pm.sample()
```

Figure 3.2 shows the graphical representation of the cs_h and cs_nh models. We can see that we have one more level for cs_h representing the hyperpriors for μ.

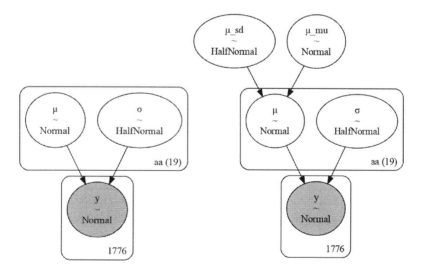

Figure 3.2: Graph representation of the non-hierarchical (left) and hierarchical (right) models for the chemical shift data. Each subfigure was generated with the pm.model_to_graphviz(.) *function*

We are going to compare the results using ArviZ's `plot_forest` function. We can pass more than one model to this function. This is useful when we want to compare the values of parameters from different models such as with the present example. In Figure 3.3, we have a plot for the 40 estimated means, one per amino acid (20) for each of the two models. We also have their 94% HDI and the inter-quantile range (the central 50% of the distribution). The vertical dashed line is the global mean according to the hierarchical model. This value is close to zero, as expected for theoretical values faithfully reproducing experimental ones.

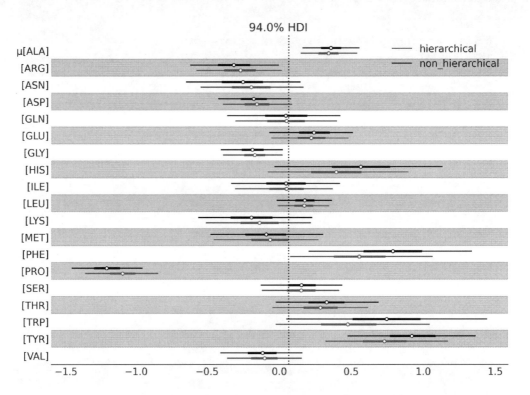

Figure 3.3: Chemical shift differences for the hierarchical and non-hierarchical models

The most relevant part of this plot is that the estimates from the hierarchical model are pulled toward the partially pooled mean, or equivalently they are shrunken in comparison to the unpooled estimates. You will also notice that the effect is more notorious for those groups farther away from the mean (such as PRO) and that the uncertainty is on par with or smaller than that from the non-hierarchical model. The estimates are partially pooled because we have one estimate for each group, but estimates for individual groups restrict each other through the hyperprior. Therefore, we get an intermediate situation between having a single group with all chemical shifts together and having 20 separate groups, one per amino acid. And that, ladies, gentlemen, and non-binary-gender-fluid people, is the beauty of hierarchical models.

Water quality

Suppose we want to analyze the quality of water in a city, so we take samples by dividing the city into neighborhoods. We may think we have two options for analyzing this data:

- Study each neighborhood as a separate entity

- Pool all the data together and estimate the water quality of the city as a single big group

You have probably already noticed the pattern here. We can justify the first option by saying we obtain a more detailed view of the problem, which otherwise could become invisible or less evident if we average the data. The second option can be justified by saying that if we pool the data, we obtain a bigger sample size and hence a more accurate estimation. But we already know we have a third option: we can do a hierarchical model!

For this example, we are going to use synthetic data. I love using synthetic data; it is a great way to understand things. If you don't understand something, simulate it! There are many uses for synthetic data. Here, we are going to imagine we have collected water samples from three different regions of the same city and measured the lead content of water; samples with concentrations of lead above recommendations from the World Health Organization are marked with zero and samples with values below the recommendations are marked with one. This is a very simple scenario. In a more realistic example, we would have a continuous measurement of lead concentration and probably many more groups. Nevertheless, for our current purposes, this example is good enough to uncover the details of hierarchical models. We can generate the synthetic data with the following code:

Code 3.3:

```
1  N_samples = [30, 30, 30]
2  G_samples = [18, 18, 18]
3  group_idx = np.repeat(np.arange(len(N_samples)), N_samples)
4  data = []
5  for i in range(0, len(N_samples)):
6      data.extend(np.repeat([1, 0], [G_samples[i], N_samples[i]-G_samples[i]]))
```

We are simulating an experiment where we have measured three groups, each one consisting of a certain number of samples; we store the total number of samples per group in the N_samples list. Using the G_samples list, we keep a record of the number of good-quality samples per group. The rest of the code is there just to generate a list of the data, filled with zeros and ones.

The model for this problem is similar to the one we used for the coin problem, except for two important features:

- We have defined two hyperpriors that will influence the Beta prior.
- Instead of setting hyperpriors on the parameters α and β, we are defining the Beta distribution in terms of μ, the mean, and ν, the concentration (or precision) of the Beta distribution. The precision is analog to the inverse of the standard deviation; the larger the value of ν, the more concentrated the Beta distribution will be. In statistical notation, our model is as follows:

$$\mu \sim \text{Beta}(\alpha_\mu, \beta_\mu)$$

$$\nu \sim \mathcal{HN}(\sigma_\nu)$$

$$\theta_i \sim \text{Beta}(\mu, \nu)$$

$$y_i \sim \text{Bernoulli}(\theta_i)$$

Notice that we are using the subscript i to indicate that the model has groups with different values for some of the parameters. Using Kruschke diagrams (see Figure 3.4), we can recognize that the new model has one additional level compared to the one from Figure 1.14. Notice also that for this model, we are parametrizing the Beta prior distribution in terms of μ and ν instead of α and β. This is a common practice in Bayesian statistics, and it is done because μ and ν are more intuitive parameters than α and β.

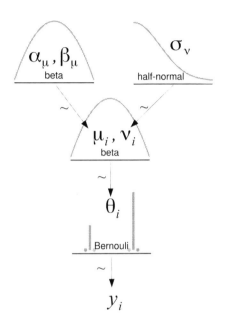

Figure 3.4: Hierarchical model

Let's write the model in PyMC:

Code 3.4:

```
1  with pm.Model() as model_h:
2      # hypyerpriors
3      μ = pm.Beta('μ', 1, 1)
4      ν = pm.HalfNormal('ν', 10)
5      # prior
6      θ = pm.Beta('θ', mu=μ, nu=ν, shape=len(N_samples))
7      # likelihood
8      y = pm.Bernoulli('y', p=θ[group_idx], observed=data)
9
10     idata_h = pm.sample()
```

Shrinkage

To show you one of the main consequences of hierarchical models, I will require your assistance, so please join me in a brief experiment. I will need you to print and save the summary computed with `az.summary(idata_h)`. Then, I want you to rerun the model two more times after making small changes to the synthetic data. Remember to save the summary after each run. In total, we will have three runs:

- One run setting all the elements of `G_samples` to 18
- One run setting all the elements of `G_samples` to 3
- One last run setting one element to 18 and the other two to 3

Before continuing, please take a moment to think about the outcome of this experiment. Focus on the estimated mean value of θ in each experiment. Based on the first two runs of the model, could you predict the outcome for the third case?

If we put the result in a table, we get something more or less like this; remember that small variations could occur due to the stochastic nature of the sampling process:

G_samples	Mean
18, 18, 18	0.6, 0.6, 0.6
3, 3, 3	0.11, 0.11, 0.11
18, 3, 3	0.55, 0.13, 0.13

Table 3.1: Sample data and corresponding means

In the first row, we can see that for a dataset of 18 good samples out of 30, we get a mean value for θ of 0.6; remember that now the mean of θ is a vector of 3 elements, 1 per group. Then, on the second row, we have only 3 good samples out of 30 and the mean of θ is 0.11. These results should not be surprising; our estimates are practically the same as the empirical means. The interesting part comes in the third row. Instead of getting a mix of the mean estimates of θ from the other two rows, such as 0.6, 0.11, and 0.11, we get different values, namely 0.55, 0.13, and 0.13.

What on Earth happened? Did we make a mistake somewhere? Nothing like that. What we are seeing is that the estimates have shrunk toward the common mean. This is totally OK; indeed this is just a consequence of our model. By using hyperpriors, we are estimating the parameters of the Beta prior distribution from the data. Each group is informing the rest, and each group is informed by the estimation of the others.

Figure 3.5 shows the posterior estimates of μ and ν plugged into a Beta distribution. In other words, this is the posterior distribution of the inferred Beta prior distribution.

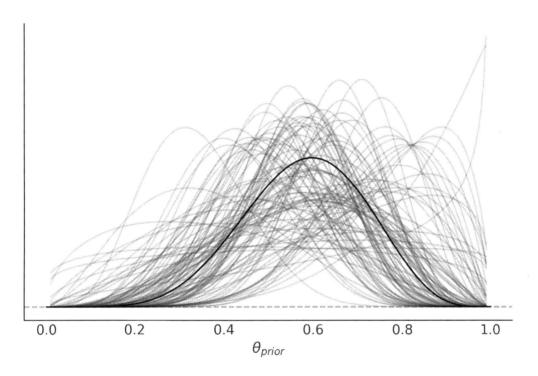

Figure 3.5: Posterior distribution of the inferred Beta prior distribution

Why is shrinkage desirable? Because it contributes to more stable inferences. This is, in many ways, similar to what we saw with the Student's t-distribution and the outliers; using a heavy-tailed distribution results in a more robust model to data points away from the mean. Introducing hyperpriors results in a more conservative model, one that is less responsive to extreme values in individual groups. Imagine that the sample sizes are different from each neighborhood, some small, some large; the smaller the sample size, the easier it is to get bogus results. At an extreme, if you take only one sample in a given neighborhood, you may just hit the only really old lead pipe in the whole neighborhood or, on the contrary, the only one made out of PVC. In one case, you will overestimate the bad quality and in the other underestimate it. Under a hierarchical model, the misestimation of one group will be ameliorated by the information provided by the other groups. A larger sample size will also do the trick but, more often than not, that is not an option.

The amount of shrinkage depends on the data; a group with more data will pull the estimate of the other groups harder than a group with fewer data points. If several groups are similar and one group is different, the similar groups are going to inform the others of their similarity and reinforce a common estimation, while pulling the estimation for the less similar group toward them; this is exactly what we saw in the previous example. The hyperpriors also have a role in modulating the amount of shrinkage. We can effectively use an informative prior distribution to shrink our estimate to some reasonable value if we have trustworthy information about the group-level distribution.

> ### Shrinkage
>
> In a hierarchical model, groups sharing a common hyperprior are effectively sharing information through the hyperprior. This results in shrinkage, that is, individual estimates are shrunk toward the common mean. By partially pooling the data, we are modeling the groups as some middle ground between the groups being independent of each other and being a single big group.

Nothing prevents us from building a hierarchical model with just two groups, but we would prefer to have several groups. Intuitively, the reason is that getting shrinkage is like assuming each group is a data point, and we are estimating the standard deviation at the group level. Generally, we do not trust an estimation with too few data points unless we have a strong prior informing our estimation. Something similar is true for a hierarchical model.

Hierarchies all the way up

Various data structures lend themselves to hierarchical descriptions that can encompass multiple levels. For example, consider professional football (soccer) players. As in many other sports, players have different positions. We may be interested in estimating some skill metrics for each player, for the positions, and for the overall group of professional football players. This kind of hierarchical structure can be found in many other domains as well:

- Medical research: Suppose we are interested in estimating the effectiveness of different drugs for treating a particular disease. We can categorize patients based on their demographic information, disease severity, and other relevant factors and build a hierarchical model to estimate the probability of cure or treatment success for each subgroup. We can then use the parameters of the subgroup distribution to estimate the overall probability of cure or treatment success for the entire patient population.

- Environmental science: Suppose we are interested in estimating the impact of a certain pollutant on a particular ecosystem. We can categorize different habitats within the ecosystem (e.g., rivers, lakes, forests, wetlands) and build a hierarchical model to estimate the distribution of pollutant levels within each habitat. We can then use the parameters of the habitat distribution to estimate the overall distribution of pollutant levels within the ecosystem.

- Market research: Suppose we are interested in understanding the purchasing behavior of consumers for a particular product across different regions. We can categorize consumers based on their demographic information (e.g., age, gender, income, education) and build a hierarchical model to estimate the distribution of purchasing behavior for each subgroup. We can then use the parameters of the subgroup distribution to estimate the distribution of purchasing behavior for the overall group of consumers.

Going back to our football players, we have collected data from the *Premier League*, *Ligue 1*, *Bundesliga*, *Serie A*, and *La Liga* over the course of four years (2017 to 2020). Let's suppose we are interested in the goals-per-shot metric. This is what statisticians usually call a *success rate*, and we can estimate it with a Binomial model where the parameter n is the number of shots and the observations y is the number of goals. This leaves us with an unknown value for p. In previous examples, we have been calling this parameter θ and we have used a Beta distribution to model it. We will do the same now, but hierarchically. See Figure 3.6 for a graphical representation of the entire model.

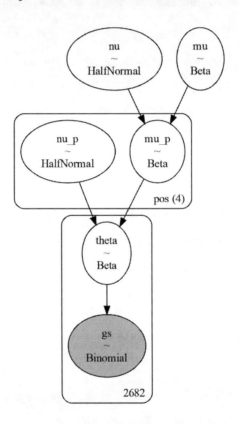

Figure 3.6: Hierarchical model for the football players example. Notice that we have one more level than in previous hierarchical models

In our model, θ represents the success rate for each player, and thus it is a vector of size n_players. We use a Beta distribution to model θ. The hyperparameters of the Beta distribution will be the vectors μ_p and ν_p, which are vectors of size 4, representing the four positions in our dataset (defender DF, midfielder MF, forward FW, and goalkeeper GK). We will need to properly index the vectors μ_p and ν_p to match the total number of players. Finally, we will have two global parameters, μ and ν, representing the professional football players.

The PyMC model is defined in the following block of code. pm.Beta('μ', 1.7, 5.8) was chosen with the help of PreliZ as a prior with 95% of the mass between 0 and 0.5. This is an example of a weakly informative prior, as there is little doubt that a success rate of 0.5 is a high value. Sports statistics are well-studied, and there is a lot of prior information that could be used to define stronger priors. For this example, we will settle on this prior. A similar justification can be done for the prior pm.Gamma('ν', mu=125, sigma=50), which we define as the maximum entropy Gamma prior with 90% of the mass between 50 and 200:

Code 3.5:

```
1  coords = {"pos": pos_codes}
2  with pm.Model(coords=coords) as model_football:
3      # Hyper parameters
4      μ = pm.Beta('μ', 1.7, 5.8)
5      ν = pm.Gamma('ν', mu=125, sigma=50)
6      # Parameters for positions
7      μ_p = pm.Beta('μ_p',
8                          mu=μ,
9                          nu=ν,
10                         dims = "pos")
11     ν_p = pm.Gamma('ν_p', mu=125, sigma=50, dims="pos")
12     # Parameter for players
13     θ = pm.Beta('θ',
14                       mu=μ_p[pos_idx],
15                       nu=ν_p[pos_idx])
16     _ = pm.Binomial('gs', n=football.shots.values, p=θ,
17                       observed=football.goals.values)
18
19     idata_football = pm.sample()
```

In the top panel of Figure 3.7, we have the posterior distribution for the global parameter μ. The posterior distribution is close to 0.1. This means that overall for a professional football player (from a top league), the probability of scoring a goal is on average 10%. This is a reasonable value, as scoring goals is not an easy task and we are not discriminating positions, i.e, we are considering players whose main role is not scoring goals. In the middle panel, we have the estimated μ_p value for the forward position; as expected, it is higher than the global parameter μ. In the bottom panel, we have the estimated θ value for Lionel Messi, with a value of 0.17, which is higher than the global parameter μ and the forward position μ_p value. This is also expected, as Lionel Messi is the best football player in the world, and his main role is scoring goals.

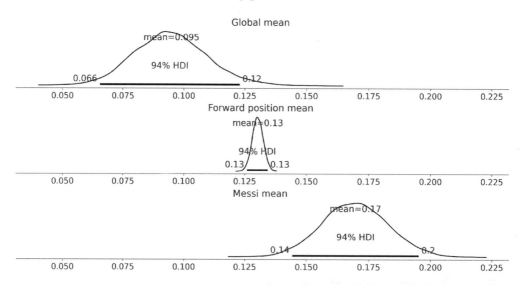

Figure 3.7: Posterior distribution for the mean global parameter (top), mean forward position (middle), and the θ parameter for Messi (bottom)

Figure 3.8 shows a forest plot for the posterior distribution for the parameter μ_p. The posterior distribution for the forward position is centered around 0.13, as we have already seen, and is the highest of the four. This makes sense as the role of the players at a forward position is scoring goals as well as assisting them. The lowest value of μ_p is for the goalkeeper position. This is expected, as the main role is to stop the opposing team from scoring, and not to score goals. The interesting aspect is that the uncertainty is very high; this is because we have very few goalkeepers scoring goals in our dataset, three to be precise. The posterior distributions for the defender and midfielder positions are somewhat in the middle, being slightly higher for the midfielder. We can explain this as the main role of a midfielder is to defend and attack, and thus the probability of scoring a goal is higher than a defender but lower than a forward.

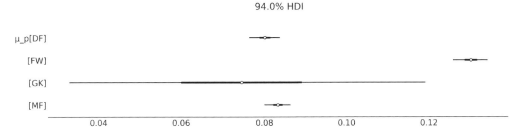

Figure 3.8: Posterior distribution for the parameter μ_p, the mean position

> **You Need to Know When to Stop**
>
> It is possible to create hierarchical models with as many levels as we want. But unless the problem necessitates additional structure, adding more levels than required does not enhance the quality of our model or inferences. Instead, we will get entangled in a web of hyperpriors and hyperparameters without the ability to assign any meaningful interpretation to them. The goal of building models is to make sense of data, and thus useful models are usually those that reflect and take advantage of the structure of the data.

Summary

In this chapter, we have presented one of the most important concepts to learn from this book: hierarchical models. We can build hierarchical models every time we can identify subgroups in our data. In such cases, instead of treating the subgroups as separate entities or ignoring the subgroups and treating them as a single group, we can build a model to partially pool information among groups. The main effect of this partial pooling is that the estimates of each subgroup will be biased by the estimates of the rest of the subgroups. This effect is known as shrinkage and, in general, is a very useful trick that helps to improve inferences by making them more conservative (as each subgroup informs the others by pulling estimates toward it) and more informative. We get estimates at the subgroup level and the group level.

Paraphrasing the Zen of Python, we can certainly say *hierarchical models are one honking great idea, let's do more of those!* In the following chapters, we will keep building hierarchical models and learn how to use them to build better models. We will also discuss how hierarchical models are related to the pervasive overfitting/underfitting issue in statistics and machine learning in Chapter 5. In Chapter 10, we will discuss some technical problems that we may find when sampling from hierarchical models and how to diagnose and fix those problems.

Exercises

1. Using your own words explain the following concepts in two or three sentences:

    -   Complete pooling
    -   No pooling
    -   Partial pooling

2. Repeat the exercise we did with model_h. This time, without a hierarchical structure, use a flat prior such as $\text{Beta}(\alpha = 1, \beta = 1)$. Compare the results of both models.

3. Create a hierarchical version of the tips example from Chapter 2, by partially pooling across the days of the week. Compare the results to those obtained without the hierarchical structure.

4. For each subpanel in Figure 3.7, add a reference line representing the empirical mean value at each level, that is, the global mean, the forward mean, and Messi's mean. Compare the empirical values to the posterior mean values. What do you observe?

5. Amino acids are usually grouped into categories such as polar, non-polar, charged, and special. Build a hierarchical model similar to cs_h but including a group effect for the amino acid category. Compare the results to those obtained in this chapter.

Join our community Discord space

Join our Discord community to meet like-minded people and learn alongside more than 5000 members at:

`https://packt.link/bayesian`

4

Modeling with Lines

In more than three centuries of science everything has changed except perhaps one thing: the love for the simple.

– Jorge Wagensberg

Music—from classical compositions to *Sheena is a Punk Rocker* by The Ramones, passing through unrecognized hits from garage bands and Piazzolla's Libertango—is made of recurring patterns. The same scales, combinations of chords, riffs, motifs, and so on appear over and over again, giving rise to a wonderful sonic landscape capable of eliciting and modulating the entire range of emotions that humans can experience. Similarly, the universe of statistics is built upon recurring patterns, small motifs that appear now and again. In this chapter, we are going to look at one of the most popular and useful of them, the **linear model** (or motif, if you want). This is a very useful model on its own and also the building block of many other models. If you've ever taken a statistics course, you may have heard of simple and multiple linear regression, logistic regression, ANOVA, ANCOVA, and so on. All these methods are variations of the same underlying motif, the linear regression model.

In this chapter, we will cover the following topics:

- Simple linear regression
- NegativeBinomial regression
- Robust regression
- Logistic regression
- Variable variance
- Hierarchical linear regression
- Multiple linear regression

Simple linear regression

Many problems we find in science, engineering, and business are of the following form. We have a variable X and we want to model or predict a variable Y. Importantly, these variables are paired like $\{(x_1, y_1), (x_2, y_2), \cdots, (x_n, y_n)\}$. In the most simple scenario, known as simple linear regression, both X and Y are uni-dimensional continuous random variables. By continuous, we mean a variable represented using real numbers. Using NumPy, you will represent these variables as one-dimensional arrays of floats. Usually, people call Y the dependent, predicted, or outcome variable, and X the independent, predictor, or input variable.

Some typical situations where linear regression models can be used are the following:

- Model the relationship between soil salinity and crop productivity. Then, answer questions such as: is the relationship linear? How strong is this relationship?
- Find a relationship between average chocolate consumption by country and the number of Nobel laureates in that country, and then understand why this relationship could be spurious.
- Predict the gas bill (used for heating and cooking) of your house by using the solar radiation from the local weather report. How accurate is this prediction?

In Chapter 2, we saw the Normal model, which we define as:

$$\mu \sim \text{some prior}$$

$$\sigma \sim \text{some other prior}$$

$$Y \sim \mathcal{N}(\mu, \sigma)$$

The main idea of linear regression is to extend this model by adding a predictor variable X to the estimation of the mean μ:

$$\alpha \sim \text{a prior}$$

$$\beta \sim \text{another prior}$$

$$\sigma \sim \text{some other prior}$$

$$\mu = \alpha + \beta X$$

$$Y \sim \mathcal{N}(\mu, \sigma)$$

This model says that there is a linear relation between the variable X and the variable Y. But that relationship is not deterministic, because of the noise term σ. Additionally, the model says that the mean of Y is a linear function of X, with **intercept** α and **slope** β. The intercept tells us the value of Y when $X = 0$ and the slope tells us the change in Y per unit change in X. Because we don't know the values of α, β, or σ we set priors distribution over them.

When setting priors for linear models we typically assume that they are independent. This assumption greatly simplifies setting priors because we then need to set three priors instead of one joint prior. At least in principle, α and β can take any value on the real line, thus it is common to use Normal priors for them. And because σ is a positive number, it is common to use a HalfNormal or Exponential prior for it.

The values the intercept can take can vary a lot from one problem to another and for different domain knowledge. For many problems I have worked on, α is usually centered around 0 and with a standard deviation no larger than 1, but this is just my experience (almost anecdotal) with a small subset of problems and not something easy to transfer to other problems. Usually, it may be easier to have an informed guess for the slope (β). For instance, we may know the sign of the slope a priori; for example, we expect the variable weight to increase, on average, with the variable height. For σ, we can set it to a large value on the scale of the variable Y, for example, two times the value for its standard deviation. We should be careful of using the observed data to guesstimate priors; usually, it is fine if the data is used to avoid using very restrictive priors. If we don't have too much knowledge of the parameter, it makes sense to ensure our prior is vague. If we instead want more informative priors, then we should not get that information from the observed data; instead, we should get it from our domain knowledge.

> **Extending the Normal Model**
>
> A linear regression model is an extension of the Normal model where the mean is computed as a linear function of a predictor variable.

Linear bikes

We now have a general idea of what Bayesian linear models look like. Let's try to cement that idea with an example. We are going to start very simply; we have a record of temperatures and the number of bikes rented in a city. We want to model the relationship between the temperature and the number of bikes rented. Figure 4.1 shows a scatter plot of these two variables from the bike-sharing dataset from the UCI Machine Learning Repository (https://archive.ics.uci.edu/ml/index.php).

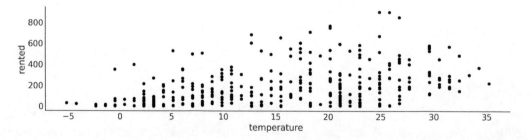

Figure 4.1: Bike-sharing dataset. Scatter plot of temperature in Celcius vs. number of rented bikes

The original dataset contains 17,379 records, and each record has 17 variables. We will only use 359 records and two variables, temperature (Celcius) rented (number of rented bikes). We are going to use temperature as our independent variable (our X) and the number of bikes rented as our dependent variable (our Y). We are going to use the following model:

Code 4.1:

```
1  with pm.Model() as model_lb:
2      α = pm.Normal("α", mu=0, sigma=100)
3      β = pm.Normal("β", mu=0, sigma=10)
4      σ = pm.HalfCauchy("σ", 10)
5      μ = pm.Deterministic("μ", α + β * bikes.temperature)
6      y_pred = pm.Normal("y_pred", mu=μ, sigma=σ, observed=bikes.rented)
7      idata_lb = pm.sample()
```

Take a moment to read the code line by line and be sure to understand what is going on. Also check Figure 4.2 for a visual representation of this model.

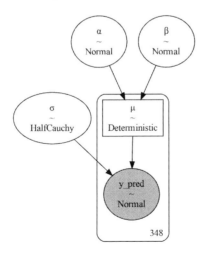

Figure 4.2: Bayesian linear model for the bike-sharing dataset

As we have previously said, this is like a Normal model, but now the mean is modeled as a linear function of the temperature. The intercept is α and the slope is β. The noise term is ϵ and the mean is μ. The only new thing here is the Deterministic variable μ. This variable is not a random variable, it is a deterministic variable, and it is computed from the intercept, the slope, and the temperature. We need to specify this variable because we want to save it in InferenceData for later use. We could have just written μ = α + β * bikes.temperature or even _ = pm.Normal('y_pred', mu=α + β * bikes.temperature, ... and the model will be the same, but we would not have been able to save μ in InferenceData. Notice that μ is a vector with the same length as bikes.temperature, which is the same as the number of records in the dataset.

Interpreting the posterior mean

To explore the results of our inference, we are going to generate a posterior plot but omit the deterministic variable μ. We commit it because otherwise, we would get a lot of plots, one for each value of temperature. We can do this by passing the names of the variables we want to include in the plot as a list to the var_names argument or we can negate the variable that we want to exclude as in the following block of code:

Code 4.2:

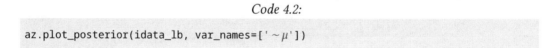

```
az.plot_posterior(idata_lb, var_names=['~μ'])
```

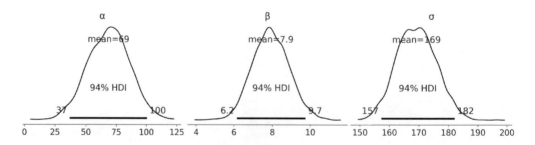

Figure 4.3: Posterior plot for the bike linear model

From Figure 4.3, we can see the marginal posterior distribution for α, β, and σ. If we only read the means of each distribution, say $\mu = 69 + 7.9X$, with this information we can say that the expected value of rented bikes when the temperature is 0 is 69, and for each degree of temperature the number of rented bikes increases by 7.9. So for a temperature of 28 degrees, we expect to rent $69 + 7.9 * 28 \approx 278$ bikes. This is our expectation, but the posterior also informs us about the uncertainty around this estimate. For instance, the 94% HDI for β is (6.1, 9.7), so for each degree of temperature the number of rented bikes could increase from 6 to about 10. Also even if we omit the posterior uncertainty and we only pay attention to the means, we still have uncertainty about the number of rented bikes because we have a value of σ of 170. So if we say that for a temperature of 28 degrees, we expect to rent 278 bikes, we should not be surprised if the actual number turns out to be somewhere between 100 and 500 bikes.

Now let's create a few plots that will help us visualize the combined uncertainty of these parameters. Let's start with two plots for the mean (see Figure 4.4). Both are plots of the mean number of rented bikes as a function of the temperature. The difference is how we represent the uncertainty. We show two popular ways of doing it. In the left subpanel, we take 50 samples from the posterior and plot them as individual lines. In the right subpanel, we instead take all the available posterior samples for μ and use them to compute the 94% HDI.

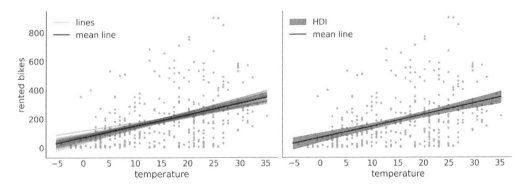

Figure 4.4: Posterior plot for the bike linear model

The plots in Figure 4.4 convey essentially the same information, but one represents uncertainty as a set of lines and the other as a shaded area. Notice that if you repeat the code to generate the plot, you will get different lines, because we are sampling from the posterior. The shaded area, however, will be the same, because we are using all the available posterior samples. If we go further and refit the model, we will not only get different lines but the shaded area could also change, and probably the difference between runs is going to be very small; if not, you probably need to increase the number of draws, or there is something funny about your model and sampling (see Chapter 10 for guidance).

Anyway, why are we showing two slightly different plots if they convey the same information? Well, to highlight that there are different ways to represent uncertainty. Which one is better? As usual, that is context-dependent. The shaded area is a good option; it is very common, and it is simple to compute and interpret. Unless there are specific reasons to show individual posterior samples, the shaded area may be your preferred choice. But we may want to show individual posterior samples. For instance, most of the lines might span a certain region, but we get a few with very high slopes. A shaded area could hide that information. When showing individual samples from the posterior it may be a good idea to animate them if you are showing them in a presentation or a video (see Kale et al. [2019] for more on this).

Another reason to show you the two plots in Figure 4.4 is that you can learn different ways of extracting information from the posterior. Please pay attention to the next block of code. For clarity, we have omitted the code for plotting and we only show the core computations:

Code 4.3:

```
1  posterior = az.extract(idata_lb, num_samples=50)
2  x_plot = xr.DataArray(
3      np.linspace(bikes.temperature.min(), bikes.temperature.max(), 50),
4      dims="plot_id"
5  )
6  mean_line = posterior["α"].mean() + posterior["β"].mean() * x_plot
7  lines = posterior["α"] + posterior["β"] * x_plot
8  hdi_lines = az.hdi(idata_lb.posterior["μ"])
9  ...
```

You can see that in the first line, we used `az.extract`. This function takes the `chain` and `draw` dimensions and stacks them in a single `sample` dimension, which can be useful for later processing. Additionally, we use the `num_samples` argument to ask for a subsample from the posterior. By default, `az.extract` will operate on the posterior group. If you want to extract information from another group, you can use the `group` argument. On the second line, we define a DataArray called `x_plot`, with equally spaced values ranging from the minimum to the maximum observed temperatures. The reason to create a DataArray is to be able to use Xarray's automatic alignment capabilities in the next two lines. If we use a NumPy array, we will need to add extra dimensions, which is usually confusing. The best way to fully understand what I mean is to define `x_plot = np.linspace(bikes.temperature.min(), bikes.temperature.max())` and try to redo the plot. In the third line of code, we compute the mean of the posterior for μ for each value of `x_plot`, and in the fourth line, we compute individual values for μ. In these two lines we could have used `posterior['`μ`']`, but instead, we explicitly rewrite the linear model. We do this with the hope that it will help you to gain more intuition about linear models.

Interpreting the posterior predictions

What if we are not just interested in the expected (mean) value, but we want to think in terms of predictions, that is, in terms of rented bikes? Well, for that, we can do posterior predictive sampling. After executing the next line of code, `idata_lb` will be populated with a new group, `posterior_predictive`, with a variable, `y_pred`, representing the posterior predictive distribution for the number of rented bikes.

Code 4.4:

```
pm.sample_posterior_predictive(idata_lb, model=model_lb, extend_inferencedata=True)
```

The black line in Figure 4.5 is the mean of the number of rented bikes. This is the same as in Figure 4.4. The new elements are the dark gray band representing the central 50% (quantiles 0.25 and 0.75) for the rented bikes and the light gray band, representing the central 94% (quantiles 0.03 and 0.97). You may notice that our model is predicting a negative number of bikes, which does not make sense. But upon reflection, this should be expected as we use a Normal distribution for the likelihood in `model_lb`. A very dirty *fix* could be to clip the predictions at values lower than 0, but that's ugly. In the next section, we will see that we can easily improve this model to avoid nonsensical predictions.

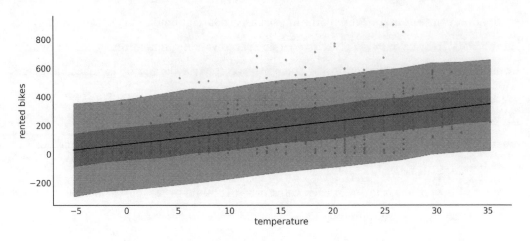

Figure 4.5: Posterior predictive plot for the bike linear model

Generalizing the linear model

The linear model we have been using is a special case of a more general model, the **Generalized Linear Model (GLM)**. The GLM is a generalization of the linear model that allows us to use different distributions for the likelihood. At a high level, we can write a Bayesian GLM like:

$$\alpha \sim \text{a prior}$$
$$\beta \sim \text{another prior}$$
$$\theta \sim \text{some prior}$$
$$\mu = \alpha + \beta X$$
$$Y \sim \phi(f(\mu), \theta)$$

ϕ is an arbitrary distribution; some common cases are Normal, Student's t, Gamma, and NegativeBinomial. θ represents any *auxiliary* parameter the distribution may have, like σ for the Normal. We also have f, usually called the inverse link function. When ϕ is Normal, then f is the identity function. For distributions like Gamma and NegativeBinomial, f is usually the exponential function. Why do we need f? Because the linear model will generally be on the real line, but the μ parameter (or its equivalent) may be defined on a different domain. For instance, μ for the NegativeBinomial is defined for positive values, so we need to transform μ. The exponential function is a good candidate for this transformation. We are going to explore a few GLMs in this book. A good exercise for you, while reading the book, is to create a table, and every time you see a new GLM, you add one line indicating what ϕ, θ, and f are and maybe some notes about when this GLM is used. OK, let's start with our first concrete example of a GLM.

Counting bikes

How can we change model_lb to better accommodate the bike data? There are two things to note: the number of rented bikes is discrete and it is bounded at 0. This is usually known as count data, which is data that is the result of counting something. Count data is sometimes modeled using a continuous distribution like a Normal, especially when the number of counts is large. But it is often a good idea to use a discrete distribution. Two common choices are the Poisson and NegativeBinomial distributions. The main difference is that for Poisson, the mean and the variance are the same, but if this is not true or even approximately true, then NegativeBinomial may be a better choice as it allows the mean and variance to be different. When in doubt, you can fit both Poisson and NegativeBinomial and see which one provides a better model. We are going to do that in Chapter 5. But for now, we are going to use NegativeBinomial.

Code 4.5:

```
1  with pm.Model() as model_neg:
2      α = pm.Normal("α", mu=0, sigma=1)
3      β = pm.Normal("β", mu=0, sigma=10)
4      σ = pm.HalfNormal("σ", 10)
5      μ = pm.Deterministic("μ", pm.math.exp(α + β * bikes.temperature))
6      y_pred = pm.NegativeBinomial("y_pred", mu=μ, alpha=σ, observed=bikes.rented)
7      idata_neg = pm.sample()
8      idata_neg.extend(pm.sample_posterior_predictive(idata_neg))
```

The PyMC model is very similar to the previous one but with two main differences. First, we use pm.NegativeBinomial instead of pm.Normal for the likelihood. The NegativeBinomial distribution has two parameters, the mean μ and a dispersion parameter α. The variance of NegativeBinomial is $\mu + \frac{\mu^2}{\alpha}$, so the larger the value of α the larger the variance. The second difference is that μ is pm.math.exp(α + β * bikes.temperature) instead of just α + β * bikes.temperature and, as we already explained, this is needed to transform the real line into the positive interval.

The posterior predictive distribution for model_neg is shown in Figure 4.6. The posterior predictive distribution is also very similar to the one we obtained with the linear model (Figure 4.5). The main difference is that now we are not predicting a negative number of rented bikes! We can also see that the variance of the predictions increases with the mean. This is expected because the variance of NegativeBinomial is $\mu + \frac{\mu^2}{\alpha}$.

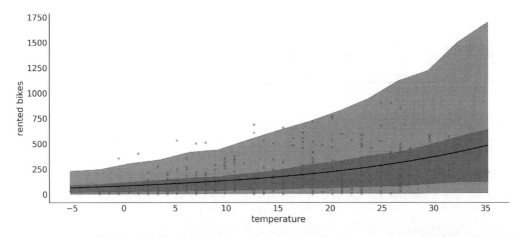

Figure 4.6: Posterior predictive plot for the bike NegativeBinomial linear model

Figure 4.7 shows the posterior predictive check for model_lb on the left and model_neg on the right. We can see that when using a Normal, the largest mismatch is that the model predicts a negative number of rented bikes, but even on the positive side we see that the fit is not that good. On the other hand, the NegativeBinomial model seems to be a better fit, although it's not perfect. Look at the right tail: it's heavier for the predictions than observations. But also notice that the probability of this very high demand is low. So, overall we can restate that the NegativeBinomial model is better than the Normal one.

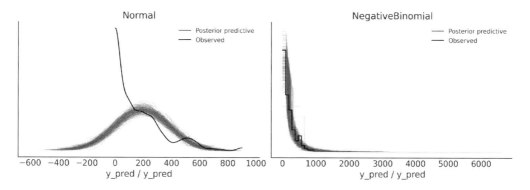

Figure 4.7: Posterior predictive check for the bike linear model

Robust regression

I once ran a complex simulation of a molecular system. At each step of the simulation, I needed it to fit a linear regression as an intermediate step. I had theoretical and empirical reasons to think that my Y was conditionally Normal given my Xs, so I decided simple linear regression should do the trick. But from time to time the simulation generated a few values of Y that were way above or below the bulk of the data. This completely ruined my simulation and I had to restart it.

Usually, these values that are very different from the bulk of the data are called outliers. The reason for the failure of my simulations was that the outliers were *pulling* the regression line away from the bulk of the data and when I passed this estimate to the next step in the simulation, the thing just halted. I solved this with the help of our good friend the Student's t-distribution, which, as we saw in Chapter 2, has heavier tails than the Normal distribution. This means that the outliers have less influence on the regression line. This is an example of a robust regression.

To exemplify the robustness that a Student's T distribution brings to linear regression, we are going to use a very simple and nice dataset: the third data group from Anscombe's quartet. If you do not know what Anscombe's quartet is, check it out on Wikipedia (https://en.wikipedia.org/wiki/Anscombe%27s_quartet).

In the following model, `model_t`, we are using a shifted exponential to avoid values close to 0. The non-shifted Exponential puts too much weight on values close to 0. In my experience, this is fine for data with none to moderate outliers, but for data with extreme outliers (or data with a few bulk points), like in Anscombe's third dataset, it is better to avoid such low values. Take this, as well as other prior recommendations, with a pinch of salt. The defaults are good starting points, but there's no need to stick to them. Other common priors are Gamma(2, 0.1) and Gamma(mu=20, sigma=15), which are somewhat similar to Exponential(1/30) but with less values closer to 0:

Code 4.6:

```
1  with pm.Model() as model_t:
2      α = pm.Normal("α", mu=ans.y.mean(), sigma=1)
3      β = pm.Normal("β", mu=0, sigma=1)
4      σ = pm.HalfNormal("σ", 5)
5      ν_ = pm.Exponential("ν_", 1 / 29)
6      ν = pm.Deterministic("ν", ν_ + 1)
7      μ = pm.Deterministic("μ", α + β * ans.x)
8      _ = pm.StudentT("y_pred", mu=μ, sigma=σ, nu=ν, observed=ans.y)
9      idata_t = pm.sample(2000)
```

In Figure 4.8, we can see the robust fit, according to `model_t`, and the non-robust fit, according to SciPy's `linregress` (this function is doing least-squares regression).

While the non-robust fit tries to *compromise* and include all points, the robust Bayesian model, `model_t`, automatically *discards* one point and fits a line that passes closer through all the remaining points. I know this is a very peculiar dataset, but the message remains the same as for other datasets; a Student's t-distribution, due to its heavier tails, gives less importance to points that are far away from the bulk of the data.

From Figure 4.9, we can see that for the bulk of the data, we get a very good match. Also, notice that our model predicts values away from the bulk to both sides and not just above the bulk (as in the observed data). For our current purposes, this model is performing just fine and it does not need further changes. Nevertheless, notice that for some problems, we

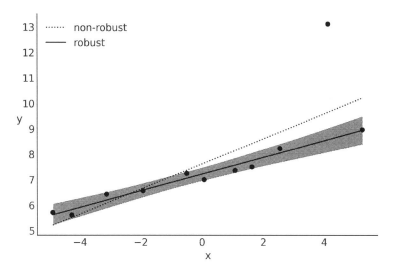

Figure 4.8: Robust regression according to `model_t`

may want to avoid this. In such a case, we should probably go back and change the model to restrict the possible values of `y_pred` to positive values using a truncated Student's t-distribution. This is left as an exercise for the reader.

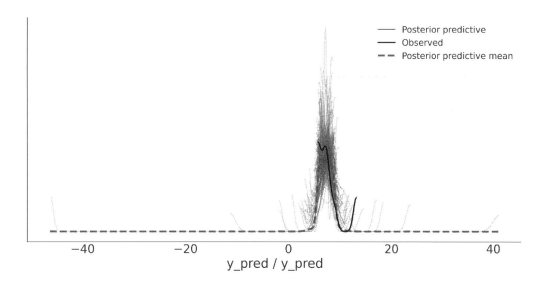

Figure 4.9: Posterior predictive check for `model_t`

Logistic regression

The logistic regression model is a generalization of the linear regression model, which we can use when the response variable is binary. This model uses the logistic function as an inverse link function. Let's get familiar with this function before we move on to the model:

$$\text{logistic}(z) = \frac{1}{1 + e^{-z}}$$

For our purpose, the key property of the logistic function is that irrespective of the values of its argument z, the result will always be a number in the [0-1] interval. Thus, we can see this function as a convenient way to compress the values computed from a linear model into values that we can feed into a Bernoulli distribution. This logistic function is also known as the sigmoid function because of its characteristic S-shaped aspect, as we can see from Figure 4.10.

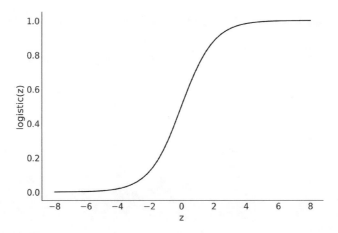

Figure 4.10: Logistic function

The logistic model

We have almost all the elements to turn a simple linear regression into a simple logistic regression. Let's begin with the case of only two classes, for example, ham/spam, safe/unsafe, cloudy/sunny, healthy/ill, or hotdog/not hotdog. First, we codify these classes by saying that the predicted variable y can only take two values, 0 or 1, that is $y \in \{0, 1\}$.

Stated this way, the problem sounds very similar to the coin-flipping one we used in previous chapters. We may remember we used the Bernoulli distribution as the likelihood. The difference with the coin-flipping problem is that now θ is not going to be generated from a beta distribution; instead, θ is going to be defined by a linear model with the logistic as the inverse link function. Omitting the priors, we have:

$$\theta = \text{logistic}(\alpha + \beta x)$$

$$y \sim \text{Bernoulli}(\theta)$$

We are going to apply logistic regression to the classic iris dataset which has measurements from flowers from three closely related species: setosa, virginica, and versicolor. These measurements are the petal length, petal width, sepal length, and sepal width. In case you are wondering, sepals are modified leaves whose function is generally related to protecting the flowers in a bud.

We are going to begin with a simple case. Let's assume we only have two classes, setosa, and versicolor, and just one independent variable or feature, sepal_length. We want to predict the probability of a flower being setosa given its sepal length.

As is usually done, we are going to encode the setosa and versicolor categories with the numbers 0 and 1. Using pandas, we can do the following:

Code 4.7:

```
1  df = iris.query("species == ('setosa', 'versicolor')")
2  y_0 = pd.Categorical(df["species"]).codes
3  x_n = "sepal_length"
4  x_0 = df[x_n].values
5  x_c = x_0 - x_0.mean()
```

As with other linear models, centering the data can help with the sampling. Now that we have the data in the right format, we can finally build the model with PyMC:

Code 4.8:

```python
with pm.Model() as model_lrs:
    α = pm.Normal("α", mu=0, sigma=1)
    β = pm.Normal("β", mu=0, sigma=5)
    μ = α + x_c * β
    θ = pm.Deterministic("θ", pm.math.sigmoid(μ))
    bd = pm.Deterministic("bd", -α / β)
    yl = pm.Bernoulli("yl", p=θ, observed=y_0)

    idata_lrs = pm.sample()
```

`model_lrs` has two deterministic variables: θ and bd. θ is the result of applying the logistic function to variable μ. bd is the boundary decision, which is the value we use to separate classes. We will discuss this later in detail. Another point worth mentioning is that instead of writing the logistic function ourselves, we are using the one provided by PyMC, `pm.math.sigmoid`.

Figure 4.11 shows the result of `model_lrs`:

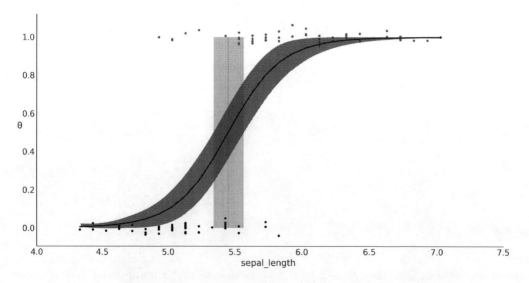

Figure 4.11: Logistic regression, result of `model_lrs`

Figure 4.11 shows the sepal length versus the probability of being versicolor θ (and if you want, also the probability of being setosa, $1 - \theta$). We have added some jitter (noise) to the binary response so the point does not overlap. An S-shaped (black) line is the mean value of θ. This line can be interpreted as the probability of a flower being versicolor, given that we know the value of the sepal length. The semitransparent S-shaped band is the 94% HDI. What about the vertical line? That's the topic of the next section.

Classification with logistic regression

My mother prepares a delicious dish called sopa seca, which is basically a spaghetti-based recipe and translates literally to "dry soup." While it may sound like a misnomer or even an oxymoron, the name of the dish makes total sense when you learn how it is cooked (you may check out the recipe in the GitHub repo for this book at `https://github.com/aloctavodia/BAP3`). Something similar happens with logistic regression, a model that, despite its name, is generally framed as a method for solving classification problems. Let's see the source of this duality.

Regression problems are about predicting a continuous value for an output variable given the values of one or more input variables. We have seen many examples of regression that include logistic regression. However, logistic regression is usually discussed in terms of classification. Classification involves assigning discrete values (representing a class, like versicolor) to an output variable given some input variables, for instance, stating that a flower is versicolor or setosa given its sepal length.

So, is logistic regression a regression or a classification method? The answer is that it is a regression method; we are regressing the probability of belonging to some class, but it can be used for classification too. The only thing we need is a decision rule: for example, we assign the class `versicolor` if $\theta \geq 0.5$ and assign `setosa` otherwise. The vertical line in Figure 4.11 is the boundary decision, and it is defined as the value of the independent variable that makes the probability of being versicolor equal to 0.5. We can calculate this value analytically, and it is equal to $-\frac{\alpha}{\beta}$. This calculation is based on the definition of the model:

$$\theta = \text{logistic}(\alpha + \beta x)$$

And from the definition of the logistic function, we have that $\theta = 0.5$ when $\alpha + \beta x = 0$.

$$0.5 = \text{logistic}(\alpha + \beta x) \Longleftrightarrow 0 = \alpha + \beta x$$

Reordering, we find that the value of x that makes $\theta = 0.5$ is $-\frac{\alpha}{\beta}$.

Because we have uncertainty in the value of α and β, we also have uncertainty about the value of the boundary decision. This uncertainty is represented as the vertical (gray) band in Figure 4.11, which goes from ≈ 5.3 to ≈ 5.6. If we were doing automatic classification of flowers based on their sepal length (or any similar problem that could be framed within this model), we could assign setosa to flowers with a sepal length below 5.3 and versicolor to flowers with sepal length above 5.6. For flowers with a sepal lengths between 5.3 and 5.6, we would be uncertain about their class, so we could either assign them randomly or use some other information to make a decision, including asking a human to check the flower.

To summarize this section:

- The value of θ is, generally speaking, $P(Y = 1 \mid X)$. In this sense, logistic regression is a true regression; the key detail is that we are regressing the probability that a data point belongs to class 1, given a linear combination of features.
- We are modeling the mean of a dichotomous variable, which is a number in the [0-1] interval. Thus, if we want to use logistic regression for classification, we need to introduce a rule to turn this probability into a two-class assignment. For example, if $P(Y = 1) > 0.5$, we assign that observation to class 1, otherwise we assign it to class 0.
- There is nothing special about the value of 0.5, other than that it is the number in the middle of 0 and 1. This boundary can be justified when we are OK with misclassifying a data point in either direction. But this is not always the case, because the cost associated with the misclassification does not need to be symmetrical. For example,

if we are trying to predict whether a patient has a disease or not, we may want to use a boundary that minimizes the number of false negatives (patients that have the disease but we predict they don't) or false positives (patients that don't have the disease but we predict they do). We will discuss this in more detail in the next section.

Interpreting the coefficients of logistic regression

We must be careful when interpreting the coefficients of logistic regression. Interpretation is not as straightforward as with simple linear models. Using the logistic inverse link function introduces a non-linearity that we have to take into account. If β is positive, increasing x will increase $p(y = 1)$ by some amount, but the amount is not a linear function of x. Instead, the dependency is non-linear on the value of x, meaning that the effect of x on $p(y = 1)$ depends on the value of x. We can visualize this fact in Figure 4.11. Instead of a line with a constant slope, we have an S-shaped line with a slope that changes as a function of x.

A little bit of algebra can give us some further insight into how much $p(y = 1)$ changes with x. The basic logistic model is:

$$\theta = \text{logistic}(\alpha + \beta x)$$

The inverse of the logistic is the logit function, which is:

$$\text{logit}(z) = \log \frac{z}{1 - z}$$

Combining these two expressions, we get:

$$\text{logit}(\theta) = \log \frac{\theta}{1 - \theta} = \alpha + \beta x$$

Remember that θ in our model is $p(y = 1)$, so we can rewrite the previous expression as:

$$\log \left(\frac{p(y = 1)}{1 - p(y = 1)} \right) = \alpha + \beta x$$

The $\frac{p(y=1)}{1-p(y=1)}$ quantity is known as the **odds** of $y = 1$. If we call $y = 1$ a *success*, then the odds of success is the ratio of the probability of success over the probability of failure. For example, while the probability of getting a 2 by rolling a fair die is $\frac{1}{6}$, the odds of getting a 2 are $\frac{1/6}{5/6} = \frac{1}{5} = 0.2$. In other words, there is one favorable event for every five unfavorable events. Odds are often used by gamblers because they provide a more intuitive tool to think about bets than raw probabilities. Figure 4.12 shows how probabilities are related to odds and log-odds.

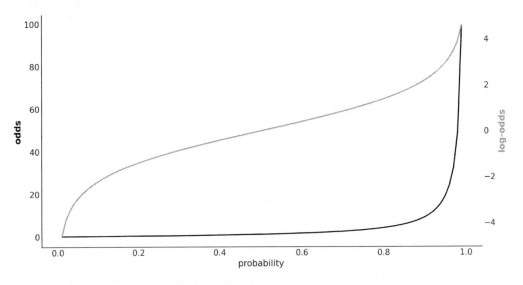

Figure 4.12: Relationship between probability, odds, and log-odds

> **Interpreting Logistic Regression**
>
> In logistic regression, the β coefficient (the *slope*) encodes the increase in log-odds units by a unit increase of the x variable.

The transformation from probability to odds is a monotonic transformation, meaning the odds increase as the probability increases, and the other way around. While probabilities are restricted to the $[0, 1]$ interval, odds live in the $[0, \infty)$ interval. The logarithm is another monotonic transformation and log-odds are in the $(-\infty, \infty)$ interval.

Variable variance

We have been using the linear motif to model the mean of a distribution and, in the previous section, we used it to model interactions. In statistics, it is said that a linear regression model presents heteroskedasticity when the variance of the errors is not constant in all the observations made. For those cases, we may want to consider the variance (or standard deviation) as a (linear) function of the dependent variable.

The World Health Organization and other health institutions around the world collect data for newborns and toddlers and design growth chart standards. These charts are an essential component of the pediatric toolkit and also a measure of the general well-being of populations to formulate health-related policies, plan interventions, and monitor their effectiveness. An example of such data is the lengths (heights) of newborn/toddler girls as a function of their age (in months):

Code 4.9:

```
1  data = pd.read_csv("data/babies.csv")
2  data.plot.scatter("month", "length")
```

To model this data, we are going to introduce three elements we have not seen before:

- σ is now a linear function of the predictor variable. Thus, we add two new parameters, γ and δ. These are direct analogs of α and β in the linear model for the mean.
- The linear model for the mean is a function of $\sqrt{X}$. This is just a simple trick to fit a linear model to a curve.
- We define a `MutableData` variable, `x_shared`. Why we want to do this will become clear soon.

Our full model is:

Code 4.10:

```
1  with pm.Model() as model_vv:
2      x_shared = pm.MutableData("x_shared", data.month.values.astype(float))
3      α = pm.Normal("α", sigma=10)
4      β = pm.Normal("β", sigma=10)
5      γ = pm.HalfNormal("γ", sigma=10)
6      δ = pm.HalfNormal("δ", sigma=10)
7
8      μ = pm.Deterministic("μ", α + β * x_shared**0.5)
9      σ = pm.Deterministic("σ", γ + δ * x_shared)
10
11     y_pred = pm.Normal("y_pred", mu=μ, sigma=σ, observed=data.length)
12
13     idata_vv = pm.sample()
```

On the left panel of Figure 4.13, we can see the mean of μ represented by a black curve, and the two semi-transparent gray bands represent one and two standard deviations. On the right panel, we have the estimated variance as a function of the length. As you can see, the variance increases with the length, which is what we expected.

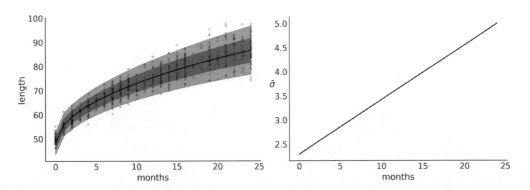

Figure 4.13: Posterior fit for model_vv *on the left panel. On the right is the mean estimated variance as a function of the length*

Now that we have fitted the model, we might want to use the model to find out how the length of a particular girl compares to the distribution. One way to answer this question is to ask the model for the distribution of the variable `length` for babies of, say, 0.5 months. We can answer this question by sampling from the posterior predictive distribution conditional on a length of 0.5. Using PyMC, we can get the answer by sampling `pm.sample_posterior_predictive`; the only problem is that by default, this function will return values of $\tilde{y}$ for the already observed values of x, i.e., the values used to fit the model. The easiest way to get predictions for unobserved values is to define a `MutableData` variable (`x_shared` in the example) and then update the value of this variable right before sampling the posterior predictive distribution, as shown in the following code block:

Code 4.11:

```
1 with model_vv:
2     pm.set_data({"x_shared": [0.5]})
3     ppc = pm.sample_posterior_predictive(idata_vv)
4     y_ppc = ppc.posterior_predictive["y_pred"].stack(sample=("chain", "draw"))
```

Now we can plot the expected distribution of lengths for 2-week-old girls and calculate other quantities, like the percentile for a girl of that length (see Figure 4.14).

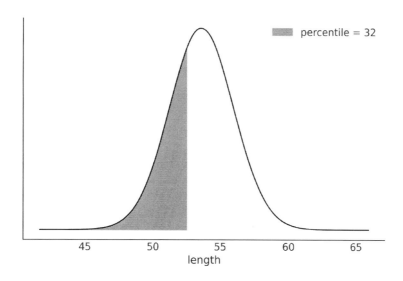

Figure 4.14: Expected distribution of length at 0.5 months. The shaded area represents 32% of the accumulated mass

Hierarchical linear regression

In Chapter 3, we learned the rudiments of hierarchical models, a very powerful concept that allows us to model complex data structures. Hierarchical models allow us to deal with inferences at the group level and estimations above the group level. As we have already seen, this is done by including hyperpriors. We also showed that groups can share information by using a common hyperprior and this provides shrinkage, which can help us to regularize the estimates.

We can apply these very same concepts to linear regression to obtain hierarchical linear regression models. In this section, we are going to walk through two examples to elucidate the application of these concepts in practical scenarios. The first one uses a synthetic dataset, and the second one uses the `pigs` dataset.

For the first example, I have created eight related groups, including one group with just one data point. We can see what the data looks like from Figure 4.15. If you want to learn more how this data was generated please check the GitHub repository `https://github.com/aloctavodia/BAP3`.

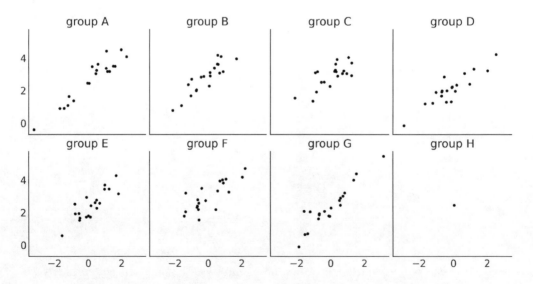

Figure 4.15: Synthetic data for the hierarchical linear regression example

First, we are going to fit a non-hierarchical model:

Code 4.12:

```
1  coords = {"group": ["A", "B", "C", "D", "E", "F", "G", "H"]}
2
3  with pm.Model(coords=coords) as unpooled_model:
4      α = pm.Normal("α", mu=0, sigma=10, dims="group")
5      β = pm.Normal("β", mu=0, sigma=10, dims="group")
6      σ = pm.HalfNormal("σ", 5)
7      _ = pm.Normal("y_pred", mu=α[idx] + β[idx] * x_m, sigma=σ, observed=y_m)
8
9      idata_up = pm.sample()
```

Figure 4.16 shows the posterior estimated values for the parameters α and β.

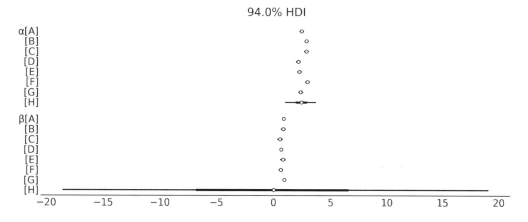

Figure 4.16: Posterior distribution for α and β for unpooled_model

As you can see from Figure 4.16 the estimates for group H are very different from the ones for the other groups. This is expected as for group H, we only have one data point, that is we do not have enough information to fit a line. We need at least two points; otherwise, the model will be over-parametrized, meaning we have more parameters than the ones we can determine from the data alone.

To overcome this situation we can provide some more information; we can do this by using priors or by adding more structure to the model. Let's add more structure by building a hierarchical model.

This is the PyMC model for the hierarchical model:

Code 4.13:

```
1  with pm.Model(coords=coords) as hierarchical_centered:
2      # hyperpriors
3      α_μ = pm.Normal("α_μ", mu=y_m.mean(), sigma=1)
4      α_σ = pm.HalfNormal("α_σ", 5)
5      β_μ = pm.Normal("β_μ", mu=0, sigma=1)
6      β_σ = pm.HalfNormal("β_σ", sigma=5)
7
8      # priors
9      α = pm.Normal("α", mu=α_μ, sigma=α_σ, dims="group")
10     β = pm.Normal("β", mu=β_μ, sigma=β_σ, dims="group")
11     σ = pm.HalfNormal("σ", 5)
12     _ = pm.Normal("y_pred", mu=α[idx] + β[idx] * x_m, sigma=σ, observed=y_m)
13
14     idata_cen = pm.sample()
```

If you run `hierarchical_centered`, you will see a message from PyMC saying something like `There were 149 divergences after tuning. Increase target_accept or reparameterize`. This message means that samples generated from PyMC may not be trustworthy. So far, we have assumed that PyMC always returns samples that we can use without issues, but that's not always the case. In Chapter 10, we further discuss why this is, along with diagnostic methods to help you identify those situations and recommendations to fix the potential issues. In that section, we also explain what divergences are. For now, we will only say that when working with hierarchical linear models, we will usually get a lot of divergences.

The easy way to solve them is to increase `target_accept`, as PyMC kindly suggests. This is an argument of `pm.sample()` that defaults to 0.8 and can take a maximum value of 1.

If you see divergences, setting this argument to values like 0.85, 0.9, or even higher can help. But if you reach values like 0.99 and still have divergences, you are probably out of luck with this simple trick and you need to do something else. And that's reparametrization. What is this? Reparametrization is writing a model in a different way, but that is mathematically equivalent to your original model: you are not changing the model, just writing it in another way. Many models, if not all, can be written in alternative ways. Sometimes, reparametrization can have a positive effect on the efficiency of the sampler or on the model's interpretability. For instance, you can remove divergences by doing a reparametrization. Let's see how to do that in the next section.

Centered vs. noncentered hierarchical models

There are two common parametrizations for hierarchical linear models, centered and non-centered. The `hierarchical_centered` model uses the centered one. The hallmark of this parametrization is that we are directly estimating parameters for individual groups; for instance, we are explicitly estimating the slope of each group. On the contrary, for the non-centered parametrization, we estimate the common slope for all groups and then a deflection for each group. It is important to notice that we are still modeling the slope of each group, but relative to the common slope, the information we are getting is the same, just represented differently. Since a model is worth a thousand words, let's check `hierarchical_non_centered`:

Code 4.14:

```
1  with pm.Model(coords=coords) as hierarchical_non_centered:
2      # hyperpriors
3      α_μ = pm.Normal("α_μ", mu=y_m.mean(), sigma=1)
4      α_σ = pm.HalfNormal("α_σ", 5)
5      β_μ = pm.Normal("β_μ", mu=0, sigma=1)
6      β_σ = pm.HalfNormal("β_σ", sigma=5)
7
8      # priors
9      α = pm.Normal("α", mu=α_μ, sigma=α_σ, dims="group")
```

```
10
11      β_offset = pm.Normal("β_offset", mu=0, sigma=1, dims="group")
12      β = pm.Deterministic("β", β_μ + β_offset * β_σ, dims="group")
13
14      σ = pm.HalfNormal("σ", 5)
15      _ = pm.Normal("y_pred", mu=α[idx] + β[idx] * x_m, sigma=σ, observed=y_m)
16
17      idata_ncen = pm.sample(target_accept=0.85)
```

The difference is that for the model `hierarchical_centered`, we defined $\beta \sim \mathcal{N}(\beta_\mu, \beta_\sigma)$, and for `hierarchical_non_centered` we did $\beta = \beta_\mu + \beta_{\text{offset}} * \beta_\sigma$. The non-centered parametrization is more efficient: when I run the model I only get 2 divergences instead of 148 as before. To remove these remaining divergences, we may still need to increase `target_accept`. For this particular case, changing it from 0.8 to 0.85 worked like magic. To fully understand why this reparametrization works, you need to understand the geometry of the posterior distribution, but that's beyond the scope of this section. Don't worry, we will discuss this in Chapter 10.

Now that our samples are divergence-free, we can go back to analyze the posterior. Figure 4.17 shows the estimated values for α and β for `hierarchical_model`.

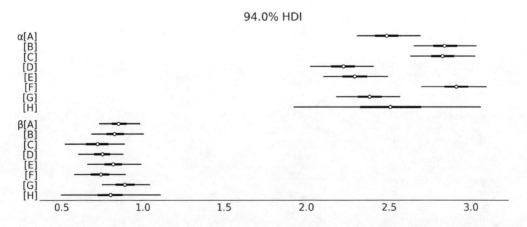

Figure 4.17: Posterior distribution for α and β for `hierarchical_non_centered`

The estimates for group H are still the ones with higher uncertainty. But the results look less crazy than those in Figure 4.16; the reason is that groups are sharing information. Hence, even when we don't have enough information to fit a line to a single point, group H *is being informed* by the other groups. Actually, all groups are informing all groups. This is the power of hierarchical models.

Figure 4.18 shows the fitted lines for each of the eight groups. We can see that we managed to fit a line to a single point. At first, this may sound weird or even fishy, but this is just a consequence of the structure of the hierarchical model. Each line is informed by the lines of the other groups, thus we are not truly adjusting a line to a single point. Instead, we are adjusting a line that's been informed by the points in the other groups to a single point.

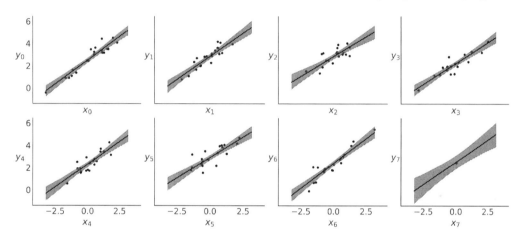

Figure 4.18: Fitted lines for `hierarchical_non_centered`

Multiple linear regression

So far, we have been working with one dependent variable and one independent variable. Nevertheless, it is not unusual to have several independent variables that we want to include in our model. Some examples could be:

- Perceived quality of wine (dependent) and acidity, density, alcohol level, residual sugar, and sulfates content (independent variables)
- A student's average grades (dependent) and family income, distance from home to

school, and mother's education level (categorical variable)

We can easily extend the simple linear regression model to deal with more than one independent variable. We call this model multiple linear regression or, less often, multivariable linear regression (not to be confused with multivariate linear regression, the case where we have multiple dependent variables).

In a multiple linear regression model, we model the mean of the dependent variable as follows:

$$\mu = \alpha + \beta_1 X_1 + \beta_2 X_2 + \cdots + \beta_k X_k$$

Using linear algebra notation, we can write a shorter version:

$$\mu = \alpha + \mathbf{X}\beta$$

$\mathbf{X}$ is a matrix of size $n \times k$ with the values of the independent variables, β is a vector of size k with the coefficients of the independent variables, and n is the number of observations.

If you are a little rusty with your linear algebra, you may want to check the Wikipedia article about the dot product between two vectors and its generalization to matrix multiplication: `https://en.wikipedia.org/wiki/Dot_product`. Basically, what you need to know is that we are just using a shorter and more convenient way to write our model:

$$\mathbf{X}\beta = \sum_{i}^{n} \beta_i X_i = \beta_1 X_1 + \beta_2 X_2 + \cdots + \beta_k X_k$$

Using the simple linear regression model, we find a straight line that (hopefully) explains our data. Under the multiple linear regression model, we find, instead, a hyperplane of dimension k. Thus, the multiple linear regression model is essentially the same as the simple linear regression model, the only difference being that now β is a vector and $\mathbf{X}$ is a matrix.

To see an example of a multiple linear regression model, let's go back to the bikes dataset. We will use the temperature and the humidity of the day to predict the number of rented bikes:

Code 4.15:

```
1  with pm.Model() as model_mlb:
2      α = pm.Normal("α", mu=0, sigma=1)
3      β0 = pm.Normal("β0", mu=0, sigma=10)
4      β1 = pm.Normal("β1", mu=0, sigma=10)
5      σ = pm.HalfNormal("σ", 10)
6      μ = pm.Deterministic("μ", pm.math.exp(α + β0 * bikes.temperature +
7                                             β1 * bikes.hour))
8      _ = pm.NegativeBinomial("y_pred", mu=μ, alpha=σ, observed=bikes.rented)
9
10     idata_mlb = pm.sample()
```

Please take a moment to compare `model_mlb`, which has two independent variables, `temperature` and `hour`, with `model_neg`, which only has one independent variable, `temperature`. The only difference is that now we have two β coefficients, one for each independent variable. The rest of the model is the same. Notice that we could have written β = `pm.Normal("β1", mu=0, sigma=10, shape=2)` and then used $\beta1[0]$ and $\beta1[1]$ in the definition of μ. I usually do that.

As you can see, writing a multiple regression model is not that different from writing a simple regression model. Interpreting the results can be more challenging, though. For instance, the coefficient of `temperature` is now β_0 and the coefficient of `hour` is β_1. We can still interpret the coefficients as the change in the dependent variable for a unit change in the independent variable. But now we have to be careful to specify which independent variable we are talking about. For instance, we can say that for a unit increase in the temperature, the number of rented bikes increases by β_0 units, while holding the value of `hour` constant. Or we can say that for a unit increase in the hour, the number of rented bikes increases by β_1 units, while holding the value of `temperature` constant. Also, the value of a coefficient for a given variable is dependent on what other variables we are including in the model. For instance, the coefficient of `temperature` will vary depending on whether we incorporate the variable `hour` into the model or not.

Figure 4.19 shows the β coefficients for models `model_neg` (only `temperature`) and for model `model_m1d` (`temperature` and `hour`).

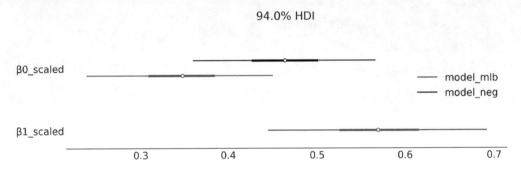

Figure 4.19: Scaled β coefficients for `model_neg` *and* `model_m1b`

We can see that the coefficient of `temperature` is different in both models. This is because the effect of `temperature` on the number of rented bikes depends on the hour of the day. Even more, the values of the β coefficients have been scaled by the standard deviation of their corresponding independent variable, so we can make them comparable. We can see that once we include `hour` in the model, the effect of `temperature` on the number of rented bikes gets smaller. This is because the effect of `hour` is already explaining some of the variations in the number of rented bikes that were previously explained by `temperature`. In extreme cases, the addition of a new variable can make the coefficient go to 0 or even change the sign. We will discuss more of this in the next chapter.

Summary

In this chapter, we have learned about linear regression, which aims to model the relationship between a dependent variable and an independent variable. We have seen how to use PyMC to fit a linear regression model and how to interpret the results and make plots that we can share with different audiences.

Our first example was a model with a Gaussian response. But then we saw that this is just one assumption and we can easily change it to deal with non-Gaussian responses, such as count data, using a NegativeBinomial regression model or a logistic regression model for binary data. We saw that when doing so we also need to set an inverse link function to map the linear predictor to the response variable. Using a Student's t-distribution as the likelihood can be useful for dealing with outliers. We spent most of the chapter modeling the mean as a linear function of the independent variable, but we learned that we can also model other parameters, like the variance. This is useful when we have heteroscedastic data. We learned how to apply the concept of partial pooling to create hierarchical linear regression models. Finally, we briefly discussed multiple linear regression models.

PyMC makes it very easy to implement all these different flavors of Bayesian linear regression by changing one or a few lines of code. In the next chapter, we will learn more about linear regression and we will learn about Bambi, a tool built on top of PyMC that makes it even easier to build and analyze linear regression models.

Exercises

1. Using the howell dataset (available at `https://github.com/aloctavodia/BAP3`), create a linear model of the weight (x) against the height (y). Exclude subjects that are younger than 18. Explain the results.

2. For four subjects, we get the weights (45.73, 65.8, 54.2, 32.59), but not their heights. Using the model from the previous exercise, predict the height for each subject, together with their 50% and 94% HDIs. Tip: Use `pm.MutableData`.

3. Repeat exercise 1, this time including those below 18 years old. Explain the results.

4. It is known for many species that weight does not scale with height, but with the logarithm of the weight. Use this information to fit the howell data (including subjects from all ages).

5. See the accompanying code `model_t2` (and the data associated with it). Experiment with priors for v, like the non-shifted Exponential and Gamma priors (they are

commented on in the code). Plot the prior distribution to ensure that you understand them. An easy way to do this is to call the `pm.sample_prior_predictive()` function instead of `pm.sample()`. You can also use PreliZ.

6. Rerun `model_lrs` using the `petal_length` variable and then the `petal_width` variable. What are the main differences in the results? How wide or narrow is the 94% HDI in each case?

7. Repeat the previous exercise, this time using a Student's t-distribution as a weakly informative prior. Try different values of v.

8. Choose a dataset that you find interesting and use it with the simple linear regression model. Be sure to explore the results using ArviZ functions. If you do not have an interesting dataset, try searching online, for example, at `http://data.worldbank.org` or `http://www.stat.ufl.edu/~winner/datasets.html`.

Join our community Discord space

Join our Discord community to meet like-minded people and learn alongside more than 5000 members at:

`https://packt.link/bayesian`

5

Comparing Models

> A map is not the territory it represents, but, if correct, it has a similar structure
> to the territory.
> – Alfred Korzybski

Models should be designed as approximations to help us understand a particular problem or a class of related problems. Models are not designed to be verbatim copies of the *real world*. Thus, all models are wrong in the same sense that maps are not the territory. But not all models are equally wrong; some models will be better than others at describing a given problem.

In the previous chapters, we focused our attention on the inference problem, that is, how to learn the values of parameters from data. In this chapter, we are going to focus on a complementary problem: how to compare two or more models for the same data. As we will learn, this is both a central problem in data analysis and a tricky one. In this chapter, we are going to keep examples super simple, so we can focus on the technical aspects of model comparison. In the forthcoming chapters, we are going to apply what we learn here to more complex examples.

In this chapter, we will explore the following topics:

- Overfitting and underfitting
- Information criteria
- Cross-validation
- Bayes factors

Posterior predictive checks

We have previously introduced and discussed posterior predictive checks as a way to assess how well a model explains the data used to fit a model. The purpose of this type of testing is not to determine whether a model is incorrect; we already know this! The goal of the exercise is to understand how well we are capturing the data. By performing posterior predictive checks, we aim to better understand the limitations of a model. Once we understand the limitations, we can simply acknowledge them or try to remove them by improving the model. It is expected that a model will not be able to reproduce all aspects of a problem and this is usually not a problem as models are built with a purpose in mind. As different models often capture different aspects of data, we can compare models using posterior predictive checks.

Let's look at a simple example. We have a dataset with two variables, x and y. We are going to fit these data with a linear model:

$$y = \alpha + \beta x$$

We will also fit the data using a quadratic model, that is, a model with one more term than the linear model. For this extra term, we just take x to the power of 2 and add a β coefficient:

$$y = \alpha + \beta_0 x + \beta_1 x^2$$

We can write these models in PyMC as usual; refer to the following code block. The only difference from all previous models we have seen so far is that we pass the argument `idata_kwargs="log_likelihood": True` to `pm.sample`. This extra step will store the log-likelihood in the `InferenceData` object, and we will use this info later:

Code 5.1:

```
1  with pm.Model() as model_1:
2      α = pm.Normal("α", mu=0, sigma=1)
3      β = pm.Normal("β", mu=0, sigma=10)
4      σ = pm.HalfNormal("σ", 5)
5
6      μ = α + β * x_c[0]
7
8      y_pred = pm.Normal("y_pred", mu=μ, sigma=σ, observed=y_c)
9
10     idata_1 = pm.sample(2000, idata_kwargs={"log_likelihood": True})
11     idata_1.extend(pm.sample_posterior_predictive(idata_1))
12
13 with pm.Model() as model_q:
14     α = pm.Normal("α", mu=0, sigma=1)
15     β = pm.Normal("β", mu=0, sigma=10, shape=order)
16     σ = pm.HalfNormal("σ", 5)
17
18     μ = α + pm.math.dot(β, x_c)
19
20     y_pred = pm.Normal("y_pred", mu=μ, sigma=σ, observed=y_c)
21
22     idata_q = pm.sample(2000, idata_kwargs={"log_likelihood": True})
23     idata_q.extend(pm.sample_posterior_predictive(idata_q))
```

Figure 5.1 shows the mean fit from both models. Visually, both models seem to provide a reasonable fit to the data. At least for me, it is not that easy to see which model is best. What do you think?

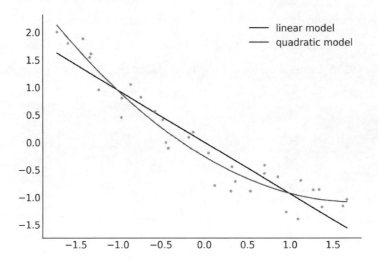

Figure 5.1: Mean fit for `model_l` *(linear) and* `model_q` *(quadratic)*

To gain further insights, we can do a posterior predictive check. Figure 5.2 shows KDEs for the observed and predicted data. Here, it is easy to see that `model_q`, the quadratic model, provides a better fit to the data. We can also see there is a lot of uncertainty, in particular at the tails of the distributions. This is because we have a small number of data points.

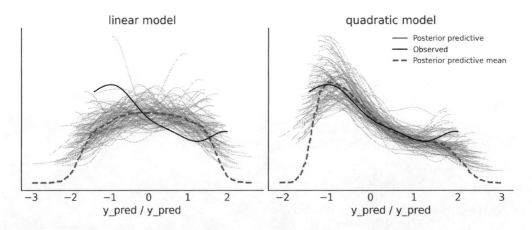

Figure 5.2: Posterior predictive checks for `model_l` *and* `model_q` *created with the* `az.plot_ppc` *function*

Posterior predictive checks are a very versatile idea. We can compare observed and predicted data in so many ways. For instance, instead of comparing the densities of the distributions, we can compare summary statistics. In the top panel of Figure 5.3, we have the distributions of means for both models. The dot over the x axis indicates the observed value. We can see that both models capture the mean very well, with the quadratic model having less variance. That both models capture the mean very well is not surprising as we are explicitly modeling the mean. In the bottom panel, we have the distributions of the interquartile range. This comparison favors the linear model instead.

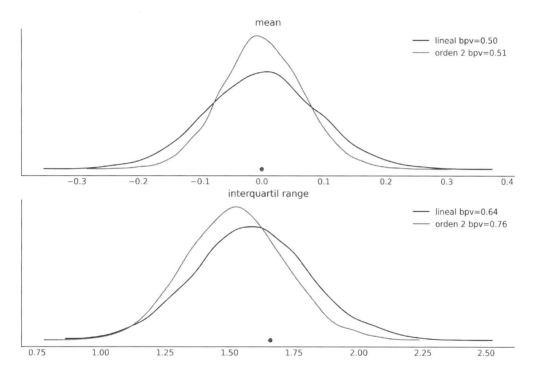

Figure 5.3: Posterior predictive checks for model_l *and* model_q *created with the* az.plot_bpv *function*

In general, a statistic that is *orthogonal* to what the model is explicitly modeling will be more informative for evaluating the model. When in doubt, it may be convenient to evaluate more than one statistic. A useful question is to ask yourself what aspects of the data you are interested in capturing.

To generate Figure 5.3, we used the az.plot_bpv ArviZ function. An excerpt of the full code to generate that figure is the following:

Code 5.2:

```
1  idatas = [idata_l, idata_q]
2
3  def iqr(x, a=-1):
4      """interquartile range"""
5      return np.subtract(*np.percentile(x, [75, 25], axis=a))
6
7  for idata in idatas:
8      az.plot_bpv(idata, kind="t_stat", t_stat="mean", ax=axes[0])
9
10 for idata in idatas:
11     az.plot_bpv(idata, kind="t_stat", t_stat=iqr, ax=axes[1])
```

Notice that we use the kind="t_stat" argument to indicate that we are going to use a summary statistic. We can pass a string as in t_stat="mean", to indicate that we want to use the mean as the summary statistic. Or, we can use a user-defined function, as in t_stat=iqr.

You may have noticed that Figure 5.3 also includes a legend with bpv values. **bpv** stands for Bayesian p-value. This is a numerical way of summarizing a comparison between simulated and observed data. To obtain them, a summary statistic T is chosen, such as the mean, median, standard deviation, or whatever you may think is worth comparing. Then T is calculated for the observed data T_{obs} and for the simulated data T_{sim}. Finally, we ask ourselves the question "what is the probability that T_{sim} is less than or equal to T_{obs}?". If the observed values agree with the predicted ones, the expected value will be 0.5. In other words, half of the predictions will be below the observations and half will be above. This quantity is known as the **Bayesian p-value**:

$$\text{Bayesian p-value} \triangleq p(T_{sim} \leq T_{obs} \mid \tilde{Y})$$

There is yet another way to compute a Bayesian p-value. Instead of using a summary statistic, we can use the entire distribution. In this case, we can ask ourselves the question "what is the probability of predicting a lower or equal value for **each observed value**?". If the model is well calibrated, these probabilities should be the same for all observed values. Because the model is capturing all observations equally well, we should expect a Uniform distribution. ArviZ can help us with the computations; this time we need to use the az.plot_bpv function with the kind="p_value" argument (which is the default). Figure 5.4 shows the results of this calculation. The white line indicates the expected Uniform distribution and the gray band shows the expected deviation given the finite size of the sample. It can be seen that these models are very similar.

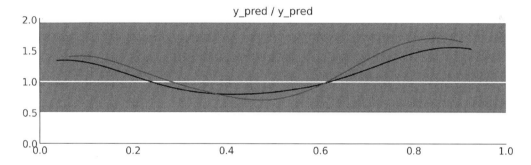

Figure 5.4: Posterior predictive checks for model_1 *and* model_q *created with the* az.plot_bpv *function*

Not Those p-values

For those who are familiar with p-values and their use in frequentist statistics, there are a couple of clarifications. What is *Bayesian* about these p-values is that we are NOT using a sampling distribution but the posterior predictive distribution. Additionally, we are not doing a null hypothesis test, nor trying to declare that a difference is "significant." We are simply trying to quantify how well the model explains the data.

Posterior predictive checks provide a very flexible framework for evaluating and comparing models, either using plots or numerical summaries such as Bayesian p-values, or a combination of both. The concept is general enough to allow an analyst to use their imagination to find different ways to explore the model's predictions and use the ones that best suit their modeling goals.

In the following sections, we will explore other methods for comparing models. These new methods can be used in combination with posterior predictive checks.

The balance between simplicity and accuracy

When choosing between alternative explanations, there is a principle known as Occam's razor. In very general terms, this principle establishes that given two or more equivalent explanations for the same phenomenon, the simplest is the preferred explanation. A common criterion of simplicity is the number of parameters in a model.

There are many justifications for this heuristic. We are not going to discuss any of them; we are just going to accept them as a reasonable guide.

Another factor that we generally have to take into account when comparing models is their accuracy, that is, how good a model is at fitting the data. According to this criterion, if we have two (or more) models and one of them explains the data better than the other, then that is the preferred model.

Intuitively, it seems that when comparing models, we tend to prefer those that best fit the data and those that are simple. But what should we do if these two principles lead us to different models? Or, more generally, is there a quantitative way to balance both contributions? The short answer is yes, and in fact, there is more than one way to do it. But first, let's see an example to gain intuition.

Many parameters (may) lead to overfitting

Figure 5.5 shows three models with an increasing number of parameters. The first one (order 0) is just a constant value: whatever the value of X, the model always predicts the same value for Y. The second model (order 1) is a linear model, as we saw in Chapter 4. The last one (order 5) is a polynomial model of order 5. We will discuss polynomial regression in more depth in Chapter 6, but for the moment, we just need to know that the core of the model has the form $\alpha + \beta_0 x + \beta_0 x^2 + \beta_0 x^3 + \beta_0 x^4 + \beta_0 x^5$.

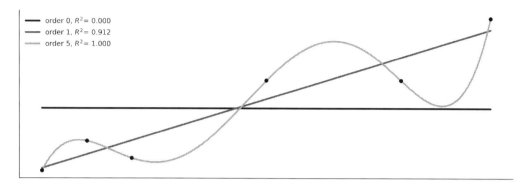

order 0, $R^2 = 0.000$
order 1, $R^2 = 0.912$
order 5, $R^2 = 1.000$

Figure 5.5: Three models for a simple dataset

In Figure 5.5, we can see that the increase in the complexity of the model (number of parameters) is accompanied by a greater accuracy reflected in the coefficient of determination R^2. This is a way to measure the fit of a model (for more information, please read `https://en.wikipedia.org/wiki/Coefficient_of_determination`). In fact, we can see that the polynomial of order 5 fits the data perfectly, obtaining $R^2 = 1$.

Why can the polynomial of order 5 capture the data without errors? The reason is that we have the same number of parameters as data, that is, six. Therefore, the model is simply acting as an alternative way of expressing the data. The model is not learning patterns about the data, it is memorizing the data! This can be problematic. The easier way to notice this is by thinking about what will happen to a model that memorizes data when presented with new, unobserved data. What do you think will happen?

Well, the performance is expected to be bad, like someone who just memorizes the questions for an exam only to find the questions have been changed at the last minute! This situation is represented in Figure 5.6; here, we have added two new data points. Maybe we got the money to perform a new experiment or our boss just sent us new data. We can see that the model of order 5, which was able to exactly fit the data, now has a worse performance than the linear model, as measured by R^2. From this simple example, we can see that a model with the best fit is not always the ideal one.

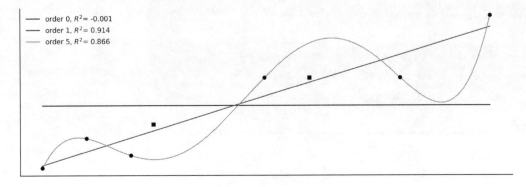

Figure 5.6: Three models for a simple dataset, plus two new points

Loosely speaking, when a model fits the dataset used to learn the parameters of that model very well but fits new datasets very poorly, we have overfitting. This is a very common problem when analyzing data. A useful way to think about overfitting is to consider a dataset as having two components: the signal and the noise. The signal is what we want to capture (or learn) from the data. If we use a dataset, it is because we believe there is a signal there, otherwise it will be an exercise in futility. Noise, on the other hand, is not useful and is the product of measurement errors, limitations in the way the data was generated or captured, the presence of corrupted data, etc. A model overfits when it is so flexible (for a dataset) that it is capable of learning noise. This has the consequence that the signal is hidden.

This is a practical justification for Occam's razor, and also a warning that, at least in principle, it is always possible to create a model so complex that it explains all the details in a dataset, even the most irrelevant ones — like the cartographers in Borges' tale, who crafted a map of the Empire as vast as the Empire itself, perfectly replicating every detail.

Too few parameters lead to underfitting

Continuing with the same example but at the other extreme of complexity, we have the model of order 0. This model is simply a Gaussian disguised as a linear model. This model is only capable of capturing the value of the mean of Y and is therefore totally indifferent to the values of X. We say that this model has underfitted the data. Models that underfit can also be misleading, especially if we are unaware of it.

Measures of predictive accuracy

"Everything should be made as simple as possible, but not simpler" is a quote often attributed to Einstein. As in a healthy diet, when modeling, we have to maintain a balance. Ideally, we would like to have a model that neither underfits nor overfits the data. We want to somehow balance simplicity and goodness of fit.

In the previous example, it is relatively easy to see that the model of order 0 is too simple, while the model of order 5 is too complex. In order to get a general approach that will allow us to rank models, we need to formalize our intuition about this balance of simplicity and accuracy.

Let's look at a couple of terms that will be useful to us:

- **Within-sample accuracy**: The accuracy is measured with the same data used to fit the model.

- **Out-of-sample accuracy**: The accuracy measured with data not used to fit the model.

The within-sample accuracy will, on average, be greater than the out-of-sample accuracy. That is why using the within-sample accuracy to evaluate a model, in general, will lead us to think that we have a better model than we really have. Using out-of-sample accuracy is therefore a good idea to avoid fooling ourselves. However, leaving data out means we will have less data to inform our models, which is a luxury we generally cannot afford. Since this is a central problem in data analysis, there are several proposals to address it. Two very popular approaches are:

- **Information criteria**: This is a general term that's used to refer to various expressions that approximate out-of-sample accuracy as in-sample accuracy plus a term that penalizes model complexity.

- **Cross-validation**: This is an empirical strategy based on dividing the available data into separate subsets that are alternatively used to fit and evaluate the models.

Let's look at both of those approaches in more detail in the following sections.

Information criteria

Information criteria are a collection of closely related tools used to compare models in terms of goodness-of-fit and model complexity. In other words, the information criteria formalize the intuition that we developed at the beginning of the chapter. The exact way in which these quantities are derived has to do with a field known as Information Theory ([MacKay, 2003]), which is fun, but we will pursue a more intuitive explanation.

One way to measure how well a model fits the data is to calculate the root mean square error between the data and the predictions made by the model:

$$\frac{1}{n} \sum_{i=1}^{n} (y_i - \mathrm{E}(y_i \mid \theta))^2$$

$\mathrm{E}(y_i \mid \theta)$ is the predicted value given the estimated parameters. It is important to note that this is essentially the average of the squared difference between the observed and predicted data. Taking the square of the errors ensures that the differences do not cancel out and emphasizes large errors compared to other alternatives such as calculating the absolute value.

The root mean square error may be familiar to you. It is a very popular measure – so popular that we may have never spent time thinking about it. But if we do, we will see that, in principle, there is nothing special about it and we could well devise other similar expressions. When we adopt a probabilistic approach, as we do in this book, a more general (and *natural*) expression is the following:

$$\sum_{i=1}^{n} \log p(y_i \mid \theta)$$

That is, we compute the likelihood for each of the n observations. We take the sum instead of the product because we are working with logarithms. Why do we say this is *natural*? Because we can think that, when choosing a likelihood for a model, we are implicitly choosing how we want to penalize deviations between the data and predictions. In fact, when $p(y_i \mid \theta)$ is a Gaussian, then the above expression will be proportional to the root mean square error.

Now, let's shift our focus to a detailed exploration of a few specific information criteria.

Akaike Information Criterion

Akaike Information Criterion (AIC) is a well-known and widely used information criterion outside the Bayesian universe and is defined as:

$$\text{AIC} = -2 \sum_{i=1}^{n} \log p(y_i \mid \hat{\theta}_{mle}) + 2k$$

k is the number of model parameters and $\hat{\theta}_{mle}$ is the maximum likelihood estimate for θ.

Maximum likelihood estimation is common practice for non-Bayesians and is, in general, equivalent to Bayesian **maximum a posteriori** (**MAP**) estimation when *flat* priors are used. It is important to note that $\hat{\theta}_{mle}$ is a point estimate and not a distribution.

The factor -2 is just a constant, and we could omit it but usually don't. What is important, from a practical point of view, is that the first term takes into account how well the model fits the data, while the second term penalizes the complexity of the model. Therefore, if two models fit the data equally well, AIC says that we should choose the model with the fewest parameters.

AIC works fine in non-Bayesian approaches but is problematic otherwise. One reason is that it does not use the posterior distribution of θ and therefore discards information. Also, AIC, from a Bayesian perspective, assumes that priors are *flat* and therefore AIC is incompatible with informative and slightly informative priors like those used in this book. Also, the number of parameters in a model is not a good measure of the model's complexity when using informative priors or structures like hierarchical structures, as these are ways of reducing the effective number of parameters, also known as *regularization*. We will return to this idea of regularization later.

Widely applicable information criteria

Widely applicable information criteria (**WAIC**) is something like the Bayesian version of AIC. It also has two terms, one that measures how good the fit is and the other that penalizes complex models. But WAIC uses the full posterior distribution to estimate both terms. The following expression assumes that the posterior distribution is represented as a sample of size S (as obtained from an MCMC method):

$$WAIC = -2 \sum_i^n \log \left(\frac{1}{S} \sum_{s=1}^S p(y_i \mid \theta^s) \right) + 2 \sum_i^n \left(V_{s=1}^S \log p(y_i \mid \theta^s) \right)$$

The first term is similar to the Akaike criterion, except it is evaluated for all the observations and all the samples of the posterior. The second term is a bit more difficult to justify without getting into technicalities. But it can be interpreted as the effective number of parameters. What is important from a practical point of view is that WAIC uses the entire posterior (and not a point estimate) for the calculation of both terms, so WAIC can be applied to virtually any Bayesian model.

Other information criteria

Another widely used information criterion is the **Deviance Information Criterion** (**DIC**). If we use the *bayes-o-meter*[TM], DIC is more Bayesian than AIC but less than WAIC. Although still popular, WAIC and mainly LOO (see the next section) have been shown to be more useful both theoretically and empirically than DIC. Therefore, we do not recommend its use.

Another widely used criterion is **Bayesian Information Criteria** (**BIC**). Like logistic regression and my mother's *dry soup*, this name can be misleading. BIC was proposed as a way to correct some of the problems with AIC and the authors proposed a Bayesian justification for it. But BIC is not really Bayesian in the sense that, like AIC, it assumes flat priors and uses maximum likelihood estimation.

But more importantly, BIC differs from AIC and WAIC in its objective. AIC, WAIC, and LOO (see next section) try to reflect which model generalizes better to other data (predictive accuracy), while BIC tries to identify which is the *correct* model and therefore is more related to Bayes factors.

Cross-validation

Cross-validation is a simple and, in most cases, effective solution for comparing models. We take our data and divide it into K slices. We try to keep the slices more or less the same (in size and sometimes also in other characteristics, such as the number of classes). We then use K-1 slices to train the model and slice to test it. This process is the systematically repeated omission, for each iteration, of a different slice from the training set and using that slice as the evaluation set. This is repeated until we have completed K fit-and-evaluation rounds, as can be seen in Figure 5.7. The accuracy of the model will be the average over the accuracy for each of the K rounds. This is known as K-fold cross-validation. Finally, once we have performed cross-validation, we use all the data for one last fit and this is the model that is used to make predictions or for any other purpose.

Figure 5.7: K-fold cross-validation

When K equals the number of data points, we get what is known as **leave-one-out cross-validation (LOOCV)**, meaning we fit the model to all but one data point each time.

Cross-validation is a routine practice in machine learning, and we have barely described the most essential aspects of this practice. There are many other variants of the schema presented here. For more information, you can read James et al. [2023] or Raschka et al. [2022].

Cross-validation is a very simple and useful idea, but for some models or for large amounts of data, the computational cost of cross-validation may be beyond our means. Many people have tried to find simpler quantities to calculate, like Information Criteria. In the next section, we discuss a method to approximate cross-validation from a single fit to all the data.

Approximating cross-validation

Cross-validation is a nice idea, but it can be expensive, particularly variants like leave-one-out-cross-validation. Luckily, it is possible to approximate it using the information from a single fit to the data! The method for doing this is called "Pareto smooth importance sampling leave-one-out cross-validation." The name is so long that in practice we call it LOO. Conceptually, what we are trying to calculate is:

$$\text{ELPD}_{\text{LOO-CV}} = \sum_{i=1}^{n} \log \int p(y_i \mid \theta) \, p(\theta \mid y_{-i}) d\theta$$

This is the Expected Log-Pointwise-predictive Density (ELPD). We add the subscript *LOO-CV* to make it explicit we are computing the ELPD using leave-one-out cross-validation. The $_{-i}$ means that we leave the observation i out.

This expression is very similar to the one for the posterior predictive distribution. The difference is that, now, we want to compute the posterior predictive distribution for observation y_i from a posterior distribution computed without the observation y_i. The first approximation we take is to prevent the explicit computation of the integral by taking samples from the posterior distribution. Thus, we can write:

$$\sum_{i}^{n} \log \left(\frac{1}{S} \sum_{j}^{s} p(y_i \mid \theta_{-i}^{j}) \right)$$

Here, the sum is over S posterior samples. We have been using MCMC samples in this book a lot. So, this approximation should not sound unfamiliar to you. The tricky part comes next.

It is possible to approximate $p(y_i \mid \theta_{-i}^j)$ using importance sampling. We are not going to discuss the details of that statistical method, but we are going to see how importance sampling is a way of approximating a target distribution by re-weighting values obtained from another distribution. This method is useful when we do not know how to sample from the target distribution but we know how to sample from another distribution. Importance sampling works best when the known distribution is *wider* than the target one.

In our case, the known distribution, once a model has been fitted, is the log-likelihood for all the observations. And we want to approximate the log-likelihood if we had dropped one observation. For this, we need to estimate the "importance" (or weight) that each observation has in determining the posterior distribution. The "importance" of a given observation is proportional to the effect the variable will produce on the posterior if removed. Intuitively, a relatively unlikely observation is more important (or carries more weight) than an expected one. Luckily, these weights are easy to compute once we have computed the posterior distribution. In fact, the weight of the observation i for the s posterior sample is:

$$w_s = \frac{1}{p(y_i \mid \theta_s)}$$

This w_s may not be reliable. The main issue is that sometimes a few w_s could be so large that they dominate our calculations, making them unstable. To tame these crazy weights, we can use Pareto smoothing. This solution consists of replacing some of these weights with weights obtained from fitting a Pareto distribution. Why a Pareto distribution? Because the theory indicates that the weights should follow this distribution.

So, for each observation, y_i, the largest weights are used to estimate a Pareto distribution, and that distribution is used to replace those weights with "smoothed" weights. This procedure gives robustness to the estimation of the ELPD and also provides a way to diagnose the approximation, i.e., to get a warning that the LOO method may be failing. For this, we need to pay attention to the values of k, which is a parameter of the Pareto distribution. Values of k greater than 0.7 indicate that we may have very influential observations.

Calculating predictive accuracy with ArviZ

Fortunately, calculating WAIC and LOO with ArviZ is very simple. We just need to be sure that the Inference Data has the log-likelihood group. When computing a posterior with PyMC, this can be achieved by doing `pm.sample(idata_kwargs="log_likelihood":` `True)`. Now, let's see how to compute LOO:

Code 5.3:

```
az.loo(idata_l)
```

```
Computed from 8000 posterior samples and 33 observations log-likelihood matrix.

          Estimate        SE
elpd_loo    -14.31      2.67
p_loo         2.40         -
------

Pareto k diagnostic values:
                        Count    Pct.
(-Inf, 0.5]   (good)       33   100.0%
 (0.5, 0.7]   (ok)          0     0.0%
  (0.7, 1]    (bad)         0     0.0%
  (1, Inf)    (very bad)    0     0.0%
```

The output of `az.loo` has two sections. In the first section, we get a table with two rows. The first row is the ELPD (`elpd_loo`) and the second one is the effective number of parameters (`p_loo`). In the second section, we have the Pareto k diagnostic. This is a measure of the reliability of the LOO approximation. Values of k greater than 0.7 indicate that we possibly have very influential observations. In this case, we have 33 observations and all of them are good, so we can trust the approximation.

To compute WAIC, you can use `az.waic`; the output will be similar, except that we will not get the Pareto k diagnostic, or any similar diagnostics. This is a downside of WAIC: we do not get any information about the reliability of the approximation.

If we compute LOO for the quadratic model, we will get a similar output, but the ELPD will be higher (around -4), indicating that the quadratic model is better.

Values of ELPD are not that useful by themselves and must be interpreted in relation to other ELPD values. That is why ArviZ provides two helper functions to facilitate this comparison. Let's look at `az.compare` first:

Code 5.4:

```
cmp_df = az.compare({"model_l": idata_l, "model_q": idata_q})
```

	rank	elpd_loo	p_loo	elpd_diff	weight	se	dse	warning	scale
model_q	0	-4.6	2.68	0	1	2.36	0	False	log
model_l	1	-14.3	2.42	9.74	3.0e-14	2.67	2.65	False	log

In the rows, we have the compared models, and in the columns, we have:

- `rank`: The order of the models (from best to worst).
- `elpd_loo`: The point estimate of the ELPD
- `p_loo`: The effective numbers parameters.
- `elpd_diff`: The difference between the ELPD of the best model and the other models.
- `weight`: The relative weight of each model. If we wanted to make predictions by combining the different models instead of choosing just one, this would be the weight that we should assign to each model. In this case, we see that the polynomial model takes all the weight.
- `se`: The standard error of the ELPD.
- `dse`: The standard error of the differences.
- `warning`: A warning about high k values.

- `scale`: The scale on which the ELPD is calculated.

The other helper function provided by ArviZ is `az.compareplot`. This function provides similar information to `az.compare`, but graphically. Figure 5.8 shows the output of this function. Notice that:

- The empty circles represent the ELPD values and the black lines are the standard error.
- The highest value of the ELPD is indicated with a vertical dashed gray line to facilitate comparison with other values.
- For all models except *the best*, we also get a triangle indicating the value of the ELPD difference between each model and the *best* model. The gray error bar indicates the standard error of the differences between the point estimates.

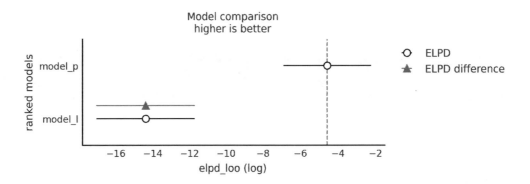

Figure 5.8: Output of `az.compareplot(cmp_df)`

The easiest way to use LOO (or WAIC) is to choose a single model. Just choose the model with the highest ELPD value. If we follow this rule, we will have to accept that the quadratic model is the best. Even if we take into account the standard errors, we can see that they do not overlap. This gives us some certainty that indeed the models are *different enough* from each other. If instead, the standard errors overlap, we should provide a more nuanced answer.

Model averaging

Model selection is attractive for its simplicity, but we might be missing information about uncertainty in our models. This is somewhat similar to calculating the full posterior and then just keeping the posterior mean; this can lead us to be overconfident about what we think we know.

An alternative is to select a single model but to report and analyze the different models together with the values of the calculated information criteria, their standard errors, and perhaps also the posterior predictive checks. It is important to put all these numbers and tests in the context of our problem so that we and our audience can get a better idea of the possible limitations and shortcomings of the models. For those working in academia, these elements can be used to add elements to the discussion section of a paper, presentation, thesis, etc. In industry, this can be useful for informing stakeholders about the advantages and limitations of models, predictions, and conclusions.

Another possibility is to average the models. In this way, we keep the uncertainty about the goodness of fit of each model. We then obtain a meta-model (and meta-predictions) using a weighted average of each model. ArviZ provides a function for this task, `az.weight_predictions`, which takes as arguments a list of InferenceData objects and a list of weights. The weights can be calculated using the `az.compare` function. For example, if we want to average the two models we have been using, we can do the following:

Code 5.5:

```
idata_w = az.weight_predictions(idatas, weights=[0.35, 0.65])
```

Figure 5.9 shows the results of this calculation. The light gray dashed line is the weighted average of the two models, the black solid line is the linear model, and the gray solid line is the quadratic one.

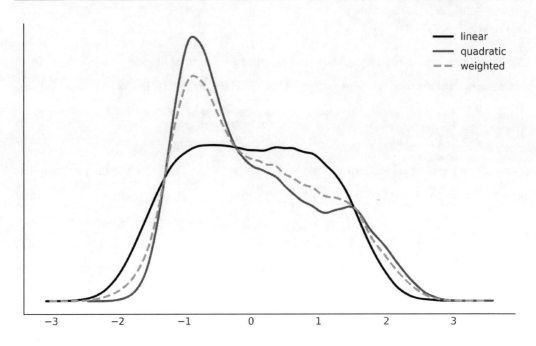

Figure 5.9: Weighted average of the linear and quadratic models

There are other ways to average models, such as explicitly building a meta-model that includes all models of interest as particular cases. For example, an order 2 polynomial contains a linear model as a particular case, or a hierarchical model is the continuous version between two extremes, a grouped model and an ungrouped model.

Bayes factors

An alternative to LOO, cross-validation, and information criteria is Bayes factors. It is common for Bayes factors to show up in the literature as a Bayesian alternative to frequentist hypothesis testing.

The *Bayesian way* of comparing k models is to calculate the **marginal likelihood** of each model $p(y \mid M_k)$, i.e., the probability of the observed data Y given the model M_k. The marginal likelihood is the normalization constant of Bayes' theorem. We can see this if we write Bayes' theorem and make explicit the fact that all inferences depend on the model.

$$p(\theta \mid Y, M_k) = \frac{p(Y \mid \theta, M_k)p(\theta \mid M_k)}{p(Y \mid M_k)}$$

where, y is the data, θ is the parameters, and M_k is a model out of k competing models.

If our main objective is to choose only one model, the *best* from a set of models, we can choose the one with the largest value of $p(y \mid M_k)$. This is fine if we assume that all models have the same prior probability. Otherwise, we must calculate:

$$p(M_k \mid y) \propto p(y \mid M_k)p(M_k)$$

If, instead, our main objective is to compare models to determine which are more likely and to what extent, this can be achieved using the Bayes factors:

$$BF_{01} = \frac{p(y \mid M_0)}{p(y \mid M_1)}$$

That is the ratio between the marginal likelihood of two models. The higher the value of BF_{01}, the *better* the model in the numerator (M_0 in this example). To facilitate the interpretation of the Bayes factors, and to put numbers into words, Harold Jeffreys proposed a scale for their interpretation, with levels of *support* or *strength* (see Table 5.1).

Bayes Factor	Support
1–3	Anecdotal
3–10	Moderate
10–30	Strong
30–100	Very Strong
>100	Extreme

Table 5.1: Support for model M_0, the one in the numerator

Keep in mind that if you get numbers below 1, then the support is for M_1, i.e., the model in the denominator. Tables are also available for those cases, but notice that you can simply take the inverse of the obtained value.

It is very important to remember that these rules are just conventions – simple guides at best. Results should always be put in the context of our problems and should be accompanied by enough detail so that others can assess for themselves whether they agree with our conclusions. The proof necessary to ensure something in particle physics, or in court, or to decide to carry out an evacuation in the face of a looming natural catastrophe is not the same.

Some observations

We will now briefly discuss some key facts about the marginal likelihood:

- The good: Occam's razor included. Models with lots of parameters have a higher penalty than models with few parameters. The intuitive reason is that the greater the number of parameters, the more the prior *extends* with respect to the likelihood. An example where it is easy to see this is with nested models: for example, a polynomial of order 2 "contains" the models polynomial of order 1 and polynomial of order 0.

- The bad: For many problems, the marginal likelihood cannot be calculated analytically. Also, approximating it numerically is usually a difficult task that in the best of cases requires specialized methods and, in the worst case, the estimates are either impractical or unreliable. In fact, the popularity of the MCMC methods is that they allow obtaining the posterior distribution without the need to calculate the marginal likelihood.

- The ugly: The marginal likelihood depends *very sensitively* on the prior distribution of the parameters in each model $p(\theta_k \mid M_k)$.

It is important to note that the *good* and the *ugly* points are related. Using marginal likelihood to compare models is a good idea because it already includes a penalty for complex models (which helps us prevent overfitting), and at the same time, a change in the prior will affect the marginal likelihood calculations. At first, this sounds a bit silly; we already know that priors affect calculations (otherwise we could just avoid them). But we are talking about changes in the prior that would have a small effect in the posterior but a great impact on the value of the marginal likelihood.

The use of Bayes factors is often a watershed among Bayesians. The difficulty of its calculation and the sensitivity to the priors are some of the arguments against it. Another reason is that, like p-values and hypothesis testing in general, Bayes factors favor dichotomous thinking over the estimation of the "effect size." In other words, instead of asking ourselves questions like: How many more years of life can a cancer treatment provide? We end up asking if the difference between treating and not treating a patient is "statistically significant." Note that this last question can be useful in some contexts. The point is that in many other contexts, this type of question is not the question that interests us; we're only interested in the one that we were taught to answer.

Calculation of Bayes factors

As we have already mentioned, marginal likelihood (and the Bayes factors derived from it) is generally not available in closed form, except for some models. For this reason, many numerical methods have been devised for its calculation. Some of these methods are so simple and naive (`https://radfordneal.wordpress.com/2008/08/17/the-harmonic-mean-of-the-likelihood-worst-monte-carlo-method-ever`) that they work very poorly in practice.

Analytically

For some models, such as the BetaBinomial model, we can calculate the marginal likelihood analytically. If we write this model as:

$$\theta \sim Beta(\alpha, \beta)$$
$$y \sim Bin(n = 1, p = \theta)$$

then the marginal likelihood will be:

$$p(y) = \binom{n}{h} \frac{B(\alpha + h, \ \beta + n - h)}{B(\alpha, \beta)}$$

B is the beta function (not to be confused with the Beta distribution), n is the number of attempts, and h is the success number.

Since we only care about the relative value of the marginal likelihood under two different models (for the same data), we can omit the binomial coefficient $\binom{n}{h}$, so we can write:

$$p(y) \propto \frac{B(\alpha + h, \ \beta + n - h)}{B(\alpha, \beta)}$$

This expression has been coded in the next code block but with a twist. We will use the betaln function, which returns the natural logarithm of the beta function, it is common in statistics to do calculations on a logarithmic scale. This reduces numerical problems when working with probabilities.

Code 5.6:

```
1  from scipy.special import betaln
2
3  def beta_binom(prior, y):
4      """
5      Calculate the marginal probability, analytically, for a BetaBinomial model.
6      prior : tuple
7          alpha and beta parameters for the beta prior
8      y : array
9          array with "1" and "0" corresponding to success and failure respectively
10     """
11     alpha, beta = prior
12     h = np.sum(y)
13     n = len(y)
14     p_y = np.exp(betaln(alpha + h, beta + n - h) - betaln(alpha, beta))
15
16     return p_y
```

Our data for this example consists of 100 coin tosses and the same number of heads and tails. We will compare two models, one with a Uniform prior and one with a *more concentrated* prior around $\theta = 0.5$:

Code 5.7:

```
1  y = np.repeat([1, 0], [50, 50])  # 50 heads, 50 tails
2  priors = ((1, 1), (30, 30))  # uniform prior, peaked prior
```

Figure 5.10 shows the two priors. The Uniform prior is the black line, and the peaked prior is the gray line.

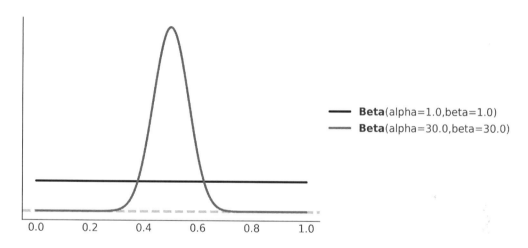

Figure 5.10: Uniform and peaked priors

Now, we can calculate the marginal likelihood for each model and the Bayes factor, which turns out to be 5:

Code 5.8:

```
1  BF = beta_binom(priors[1], y) / beta_binom(priors[0], y)
2  print(round(BF))
   5
```

We see that the model with the prior beta$(30, 30)$, more concentrated, has ≈ 5 times more support than the model with the beta$(1, 1)$. This is to be expected since the prior for the first case is concentrated around $\theta = 0.5$ and the data Y have the same number of heads and tails, that is, they agree with a value of θ around 0.5.

Sequential Monte Carlo

The **Sequential Monte Carlo (SMC)** method is a sampling method that works by progressing through a series of successive stages that bridge one distribution that is easy to sample from and the posterior of interest. In practice, the starting distribution is usually the prior. A byproduct of the SMC sampler is the estimate of the marginal likelihood.

Code 5.9:

```
1  models = []
2  idatas = []
3  for alpha, beta in priors:
4      with pm.Model() as model:
5          a = pm.Beta("a", alpha, beta)
6          yl = pm.Bernoulli("yl", a, observed=y)
7          idata = pm.sample_smc(random_seed=42)
8          models.append(model)
9          idatas.append(idata)
10
11 BF_smc = np.exp(
12     idatas[1].sample_stats["log_marginal_likelihood"].mean()
13     - idatas[0].sample_stats["log_marginal_likelihood"].mean()
14 )
15 print(np.round(BF_smc).item())
```
```
5.0
```

As we can see from the preceding code block, SMC also gives us a Bayes factor of 5, the same answer as the analytical calculation! The advantage of using SMC to calculate marginal likelihood is that we can use it for a wider range of models since we no longer need to know an expression in closed form. The price we pay for this flexibility is a higher computational cost. Also, keep in mind that SMC (with an independent Metropolis-Hastings kernel, as implemented in PyMC) is not as efficient as NUTS. As the dimensionality of the problem increases, a more precise estimate of the posterior and the marginal likelihood will require a larger number of samples of the posterior.

> ### Log Space
>
> In computational statistics, we usually perform computations in log space. This helps provide numerical stability and computational efficiency, among other things. See, for example, the preceding code block; you can see that we calculated a difference (instead of a division) and then we took the exponential before returning the result.

Savage–Dickey ratio

For the above examples, we have compared two BetaBinomial models. We could have compared two completely different models, but there are times when we want to compare a null hypothesis H_0 (or null model) against an alternative H_1 hypothesis. For example, to answer the question "Is this coin biased?", we could compare the value $\theta = 0.5$ (representing no bias) with the output of a model in which we allow θ to vary. For this type of comparison, the null model is nested within the alternative, which means that the null is a particular value of the model we are building. In those cases, calculating the Bayes factor is very easy and does not require any special methods. We only need to compare the prior and posterior evaluated at the null value (for example, $\theta = 0.5$) under the alternative model. We can see that this is true from the following expression:

$$
BF_{01} = \frac{p(y \mid H_0)}{p(y \mid H_1)} \frac{p(\theta = 0.5 \mid y, H_1)}{p(\theta = 0.5 \mid H_1)}
$$

This is true only when H_0 is a particular case of H_1, (https://statproofbook.github.io/P/bf-sddr). Next, let's do it with PyMC and ArviZ. We only need to sample the prior and posterior for a model. Let's try the BetaBinomial model with a Uniform prior:

Code 5.10:

```
1  with pm.Model() as model_uni:
2      a = pm.Beta("a", 1, 1)
3      yl = pm.Bernoulli("yl", a, observed=y)
4      idata_uni = pm.sample(2000, random_seed=42)
5      idata_uni.extend(pm.sample_prior_predictive(8000))
6
7  az.plot_bf(idata_uni, var_name="a", ref_val=0.5)
```

The result is shown in Figure 5.11. We can see one KDE for the prior (black) and one for the posterior (gray). The two black dots show that we evaluated both distributions at the value 0.5. We can see that the Bayes factor in favor of the null hypothesis, BF_01, is ≈ 8, which we can interpret as *moderate evidence* in favor of the null hypothesis (see Table 5.1).

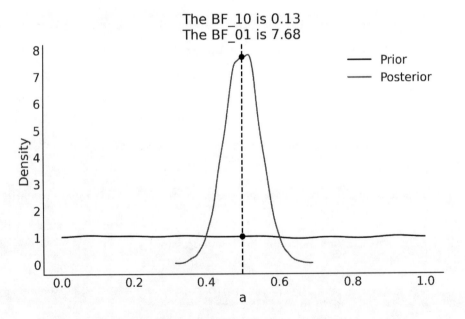

Figure 5.11: Bayes factor for the BetaBinomial model with Uniform prior

As we have already discussed, the Bayes factors measure which model, as a whole, is better at explaining the data. This includes the prior, even if the prior has a relatively low impact on the computation of the posterior. We can also see this prior effect by comparing a second model to the null model.

If, instead, our model were a BetaBinomial with a Beta prior (30, 30), the `BF_01` would be lower (*anecdotal* on the Jeffrey scale). This is because, according to this model, the value of $\theta = 0.5$ is much more likely a priori than for a Uniform prior, and therefore the prior and posterior will be much more similar. That is, it is not very *surprising* to see that the posterior is concentrated around 0.5 after collecting data. Don't just believe me, let's calculate it:

Code 5.11:

```
1  with pm.Model() as model_conc:
2      a = pm.Beta("a", 30, 30)
3      yl = pm.Bernoulli("yl", a, observed=y)
4      idata_conc = pm.sample(2000, random_seed=42)
5      idata_conc.extend(pm.sample_prior_predictive(8000))
6
7  az.plot_bf(idata_conc, var_name="a", ref_val=0.5)
```

Figure 5.12 shows the result. We can see that the `BF_01` is ≈ 1.6, which we can interpret as *anecdotal evidence* in favor of the null hypothesis (see the Jeffreys' scale, discussed earlier).

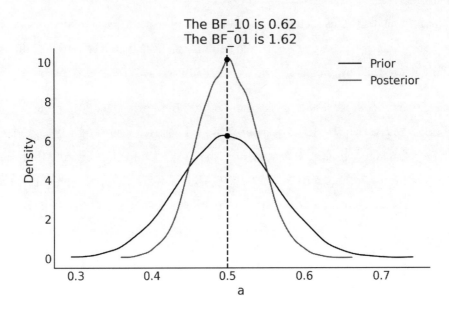

Figure 5.12: Bayes factor for the BetaBinomial model with peaked prior

Bayes factors and inference

So far, we have used Bayes factors to judge which model seems to be better at explaining the data, and we found that one of the models is ≈ 5 times *better* than the other.

But what about the posterior we get from these models? How different are they? Table 5.2 summarizes these two posteriors:

	mean	sd	hdi_3%	hdi_97%
uniform	0.5	0.05	0.4	0.59
peaked	0.5	0.04	0.42	0.57

Table 5.2: Statistics for the models with uniform and peaked priors computed using the ArviZ summary function

We can argue that the results are quite similar; we have the same mean value for θ and a slightly wider posterior for `model_0`, as expected since this model has a wider prior. We can also check the posterior predictive distribution to see how similar they are (see Figure 5.13).

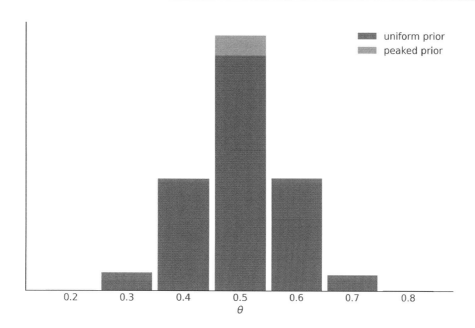

Figure 5.13: Posterior predictive distributions for models with uniform and peaked priors

In this example, the observed data is more consistent with model_1, because the prior is concentrated around the correct value of θ, while model_0, assigns the same probability to all possible values of θ. This difference between the models is captured by the Bayes factor. We could say that the Bayes factors measure which model, as a whole, is better for explaining the data. This includes the details of the prior, no matter how similar the model predictions are. In many scenarios, this is not what interests us when comparing models, and instead, we prefer to evaluate models in terms of how similar their predictions are. For those cases, we can use LOO.

Regularizing priors

Using informative and weakly informative priors is a way of introducing bias in a model and, if done properly, this can be really good because bias prevents overfitting and thus contributes to models being able to make predictions that generalize well. This idea of adding a bias element to reduce generalization errors without affecting the ability of the model to adequately model a problem is known as **regularization**. This regularization often takes the form of a term penalizing certain values for the parameters in a model, like too-big coefficients in a regression model. Restricting parameter values is a way of reducing the data a model can represent, thus reducing the chances that a model will capture noise instead of the signal.

This regularization idea is so powerful and useful that it has been discovered several times, including outside the Bayesian framework. For regression models, and outside Bayesian statistics, two popular regularization methods are ridge regression and lasso regression. From the Bayesian point of view, ridge regression can be interpreted as using Normal distributions for the β coefficients of a linear model, with a small standard deviation that pushes the coefficients toward zero. In this sense, we have been doing something very close to ridge regression for every single linear model in this book (except the examples in this chapter that use SciPy!).

On the other hand, lasso regression can be interpreted from a Bayesian point of view as the MAP of the posterior computed from a model with Laplace priors for the β coefficients. The Laplace distribution looks similar to the Gaussian distribution but with a sharp peak at zero. You can also interpret it as two *back-to-back* Exponential distributions (try `pz.Laplace(0, 1).plot_pdf()`). The Laplace distribution concentrates its probability mass much closer to zero compared to the Gaussian distribution. The idea of using such a prior is to provide both regularization and variable selection. The idea is that since we have this peak at zero, we expect the prior distribution to induce sparsity, that is, we create a model with a lot of parameters and the prior will automatically make most of them zero, keeping only the relevant variables contributing to the output of the model.

Unfortunately, contrary to ridge regression, this idea does not directly translate from the frequentist realm to the Bayesian one. Nevertheless, there are Bayesian priors that can be used for inducing sparsity and performing variable selection, like the horseshoe prior. If you want to learn more about the horseshoe and other shrinkage priors, you may find the article by Piironen and Vehtari [2017] at `https://arxiv.org/abs/1707.01694` very interesting. In the next chapter, we will discuss more about variable selection. Just one final note: it is important to notice that the classical versions of ridge and lasso regressions correspond to single-point estimates, while the Bayesian versions yield full posterior distributions.

Summary

In this chapter, we have seen how to compare models using posterior predictive checks, information criteria, approximated cross-validation, and Bayes factors.

Posterior predictive check is a general concept and practice that can help us understand how well models are capturing different aspects of the data. We can perform posterior predictive checks with just one model or with many models, and thus we can use it as a method for model comparison. Posterior predictive checks are generally done via visualizations, but numerical summaries like Bayesian values can also be helpful.

Good models have a good balance between complexity and predictive accuracy. We exemplified this feature by using the classical example of polynomial regression. We discussed two methods to estimate the out-of-sample accuracy without leaving data aside: cross-validation and information criteria. From a practical point of view, information criteria is a family of theoretical methods looking to balance two contributions: a measurement of how well a model fits the data and a penalization term for complex models. We briefly discussed AIC, for its historical importance, and then WAIC, which is a better method for Bayesian models as it takes into account the entire posterior distribution and uses a more sophisticated method to compute the effective number of parameters.

We also discussed cross-validation, and we saw we can approximate leave-one-out cross-validation using LOO. Both WAIC and LOO tend to produce very similar results, but LOO can be more reliable. So we recommend its use. Both WAIC and LOO can be used for model selection and model averaging. Instead of selecting a single best model, model averaging is about combining all available models by taking a weighted average of them.

A different approach to model selection, comparison, and model averaging is Bayes factors, which are the ratio of the marginal likelihoods of two models. Bayes factor computations can be really challenging. In this chapter, we showed two routes to compute them with PyMC and ArviZ: using the sampling method known as Sequential Monte Carlo and using the Savage–Dickey ratio. The first method can be used for any model as long as Sequential Monte Carlo provides a good posterior. With the current implementation of SMC in PyMC, this can be challenging for high-dimensional models or hierarchical models. The second method can only be used when the null model is a particular case of the alternative model. Besides being computationally challenging, Bayes factors are problematic to use given that they are very (overly) sensitive to prior specifications.

We have shown that Bayes factors and LOO/WAIC are the answers to two related but different questions. The former is focused on identifying the right model and the other is on identifying the model with lower generalization loss, i.e., the model making the best predictions. None of these methods are free of problems, but WAIC, and in particular LOO, are much more robust than the others in practice.

Exercises

1. This exercise is about regularization priors. In the code that generates the `x_c`, `y_c` data (see `https://github.com/aloctavodia/BAP3`), change `order=2` to another value, such as `order=5`. Then, fit `model_q` and plot the resulting curve. Repeat this, but now using a prior for β with `sd=100` instead of `sd=1` and plot the resulting curve. How do the curves differ? Try this out with `sd=np.array([10, 0.1, 0.1, 0.1, 0.1])`, too.

2. Repeat the previous exercise but increase the amount of data to 500 data points.

3. Fit a cubic model (order 3), compute WAIC and LOO, plot the results, and compare them with the linear and quadratic models.

4. Use `pm.sample_posterior_predictive()` to rerun the PPC example, but this time, plot the values of y instead of the values of the mean.

5. Read and run the posterior predictive example from PyMC's documentation at `https://www.pymc.io/projects/docs/en/stable/learn/core_notebooks/posterior_predictive.html`. Pay special attention to the use of shared variables and `pm.MutableData`.

6. Go back to the code that generated Figure 5.5 and Figure 5.6 and modify it to get new sets of six data points. Visually evaluate how the different polynomials fit these new datasets. Relate the results to the discussions in this book.

7. Read and run the model averaging example from PyMC's documentation at `https://www.pymc.io/projects/examples/en/latest/diagnostics_and_criticism/model_averaging.html`.

8. Compute the Bayes factor for the coin problem using a uniform prior, Beta(1, 1), and priors such as Beta(0.5, 0.5). Set 15 heads and 30 coins. Compare this result with the inference we got in the first chapter of this book.

9. Repeat the last example where we compare Bayes factors and Information Criteria, but now reduce the sample size.

Join our community Discord space

Join our Discord community to meet like-minded people and learn alongside more than 5000 members at:

`https://packt.link/bayesian`

6

Modeling with Bambi

A good tool improves the way you work. A great tool improves the way you think.

– Jeff Duntemann

In Chapter 4, we described the basic ingredients of linear regression models and how to generalize them to better fit our needs. In this chapter, we are going to keep learning about linear models, but this time, we are going to work with Bambi [Capretto et al., 2022], a high-level Bayesian model-building interface written on top of PyMC. Bambi is designed to make it extremely easy to fit linear models, including hierarchical ones. We will see that Bambi's domain is more comprehensive than just linear models.

We are going to learn about:

- Using Bambi to build and fit models
- Analyzing results with Bambi
- Polynomial regression and splines
- Distributional models

- Categorical predictors
- Interactions
- Variable selection with Kulprit

One syntax to rule them all

PyMC has a very simple and expressive syntax that allows us to build arbitrary models. That's usually a blessing, but it can be a burden too. Bambi instead focuses on regression models, and this restriction leads to a more focused syntax and features, as we will see.

Bambi uses a Wilkinson-formula syntax similar to the one used by many R packages like nlme, lme4, and brms. Let's assume `data` is a pandas DataFrame like the one shown in Table 6.1.

	y	x	z	g
0	-0.633494	-0.196436	-0.355148	Group A
1	2.32684	0.0163941	-1.22847	Group B
2	0.999604	0.107602	-0.391528	Group C
3	-0.119111	0.804268	0.967253	Group A
4	2.07504	0.991417	0.590832	Group B
5	-0.412135	0.691132	-2.13044	Group C

Table 6.1: A dummy pandas DataFrame

Using this data, we want to build a linear model that predicts y from x. Using PyMC, we would do something like the model in the following code block:

Code 6.1:

```
1  with pm.Model() as lm:
2      Intercept = pm.Normal("Intercept", 0, 1)
3      x = pm.Normal("x", 0, 1)
4      y_sigma = pm.HalfNormal("sigma", 1)
5      y_mean = Intercept + x * data["x"]
6      y = pm.Normal("y", y_mean, y_sigma, observed=data["y"])
```

The formula syntax used by Bambi allows us to define an equivalent model in a much more compact way:

Code 6.2:

```
a_model = bmb.Model("y ~ x", data)
```

On the left side of the tilde (~), we have the dependent variable, and on the right side, the independent variable(s). With this syntax, we are just specifying the mean (μ in the PyMC's model lm). By default, Bambi assumes the likelihood is Gaussian; you can change this with the family argument. The formula syntax does not specify priors distribution, just how the dependent and independent variables are related. Bambi will automatically define (very) weakly informative priors for us. We can get more information by printing a Bambi model. If you print a_model, you should get something like this:

```
    Formula: y ~ x
    Family: gaussian
        Link: mu = identity
Observations: 117
    Priors:
target = mu
    Common-level effects
        Intercept ~ Normal(mu: 0.02, sigma: 2.8414)
        x ~ Normal(mu: 0.0, sigma: 3.1104)

    Auxiliary parameters
        sigma ~ HalfStudentT(nu: 4.0, sigma: 1.1348)
```

The first line shows the formula we used to define the model, and the second line is the likelihood. The third line is the link function. Then we have the number of observations used to fit the model, and the next is telling us we are linearly modeling the parameter mu of the Gaussian. The latter part of the output shows the model structure: the common-level effects, in this case, the intercept (Intercept) and the slope (x), and the auxiliary parameters, i.e., all the parameters not linearly modeled, in this case, the standard deviation of the Gaussian.

You can override the default priors by passing a dictionary to the `priors` argument to `bmb.Model`. For instance, if we want to define a custom prior for the coefficient of the variable x and also for the auxiliary parameter `sigma`, we can do this:

Code 6.3:

```
1 priors = {"x": bmb.Prior("HalfNormal", sigma=3),
2           "sigma": bmb.Prior("Gamma",  mu=1, sigma=2),
3          }
4 a_model_wcp = bmb.Model("y ~ x", data, priors=priors)
```

As a result, we will get the following model specifications:

```
      Formula: y ~ x
       Family: gaussian
         Link: mu = identity
 Observations: 117
       Priors:
   target = mu
       Common-level effects
           Intercept ~ Normal(mu: 0.02, sigma: 2.837)
           x ~ HalfNormal(sigma: 3.0)

       Auxiliary parameters
           sigma ~ Gamma(mu: 1.0, sigma: 2.0)
```

If you want to omit the intercept from your model, you can do it like this:

Code 6.4:

```
no_intercept_model = bmb.Model("y ~ 0 + x", data)
```

Or even like this:

Code 6.5:

```
no_intercept_model = bmb.Model("y ~ -1 + x", data)
```

Print the model `no_intercept_model`, and you will see that the intercept is not there anymore.

What if we want to include more variables? We can do it like this:

Code 6.6:

```
model_2 = bmb.Model("y ~ x + z", data)
```

We can also include group-level effects (hierarchies); for example, if we want to use the variable g to partially pool the estimates of x, we can do it like this:

Code 6.7:

```
model_h = bmb.Model("y ~ x + z + (x | g)", data)
```

We can see a visual representation of this model in Figure 6.1. Notice the variables 1|g_offset and x|g_offset. By default, Bambi fits a noncentered hierarchical model; you can change this with the argument noncentered.

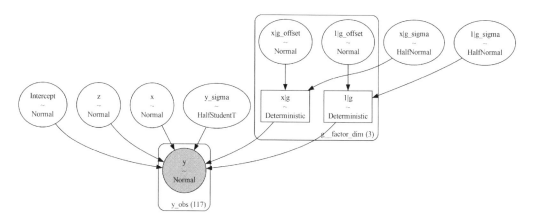

Figure 6.1: A visual representation of model_h

The formula syntax is very simple, but it is also very powerful. We have just scratched the surface of what we can do with it. Instead of describing the syntax all at once, we are going to show it by example. If you want to go deeper, you can check Formulae documentation https://bambinos.github.io/formulae/. formulae is the Python package in charge of parsing Wilkinson's formulas for Bambi.

The bikes model, Bambi's version

The first model we are going to use to illustrate how to use Bambi is the bikes model from Chapter 4. We can load the data with:

Code 6.8:

```
bikes = pd.read_csv("data/bikes.csv")
```

Now we can build and fit the model:

Code 6.9:

```
1  model_t = bmb.Model("rented ~ temperature", bikes, family="negativebinomial")
2  idata_t = model_t.fit()
```

Figure 6.2 shows a visual representation of the model. If you want to visually inspect the priors, you can use `model.plot_priors()`:

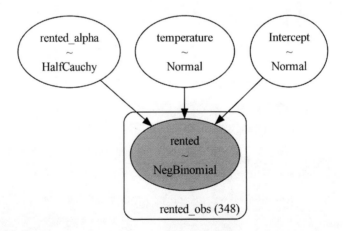

Figure 6.2: A visual representation of the bikes model, computed with the command `model.graph()`

Let's now plot the posterior mean and the posterior predictive distribution (predictions). Omitting some details needed to make the plots look nice, the code to do this is:

Code 6.10:

```
1  _, axes = plt.subplots(1, 2, sharey=True, figsize=(12, 4))
2  bmb.interpret.plot_predictions(model_t, idata_t,
3                                 "temperature", ax=axes[0])
4  bmb.interpret.plot_predictions(model_t, idata_t,
5                                 "temperature", pps=True, ax=axes[1])
```

plot_predictions is a function from Bambi's submodule interpret. This function helps to analyze regression models by plotting conditional adjusted predictions, visualizing how a parameter of the (conditional) response distribution varies as a function of (some) interpolated explanatory variables. We can see the result of this code in Figure 6.3. The left panel shows the posterior mean and the 94% HDI, while the right panel shows the posterior predictive distribution (the predicted distribution of the rented bikes). Notice that the uncertainty for the predictions is much larger than the uncertainty for the mean (pps=False). This is because the posterior predictive distribution accounts for the uncertainty in the model parameters and the uncertainty in the data, whereas the posterior distribution of the mean only accounts for the uncertainty in the intercept and slope parameters.

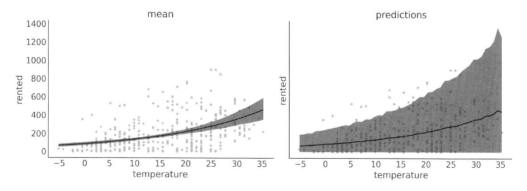

Figure 6.3: Posterior mean and posterior predictive distribution for the bikes model

The utility of plot_cap becomes more evident when we have more than one explanatory variable. For example, let's fit a model that uses both temperature and humidity to predict the number of rented bikes:

Code 6.11:

```
1  model_th = bmb.Model("rented ~ temperature + humidity", bikes,
2                          family="negativebinomial")
3
4  idata_th = model_th.fit()
5
6  bmb.interpret.plot_predictions(model_th, idata_th, ["temperature", "humidity"],
7                          subplot_kwargs={"group":None, "panel":"humidity"})
```

In Figure 6.4, we can see five panels, each one showing the change of the number of rented bikes with the temperature at different values of humidity. As you can see, the number of rented bikes increases with temperature, but the slope is larger when humidity is low.

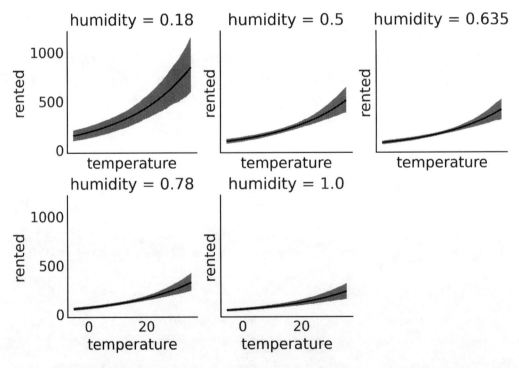

Figure 6.4: Posterior mean for the bikes model with temperature and humidity

Polynomial regression

One way to fit curves using a linear regression model is by building a polynomial, like this:

$$\mu = \beta_0 + \beta_1 x + \beta_2 x^2 + \beta_3 x^3 + \beta_4 x^4 \ldots \beta_m x^m$$

We call m the degree of the polynomial.

There are two important things to notice. First, polynomial regression is still linear regression; the linearity refers to the coefficients (the βs), not the variables (the xs). The second thing to note is that we are creating new variables out of thin air. The only observed variable is x, the rest are just powers of x. Creating new variables from observed ones is a perfectly valid "trick" when doing regression; sometimes the transformation can be motivated or justified by theory (like taking the square root of the length of babies), but sometimes it is just a way to fit a curve. The intuition with polynomials is that for a given value of x, the higher the degree of the polynomial, the more flexible the curve can be. A polynomial of degree 1 is a line, a polynomial of degree 2 is a curve that can go up or down, a polynomial of degree 3 is a curve that can go up and then down (or the other way around), and so on. Notice I said "can" because if we have a polynomial of degree 3, like $\beta_0 + \beta_1 x + \beta_2 x^2 + \beta_3 x^3$, but the coefficients β_2 and β_3 are 0 (or practically 0), then the curve will be a line.

There are two ways to define a polynomial regression with Bambi. We can write the *raw* polynomials:

Code 6.12:

```
"y ~ x + I(x ** 2) + I(x ** 3) + I(x ** 4)"
```

Here, we use the identity function I() to make it clear that we want to elevate x to some power. We need this because the ** operator has a special meaning for Bambi. If we use this syntax, we are telling Bambi to model the mean of y as $\alpha + \beta_0 x + \beta_0 x^2 + \beta_0 x^3 + \beta_0 x^4$.

Alternatively, we can write:

Code 6.13:

```
"y ~ poly(x, 4)"
```

This will also generate a polynomial of degree 4, but the polynomial terms will be orthogonal to each other, meaning the correlation between the terms is reduced. Without going into the mathematical details, this has at least two important consequences with respect to the *standard* polynomial. First, the estimation can be numerically more stable, and second, the interpretation of the coefficients is different. In standard polynomial regression, the coefficients can be difficult to interpret, as changing the value of one coefficient affects the entire polynomial. In contrast, orthogonal polynomials allow you to interpret the effect of each term more clearly, as they are independent of each other. While the interpretation of the coefficients is different, other results remain the same. For instance, you should get the same predictions with both approaches.

Let's build an orthogonal polynomial of degree 4 to model the bike data. For this example, we are going to use the hour variable:

Code 6.14:

```
1 model_poly4 = bmb.Model("rented ~ poly(temperature, degree=4)", bikes,
2                         family="negativebinomial")
3 idata_poly4 = model_poly4.fit()
```

Figure 6.5 shows the posterior mean and the posterior predictive distribution. On the first row, you will see a polynomial of degree 1, which is equivalent to a linear model. On the second row, you will see a polynomial of degree 4.

One problem with polynomials is that they act *globally*. When we apply a polynomial of degree m, we are saying that the relationship between the independent and dependent variables is of degree m for the entire dataset. This can be problematic when different regions of our data need different levels of flexibility. This could lead, for example, to curves that are too flexible. As the degree increases, the fit becomes more sensitive to the removal of points, or equivalently to the addition of future data. In other words, as the degree

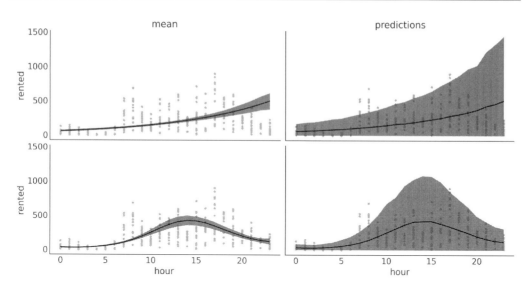

Figure 6.5: Posterior mean and posterior predictive distribution for the bikes model with temperature and humidity

increases, the model becomes more prone to overfitting. Bayesian polynomial regression usually suffers less of this "excess" of flexibility because we usually don't use flat priors, and we do not compute a single set of coefficients, but the entire posterior distribution. Still, we can do better.

Splines

A general way to write very flexible models is to apply functions B_m to X_m and then multiply them by coefficients β_m:

$$\mu = \beta_0 + \beta_1 B_1(X_1) + \beta_2 B_2(X_2) + \cdots + \beta_m B_m(X_m)$$

We are free to pick B_m as we wish; for instance, we can pick polynomials. But we can also pick other functions. A popular choice is to use B-splines; we are not going to discuss their definition, but we can think of them as a way to create smooth curves in such a way that we get flexibility, as with polynomials, but less prone to overfitting. We achieve this by using piecewise polynomials, that is, polynomials that are restricted to affect only a portion of the data. Figure 6.6 shows three examples of piecewise polynomials of increasing degrees. The dotted vertical lines show the "knots," which are the points used to restrict the regions, the dashed gray line represents the function we want to approximate, and the black lines are the piecewise polynomials.

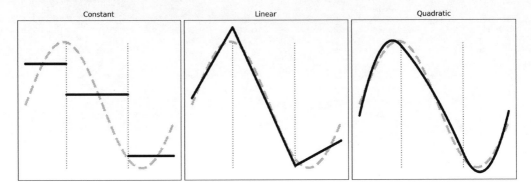

Figure 6.6: Piecewise polynomials of increasing degrees

Figure 6.7 shows examples of splines of degree 1 and 3; the dots at the bottom represent the knots, and the dashed lines are the B-splines. At the top, we have all the B-splines with equal weight; we use grayscale to highlight that we have many B-splines. On the bottom panel, each B-spline is weighted differently (we multiply them by β_m coefficients); if we sum the weighted B-splines, we get the black line as a result. This black line is what we usually call "the spline." We can use Bayesian statistics to find the proper weights for the B-splines.

We can use B-splines with Bambi by using the bs function. For example, let's fit a spline of degree 3 to the bikes data:

Code 6.15:

```
1  num_knots = 6
2  knots = np.linspace(0, 23, num_knots+2)[1:-1]
3  model_spline = bmb.Model("rented ~ bs(hour, degree=3, knots=knots)", bikes,
4                           family="negativebinomial")
5  idata_spline = model_spline.fit()
```

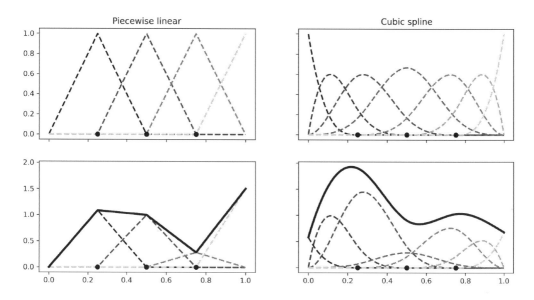

Figure 6.7: B-splines of degree 1 (piecewise linear) or 3 (cubic spline) and the resulting splines.

Figure 6.8 shows that the number of rental bikes is at the lowest number late at night. There is then an increase, probably as people wake up and go to work or school, or do other activities. We have a first peak at around hour 8, then a slight decline, followed by the second peak at around hour 18, probably because people commute back home, after which there is a steady decline. Notice that the curve is not very smooth; this is not because of the spline but because of the data. We have measurements at discrete times (every hour).

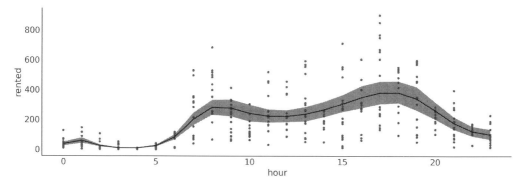

Figure 6.8: Posterior mean for the spline model

When working with splines, one important decision we must make is determining the number and placement of knots. This can be a somewhat daunting task since the optimal number of knots and their spacing are not immediately apparent. A useful suggestion for determining the knot locations is to consider placing them based on quantiles rather than uniformly – something like `knots = np.quantile(bikes.hour, np.linspace(0, 1, num_knots))`. By doing so, we would position more knots in areas where we have a greater amount of data, while placing fewer knots in areas with less data. This results in a more adaptable approximation that effectively captures the variability in regions with a higher density of data points. Additionally, we may want to fit splines with varying numbers of knots and positions and then evaluate the results, using tools such as LOO, as we saw in Chapter 5.

Distributional models

We saw earlier that we can use linear models for parameters other than the mean (or location parameter). For example, we can use a linear model for the mean and a linear model for the standard deviation of a Gaussian distribution. These models are usually called distributional models. The syntax for distributional models is very similar; we just need to add a line for the auxiliary parameters we want to model. For instance, σ for a Gaussian, or α for a NegativeBinomial.

Let's now reproduce an example from Chapter 4, the babies example:

Code 6.16:

```
1  formula = bmb.Formula(
2      "length ~ np.sqrt(month)",
3      "sigma ~ month"
4  )
5  model_dis = bmb.Model(formula, babies)
6  idata_dis = model_dis.fit()
```

Figure 6.9 shows the posterior distribution values of sigma for `model_dis` (varying sigma) and for a model with constant sigma. We can see that when sigma is allowed to vary, we obtain values below and above the estimate for a constant sigma, meaning that we are both under- and over-estimating this parameter when we don't allow it to change.

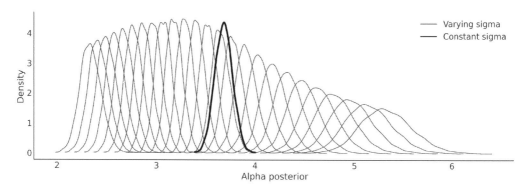

Figure 6.9: Constant and varying sigma for the babies data

Figure 6.10 shows the posterior fit for model_dis. Notice that the model can capture the increase in variability as the babies grow. This figure is very similar to Figure4.13.

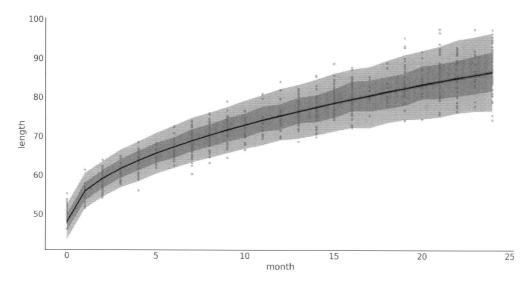

Figure 6.10: Posterior fit for model_dis

When working with PyMC, we saw that sampling from the posterior predictive distribution, at not observed values, requires us to define the "Xs" as Mutable data and then update the variable before computing the posterior predictive distribution. With Bambi, this is not necessary. We can use the `predict` method to predict new values by passing the new values to the `data` argument. For example, let's predict the length of a baby at 0.5 months (15 days):

Code 6.17:

```
model_dis.predict(idata_dis, kind="pps", data=pd.DataFrame({"month":[0.5]}))
```

Categorical predictors

A categorical variable represents distinct groups or categories that can take on a limited set of values from those categories. These values are typically labels or names that don't possess numerical significance on their own. Some examples are:

- Political affiliation: conservative, liberal, or progressive.
- Sex: female or male.
- Customer satisfaction level: very unsatisfied, unsatisfied, neutral, satisfied, or very satisfied.

Linear regression models can easily accommodate categorical variables; we just need to encode the categories as numbers. There are a few options to do so. Bambi can easily handle the details for us. The devil is in the interpretation of the results, as we will explore in the next two sections.

Categorical penguins

For the current example, we are going to use the palmerpenguins dataset, Horst et al. [2020], which contains 344 observations of 8 variables. For the moment, we are interested in modeling the mass of the penguins as a function of the length of their bills. It is expected that the mass of the penguins increases as the bill length increases. The novelty of this example is that we are going to consider the categorical variable, species. In this dataset, we have 3 categories or levels for the species variable, namely, Adelie, Chinstrap, and Gentoo. Figure 6.11 shows a scatter plot for the variables we want to model.

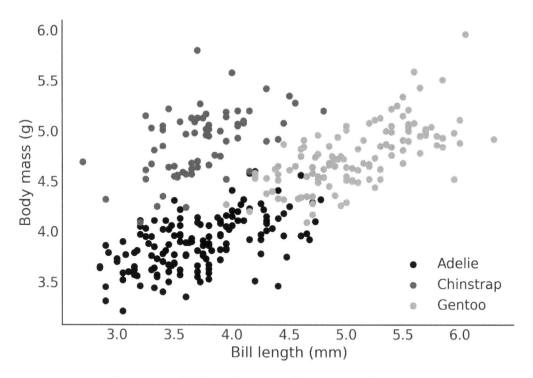

Figure 6.11: Bill length vs mass for 3 species of penguins

Let's load the data and fit the model:

Code 6.18:

```
1  penguins = pd.read_csv("data/penguins.csv").dropna()
2
3  model_p = bmb.Model("body_mass ~ bill_length + species", data=penguins)
4  idata_p = model_p.fit()
```

Notice that there is no special syntax to define Bambi's model for categorical variables. Bambi can detect and handle them automatically.

Figure 6.12 show a forest plot for `model_p`. Notice something unexpected? There are no posterior values for Adelie. This is no mistake. By default, Bambi encodes categorical variables with N levels (3 species) as N-1 dummy variables (2 species). Thus the coefficients species-Chinstrap and species-Gentoo are modeled as deflections from the baseline model:

$$\text{mass} = \beta_0 + \beta_1 \text{bill length}$$

To make this more clear, let's check a couple of plots. We can read Figure 6.12 as saying that the body mass of Chinstrap is, on average, -0.89 relative to Adelie's body mass. The same goes for Gentoo, but this time, we have to add 0.66 to the mean of the baseline model.

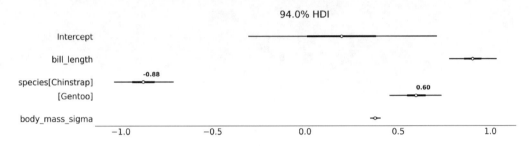

Figure 6.12: Forest plot from `model_p`

You can check that these two statements are true by looking at Figure 6.13. See how the three lines are essentially parallel to each other with Adelie in the middle, Chinstrap below (-0.89), and Gentoo above (0.58).

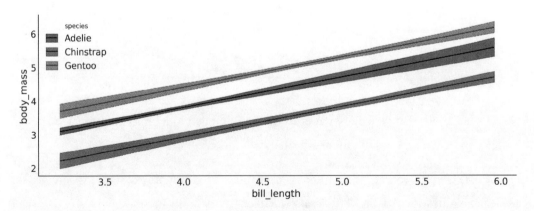

Figure 6.13: Mean in-sample predictions from `model_p`

Relation to hierarchical models

In Chapter 3, we discussed and contrasted pooled and hierarchical (or partially pooled) models. There we showed that it is often the case that we take advantage of the structure or hierarchies in data. Following the logic of that chapter, you could argue that Adelie, Gentoo, and Chinstrap, while being different species, are all penguins. So modeling their body masses hierarchically may be a good idea. And you would be right to think so. So what is the difference between such a model and the one we used in this section?

The distinguishing factor lies in the subtleties of the slope and intercept components. In the case of the latter, the slope remains the same across all three penguin species, while the intercepts can vary: `Intercept + 0` for Adelie, `Intercept + species[Chinstrap]` for Chinstrap, and `Intercept + species[Gentoo]` for Gentoo. Thus, this model highlights the distinct intercepts while keeping the slope uniform.

If instead we had built the hierarchical model `body_mass ~(bill_length|species)`, we would have been asking for a partially pooled slope and intercept. And if instead we had modeled `body_mass ~(0 + bill_length | species)`, we would have been asking for a partially pooled slope and a common intercept.

Besides these particular models, when thinking about using a predictor as a grouping variable or as a categorical predictor, it is usually useful to ask if the variable includes all possible categories (like all days of the week, all species, and so on) or only a subgroup (some schools, or a few musical genres). If we have all possible categories, then we may prefer to model it as a categorical predictor, otherwise, as a grouping variable.

As we already discussed, we often create more than one model before deciding which one we like the most. The *best* model is the one that aligns with the goals of your analysis, provides meaningful insights, and accurately represents the underlying patterns in your data. It's often a good idea to explore multiple models, compare their performance using appropriate criteria (such as those discussed in Chapter 5), and consider the practical implications of each model for your research or decision-making process.

Interactions

An interaction effect, or statistical interaction, happens when the effect of an independent variable on the response changes depending on the value of another independent variable. An interaction can occur between two or more variables. Some examples are:

- **Education level and income impact**: Higher education may have a stronger positive effect on income for one gender compared to the other, resulting in an interaction between education and gender.
- **Medication efficacy and age**: A drug that works better for older individuals than younger ones.
- **Exercise and diet effects on weight loss**: It could be that the diet's effect on weight loss is small for people who do little or no exercise and large for people who do moderate exercise.
- **Temperature and humidity for crop growth**: Some crops could thrive in hot and humid conditions, while others might perform better in cooler and less humid environments.

We have an interaction when the combined effect of two or more variables acting together is not equal to the sum of their individual effects. So we cannot model an interaction if we have a model like the following:

$$\mu = \alpha + \beta_0 X_0 + \beta_1 X_1$$

The most common way to model an interaction effect is by multiplying two (or more) variables. Take, for example, a model like the following:

$$\mu = \alpha + \overbrace{\beta_0 X_0 + \beta_1 X_1}^{\text{main terms}} + \underbrace{\beta_2 X_0 X_1}_{\text{interaction term}}$$

It is common when modeling interaction effects to also include the main effect/terms.

> **New predictors**
>
> Multiplying two variables can be seen as a trick, similar to the one we use for polynomial regression (or any transformation of a given variable). Instead of multiplying a predictor with itself, we multiply two different predictors and obtain a new one.

Defining an interaction between two variables is easy for a PyMC model; we just need to multiply the two predictors together and also add a coefficient. For a Bambi model, it is even easier; we use the : operator. To make the difference crystal clear, let's look at an example of a model with and without interactions:

Code 6.19:

```
1  # No interaction
2  model_noint = bmb.Model("body_mass ~ bill_depth + bill_length",
3                          data=penguins)
4
5  #Interaction
6  model_int = bmb.Model("body_mass ~ bill_depth + bill_length +
7                          bill_depth:bill_length",
8                          data=penguins)
9
10 idata_noint = model_noint.fit()
11 idata_int = model_int.fit()
```

We now use Bambi's plot_prediction to compare how different values of bill_length affect body_mass as a function of bill_depth generate. Figure 6.14 shows the result. We have the mean regression fit for bill_depth evaluated at 5 fixed values of bill_length. On the left, we have the result for model_noint (no interactions), and on the right, for model_int (with interactions). We can see that when we don't have interactions, the fitted lines for bill_depth are parallel at different levels of bill_length. Instead, when we have interactions, the lines are no longer parallel, precisely because the effect of changing `bill_depth` on how much `body_mass` changes is no longer constant but modulated by the values of `bill_length`.

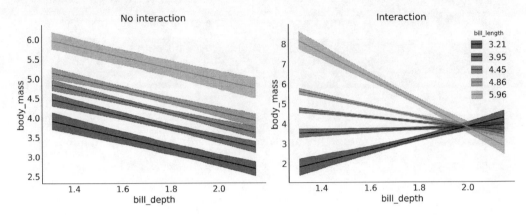

Figure 6.14: Mean in-sample predictions from `model_noint` *(left) and* `model_int` *(right)*

If you generate a figure like Figure 6.14, but instead of fixing `bill_length`, you decide to fix `bill_depth`, you will observe a similar behavior.

In the GitHub repository for this book (`https://github.com/aloctavodia/BAP3`), you are going to find the file `interactions.ipynb`. This script generates a figure in 3D, which I hope will help you build intuition about what we are doing when adding interactions. If you run it, you will see that when there are no interactions, we are fitting a 2D plane, a flat surface like a sheet of paper. But when adding interactions, you are fitting a curved surface. Compare the result of `interactions.ipynb` with Figure 6.14.

We have just seen visually that interpreting linear models with interactions is not as easy as interpreting linear models without them. Let's see this mathematically.

Let's assume we have a model with 2 variables, X_0 and X_1, and an interaction between them:

$$\mu = \alpha + \beta_0 X_0 + \beta_1 X_1 + \beta_2 X_0 X_1$$

We can rewrite this model as:

$$\mu = \alpha + \underbrace{(\beta_0 + \beta_2 X_1)}_{\text{slope of } X_0} X_0 + \beta_1 X_1$$

Or even like this:

$$\mu = \alpha + \beta_0 X_0 + \underbrace{(\beta_1 + \beta_2 X_0)}_{\text{slope of } X_1} X_1$$

From this expression, we can see that:

- The interaction term can be understood as a linear model inside a linear model.
- The interaction is symmetric; we can think of it as the slope of X_0 as a function of X_1 and at the same time as the slope of X_1 as a function of X_0. This can also be seen from the interactive figure.
- We know from before that the β_0 coefficient can be interpreted as the amount of change of μ per unit change of X_0 (that is why we call it the slope). If we add an interaction term, then this is only true at $X_1 = 0$. Try using the interactive figure to see this by yourself. Mathematically, this is true because when $X_1 = 0$, then $\beta_2 X_1 = 0$, and thus the slope of X_0 reduces to $\beta_0 X_0$. By symmetry, the same reasoning can be applied to β_1.

Interpreting models with Bambi

We have been using `bmb.interpret_plot_predictions` a lot in this chapter. But that's not the only tool that Bambi offers us to help us understand models. One of them is `bmb.interpret_plot_comparisons`. This tool helps us answer the question, "What is the expected predictive difference when we compare two values of a given variable while keeping all the rest at constant values?".

Let's use `model_int` from the previous section, so we don't need to fit a new model. We use the following code block to generate Figure 6.15:

Code 6.20:

```
1  bmb.interpret.plot_comparisons(model_int, idata_int,
2                                 contrast={"bill_depth":[1.4, 1.8]},
3                                 conditional={"bill_length":[3.5, 4.5, 5.5]})
```

Figure 6.15 shows that when comparing a hypothetical penguin with `bill_depth` of 1.8 against one with `bill_depth` of 1.4, the expected difference is:

- Approx 0.8 kg for a bill length of 3.5 cm

- -0.6 kg for a bill length of 4.5 cm

- Approx -2 kg for a bill length of 5.5 cm

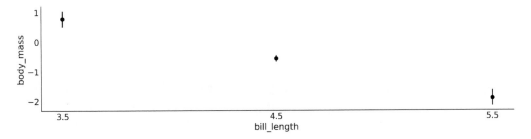

Figure 6.15: Contrast of `bill_depth` *from 1.8 to 1.4 cm for 3 fixed values of* `bill_length`

If you want the information in tabular form, use the function `bmb.interpret.comparisons` and you will get a DataFrame instead of a plot.

Another useful function is `bmb.interpret_plot_slopes`, which can be used to compute the "instant rate of change" or slope at a given value. We use the following code block to generate Figure 6.16:

Code 6.21:

```
1  bmb.interpret.plot_slopes(model_int, idata_int,
2                            wrt={"bill_depth":1.8},
3                            conditional={"bill_length":[3.5, 4.5, 5.5]},
```

Figure 6.16 shows that the slopes at a `bill_depth` of 1.8 are:

- $\approx$ 2 kg/cm for a bill length of 3.5 cm

- -1.4 kg/cm for a bill length of 4.5 cm

- $\approx$ -5 kg/cm for a bill length of 5.5 cm

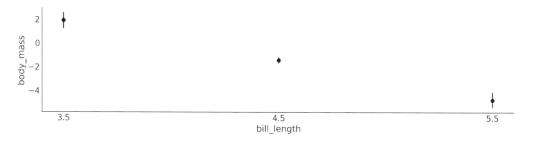

Figure 6.16: Slopes of `bill_depth` *at 1.8 cm for 3 fixed values of* `bill_length`

If you want the information in tabular form, use the function `bmb.interpret.slopes` and you will get a DataFrame instead of a plot.

In this section, we have just scratched the surface of what we can do with the tools in the `bmb.interpret` module. This module is a very useful feature of Bambi, especially for models with interactions and/or models with link functions other than the identity function. I highly recommend you read the Bambi documentation for more examples and details not covered here.

Variable selection

Variable selection refers to the process of identifying the most relevant variables in a model from a larger set of potential predictors. We perform variable selection under the assumption that only a subset of variables have a considerable impact on the outcome of interest, while others contribute little or no additional value.

Arguably the "most Bayesian thing to do" when building a model is to include all the variables that we may think of in a single model and then use the posterior from that model to make predictions or gain an understanding of the relationships of the variables. This is the "most Bayesian" approach because we are using as much data as possible and incorporating in the posterior the uncertainty about the importance of the variables. However, being *more Bayesian than Bayes* is not always the best idea. We already saw in Chapter 5 that Bayes factors can be problematic, even when they are a direct consequence of Bayes' theorem.

Performing variable selection is a good idea when:

- We need to reduce the measurement cost. For instance, in medicine, we may have the money and resources to run a pilot study and measure 30 variables for 200 patients. But we cannot do the same for thousands. Or we may be able to place a lot of sensors in an open field to better model crop gains, but we cannot extend that to the size of a country. Reducing costs is not always about money or time; when working with humans or other animals, reducing pain and discomfort is important too. For example, we may want to predict the risk of a patient having a heart attack. We can do this by measuring a lot of variables, but we can also do it by measuring just a few variables that are less invasive.

- We want to reduce the computational cost. This is not a problem for small and simple models, but when we have a lot of variables, a lot of data, or both, the computational cost can be prohibitive.

- We seek a better understanding of significant correlation structures. That is, we are interested in understanding which variables provide better predictions. It is important to state that we are not talking about causality. While statistical models, in particular, GLMS, can be used to infer causality, doing so requires extra steps and assumptions. In this book, we do not discuss how to perform causal inference. For a very gentle introduction to causal inference, please see this video: `https://www.youtube.com/watch?v=gV6wzTk3o1U`. If you are more serious, you can check out the online book Causal Inference: The Mixtape by Scott Cunningham [Cunningham, 2021]`https://mixtape.scunning.com/`.

- When we desire a model that is more resilient to changes in the data-generating distribution, we can see variable selection as a method to make the model more robust against unrepresentative data.

Projection predictive inference

There are many methods to perform variable selection. In this section, we will focus on one of them called projection predictive inference [Piironen et al., 2020, McLatchie et al., 2023]. The main reason we are focusing on this single method is that it has shown very good performance across a broad range of fields.

The main steps of projective prediction inference are:

1. Generate a reference model, i.e., a model with all the variables you think can be relevant and/or you were able to measure.

2. Generate a set of submodels, i.e., models that only include some subset of the variables in the reference model.

3. Project the reference model's posterior distribution into the submodels.

4. Pick the smallest model that makes predictions close enough to the reference model.

When doing projection predictive inference, we only need to perform Bayesian inference once, just for the reference model. For the submodels, the posteriors are projected. Without going into the technical details, the projection consists of finding the parameters for the submodels in such a way that the predictions of the submodels are as close as possible to the predictions of the reference model. The projection can be done in a computationally efficient way so the cost of estimating a posterior is orders of magnitude cheaper than with MCMC methods. This is relevant because the total number of possible submodels explodes as we increase the number of variables in the reference model. Consider that we need to evaluate all possible combinations, without repeating variables. For instance, say we have four variables (A, B, C, and D) and we need to evaluate 7 models, namely, A, B, C, AB, BC, AC, and the reference model ABC. Seven does not sound like a lot, but by the time we reach 8 variables, we will need to evaluate 92 different models. See, we double the number of variables, and the number of models increases more than 10 times!

Of course, there are ways to reduce the total number of submodels to explore. For instance, we could use some cheap method to filter out the most promising variables and only do projection predictive inference on those. Another alternative is known as forward search; that is, we first fit as many models as the variables we have. We then select one model/variable, the one generating the closest predictions to the reference model. We then generate all the submodels with 2 variables that included the variable selected in the previous step and so on. If we do this forward procedure for a reference model with 8 variables instead of 92 different models, we will need to evaluate just 36.

Another aspect that is relevant to consider when doing projection predictive inference is that we only provided priors for the reference model. The submodels don't have explicit priors; they just inherit, somehow, the priors of the reference model through the projection procedure.

One reason projective prediction works in practice is thanks to the use of a reference model. By fitting the submodels to the in-sample predictions made by the reference model, instead of the observed data, we are filtering out the noise in the data. This helps separate the more relevant variables from the less relevant ones. Another factor is the use of cross-validation in selecting the submodels, as discussed in Chapter 5.

Projection predictive with Kulprit

Kulprit is a Python package for projection predictive inference. It works with Bambi, as we can pass a reference model built with it and Kulprit will do all the hard work for us. To illustrate how to use Kulprit, we are going to use the body fat dataset [Penrose et al., 1985]. This dataset has measurements from 251 individuals, including their age, weight, height, the circumference of the abdomen, etc. Our purpose is to predict the percentage of body fat (as estimated by the `siri` variable). Since obtaining accurate measurements of body fat is expensive and potentially annoying for patients, we want to reduce the measurements while keeping a good predictive accuracy for `siri`. The original dataset included 13 variables; to keep this example really simple, I have preselected 6.

The first thing we need to do is to define and fit a Bambi model, as usual. We have to be sure that we include the argument `idata_kwargs='log_likelihood':True`. Internally, Kulprit computes the ELPD, and as we discussed in Chapter 5, we need the log likelihood in the InferenceData object to be able to estimate the ELPD:

Code 6.22:

```
1 model = bmb.Model("siri ~ age + weight + height + abdomen + thigh + wrist",
2                   data=body)
3 idata = model.fit(idata_kwargs={'log_likelihood': True})
```

After this, we are ready to use Kulprit. First, we need to call the `ProjectionPredictive` class and pass the Bambi model and the idata resulting from the fit of that model. Then we ask Kulprit to perform a search; by default, it will do a forward search:

Code 6.23:

```
1 ppi = kpt.ProjectionPredictive(model, idata)
2 ppi.search()
```

After the search has finished, we can ask Kulprit to compare the submodels in terms of the ELPD. The submodels will show ordered from lowest ELPD to highest, as in Figure 6.17. On the x-axis, we have the submodel size, i.e., number of variables; we start at zero because we include the intercept-only model. The dashed gray line corresponds to the ELPD for the reference model.

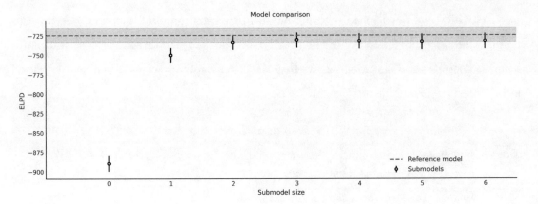

Figure 6.17: Comparison of the submodels obtained with Kulprit. Generated with
`ppi.plot_compare`

We can see then that a submodel of size 3 is practically equivalent to the reference model. But what variables are exactly included in this and the other submodels? If we print the ppi object, after performing a search, we will get an ordered list of the formulas for the submodels matching the order in the plot obtained with the command `ppi.plot_compare`:

Code 6.24:

```
print(ppi)
```

```
0 siri ~ 1
1 siri ~ abdomen
2 siri ~ abdomen + wrist
3 siri ~ abdomen + wrist + height
4 siri ~ abdomen + wrist + height + age
5 siri ~ abdomen + wrist + height + age + weight
6 siri ~ abdomen + wrist + height + age + weight + thigh
```

Then we can see that the model of size 3 is the one including the variables abdomen, wrist, and height. This result tells us that if we want to choose a model with fewer variables than the reference model but with similar predictive accuracy, then this is a good choice. Depending on the context, other submodels may also be a good idea. For instance, we may argue that the difference between the submodel of sizes 2 and 3 is rather small. Thus, we may be willing to sacrifice some accuracy in favor of an even smaller model. For this example, measuring the height of patients may not be that problematic, but for other scenarios, adding a third variable could be expensive, annoying, dangerous, etc.

Another way to interpret Figure 6.17 is by noticing how close the ELPDs are for models with size 3 or larger. It may be the case that if we repeat the analysis with a slightly different dataset, or even the same dataset but with more posterior samples, we could get a slightly different order. Thus, if we have many models of size 3 with potentially the same practical predictive accuracy, we could justify the selection of the third variable by external factors such as how easy or cheap it is to measure, or which one will be less painful for patients, etc. In summary, as with other statistical tools, results should not be taken blindly but in context; you should have the final word and the tools should help you inform your decisions.

OK, let's say that we are indeed interested in the submodel of size 3 computed by Kulprit; we can get it with:

Code 6.25:

```
submodel = ppi.project(3)
```

From the `submodel` object, we can then retrieve some useful information like Bambi's model `submodel.model` or the InferenceData object `submodel.idata`.

One word of caution about interpreting these two objects—`submodel.model` is a Bambi model generated from a formula. Thus, its priors will be those automatically computed by Bambi. But, the posterior that Kulprit computes, which is stored in `submodel.idata.posterior`, does not come directly from this model. Instead, it is computed using projection predictive inference (not MCMC) with priors that are implicitly inherited during the projection step (not explicit priors). Figure 6.18 shows such a projected posterior.

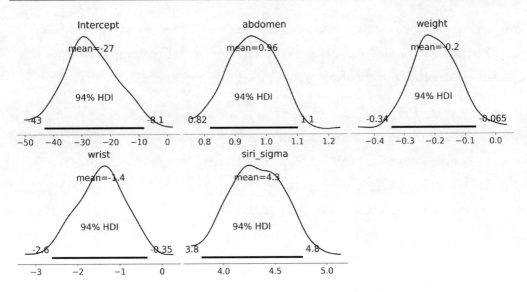

Figure 6.18: Projected posterior for submodel of size 3

Can we trust projected posteriors? Under very general conditions this should be a valid posterior so we can trust it. It should be enough to give you an approximate idea of the values of the parameters and, of course, it is enough for variable selection. The lack of explicit priors could make the interpretation of the model more difficult, but if you only care about predictions, that should not be an issue. Of course, you can always use Bambi (or PyMC) to explicitly compute the full posterior as usual and specify the priors yourself if needed. Figure 6.19 shows a forest plot for the posterior of the submodel as computed with Bambi (True) and approximated with Kulprit (Projected). Notice that there are two possible sources of differences here: the intrinsic differences between MCMC and projection predictive methods and the different priors for both models.

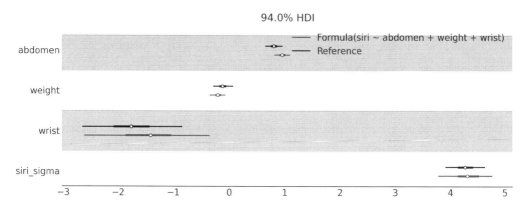

Figure 6.19: Comparison of the posterior of the submodel (`siri ~abdomen + wrist + height`) as computed by Kulprit and the reference model as computed by Bambi; variables not shared by both models have been omitted

Kulprit is a very new library that will keep evolving, and users can expect numerous enhancements and refinements shortly. If Kulprit interests you, you can help with its development by reporting issues, suggesting ideas, improving the documentation, or working on its codebase at `https://github.com/bambinos/kulprit`.

Summary

In this chapter, we have seen how to use Bambi to fit Bayesian models as an alternative to the pure PyMC model. We start with the simplest case, a model with a single predictor, and then move to more complex models, including polynomials, splines, distributional models, models with categorical predictors, and interactions.

The main advantage of Bambi is that it is very easy to use; it is very similar to R's `formula` syntax. And internally, Bambi defines weakly informative priors and handles details that can be cumbersome for complex models. The main disadvantage is that it is not as flexible as PyMC. The range of models that Bambi can handle is a small subset of those from PyMC. Still, this subset contains many of the most commonly used statistical models in both industry and academia. The strength of Bambi is not just easy model building, but easier model interpretation. Across the chapter, we have seen how to use Bambi's `interpret` module to gain a better understanding of the models we fit. Finally, we have seen how to use Kulprit to perform projection predictive inference and perform variable selection. Projection predictive inference offers a promising approach to variable selection, and Kulprit is a promising Pythonic way of doing it.

Exercises

1. Read the Bambi documentation (`https://bambinos.github.io/bambi/`) and learn how to specify custom priors.

2. Apply what you learned in the previous point and specify a HalfNormal prior for the slope of `model_t`.

3. Define a model like `model_poly4`, but using `raw` polynomials, compare the coefficients and the mean fit of both models.

4. Explain in your own words what a distributional model is.

5. Expand `model_spline` to a distributional model. Use another spline to model the α parameter of the NegativeBinomial family.

6. Create a model named `model_p2` for the `body_mass` with the predictors `bill_length`, `bill_depth`, `flipper_length`, and `species`.

7. Use LOO to compare the model in the previous point and `model_p`.

8. Use the functions in the `interpret` module to interpret `model_p2`. Use both plots and tables.

Join our community Discord space

Join our Discord community to meet like-minded people and learn alongside more than 5000 members at:

https://packt.link/bayesian

7

Mixture Models

...the father has the form of a lion, the mother of an ant; the father eats flesh and the mother herbs. And these breed the ant-lion...
−The Book of Imaginary Beings

The River Plate (also known as La Plata River or Río de la Plata) is the widest river on Earth and a natural border between Argentina and Uruguay. During the late 19th century, the port area along this river was a place where indigenous people mixed with Africans (most of them slaves) and European immigrants. One consequence of this encounter was the mix of European music, such as the waltz and mazurka, with the African candombe and Argentinian milonga (which, in turn, is a mix of Afro-American rhythms), giving origin to the dance and music we now call the tango.

Mixing previously existing elements is a great way to create new things, not only in the context of music. In statistics, mixture models are one common approach to model building. These models are built by mixing simpler distributions to obtain more complex ones. For example, we can combine two Gaussians to describe a bimodal distribution or many Gaussians to describe arbitrary distributions. While using Gaussians is very common, in principle we can mix any family of distributions we want. Mixture models are used for different purposes, such as directly modeling sub-populations or as a useful trick for handling complicated distributions that cannot be described with simpler distributions.

In this chapter, we will cover the following topics:

- Finite mixture models
- Zero-inflated and hurdle models
- Infinite mixture models
- Continuous mixture models

Understanding mixture models

Mixture models naturally arise when the overall population is a combination of distinct sub-populations. A familiar example is the distribution of heights in a given adult human population, which can be described as a mixture of female and male sub-populations. Another classical example is the clustering of handwritten digits. In this case, it is very reasonable to expect 10 sub-populations, at least in a base 10 system! If we know to which sub-population each observation belongs, it is generally a good idea to use that information to model each sub-population as a separate group. However, when we do not have direct access to this information, mixture models come in handy.

> **Blends of Distributions**
>
> Many datasets cannot be properly described using a single probability distribution, but they can be described as a mixture of such distributions. Models that assume data comes from a mixture of distributions are known as mixture models.

When building a mixture model, it is not necessary to believe we are describing true sub-populations in the data. Mixture models can also be used as a statistical trick to add flexibility to our toolbox. Take, for example, the Gaussian distribution. We can use it as a reasonable approximation for many unimodal and approximately symmetrical distributions.

But what about multimodal or skewed distributions? Can we use Gaussian distributions to model them? Yes, we can, if we use a mixture of Gaussians.

In a Gaussian mixture model, each component will be a Gaussian with a different mean and, generally (but not necessarily), a different standard deviation. By combining Gaussians, we can add flexibility to our models and fit complex data distributions. In fact, we can approximate practically any distribution we want by using a proper combination of Gaussians. The exact number of distributions will depend on the accuracy of the approximation and the details of the data. Actually, we have been using this idea in many of the plots throughout this book. The Kernel Density Estimation (KDE) technique is a non-Bayesian implementation of this idea. Conceptually, when we call `az.plot_kde`, the function places a Gaussian, with a fixed variance, on top of each data point and then sums all the individual Gaussians to approximate the empirical distribution of the data. Figure 7.1 shows an example of how we can mix 8 Gaussians to represent a complex distribution, like a boa constrictor digesting an elephant, or a hat, depending on your perspective.

In Figure 7.1, all Gaussians have the same variance and they are centered at the gray dots, which represent sample points from a possible unknown population. If you look carefully, you may notice that two of the Gaussians are on top of each other.

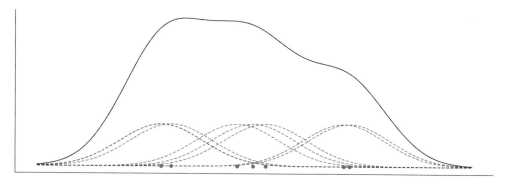

Figure 7.1: Example of a KDE as a Gaussian mixture model

Whether we believe in sub-populations or use them for mathematical convenience (or even something in the middle), mixture models are a useful way of adding flexibility to our models by using a mixture of distributions to describe the data.

Finite mixture models

One way to build mixture models is to consider a finite weighted mixture of two or more distributions. Then the probability density of the observed data is a weighted sum of the probability density of K subgroups:

$$p(y) = \sum_{i=1}^{K} w_i p(y \mid \theta_i)$$

We can interpret w_i as the probability of the component i, and thus its values are restricted to the interval $[0, 1]$ and they need to sum up to 1. The components $p(y \mid \theta_i)$ are usually simple distributions, such as a Gaussian or a Poisson. If K is finite, we have a finite mixture model. To fit such a model, we need to provide a value of K, either because we know the correct value beforehand or because we can make an educated guess.

Conceptually, to solve a mixture model, all we need to do is properly assign each data point to one of the components. In a probabilistic model, we can do this by introducing a random variable, whose function is to specify to which component a particular observation is assigned. This variable is generally referred to as a **latent variable** because we cannot directly observe it.

For a mixture of only two components ($K = 2$), we can use the coin-flipping problem model as a building block. For that model, we have two possible outcomes and we use the Bernoulli distribution to describe them. Since we do not know the probability of getting heads or tails, we use a Beta distribution as a prior distribution. If instead of head or tails, we think of any two groups (or components or classes), we can assign the observation to one group if we get 0 and to the other if we get 1. This is all very nice, but in a mixture model, we can have two or more groups, so we need to make this idea more general. We can do it by noticing that the generalization of the Bernoulli distribution to K outcomes is the Categorical distribution and the generalization of the Beta distribution to higher dimensions is the Dirichlet distribution. If the components we are assigning are Gaussians, like in Figure 7.1, then Figure 7.2 shows a Kruschke-style diagram of such a model. The rounded-corner box indicates that we have K components and the Categorical variables decide which of them we use to describe a given data point. Notice that only μ_k depends on the different components, while σ_μ and σ_σ are shared for all of them. This is just a modeling choice; if necessary, we can change it and allow other parameters to be conditioned on each component.

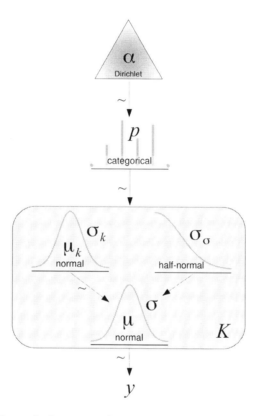

Figure 7.2: Kruschke-style diagram of a mixture model with Gaussian components

We are going to implement this model in PyMC, but before doing that, let me introduce the Categorical and Dirichlet distributions. If you are already familiar with these distributions, you can skip the next two sections and jump to the example.

The Categorical distribution

The Categorical distribution is the most general discrete distribution and is parameterized by a vector where each element specifies the probabilities of each possible outcome. Figure 7.3 represents two possible instances of the Categorical distribution. The dots represent the values of the Categorical distribution, while the continuous dashed lines are a visual aid to help us easily grasp the *shape* of the distribution:

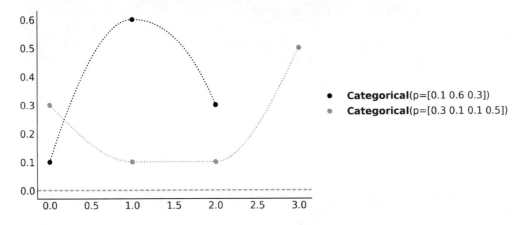

Figure 7.3: Two members of the Categorical distribution family. The dashed lines are just a visual aid.

The Dirichlet distribution

The Dirichlet distribution lives in the simplex, which you can think of as an n-dimensional triangle; a 1-simplex is a line, a 2-simplex is a triangle, a 3-simplex is a tetrahedron, and so on. Why a simplex? Intuitively, because the output of this distribution is a K-length vector, whose elements are restricted to be on the interval $[0, 1]$ and sum up to 1. As we said, the Dirichlet distribution is the generalization of the Beta distribution. Thus, a good way to understand the former is to compare it to the latter. We use the Beta for problems with two outcomes: one with probability p and the other $1 - p$. As we can see, $p + (1 - p) = 1$. The Beta returns a two-element vector, $(p, q = 1 - p)$, but in practice, we omit q as the outcome is entirely determined once we know the value of p. If we want to extend the Beta distribution to three outcomes, we need a three-element vector (p, q, r), where each element is in the interval $[0, 1]$ and their values sum up to 1. Similar to the Beta distribution, we could use three scalars to parameterize such a distribution, and we may call them α, β, and γ; however, we could easily run out of Greek letters as there are only 24 of them. Instead, we can just use a vector named α of length K. Note that we can think of the Beta and Dirichlet as distributions over proportions. Figure 7.4 shows 4 members of the Dirichlet distribution when $K = 3$. On the top, we have the pdf and on the bottom, we have samples from the distribution.

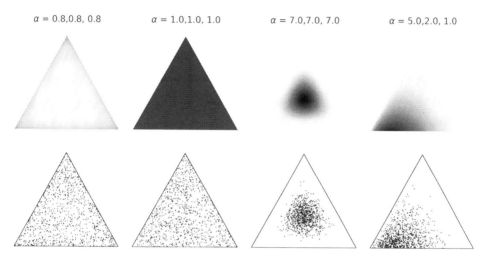

Figure 7.4: Four members of the Dirichlet distribution family

Okay, now we have all the *components* to implement our first mixture model.

Chemical mixture

To keep things very concrete, let's work on an example. We are going to use the chemical shifts data we already saw in Chapter 2. Figure 7.5 shows a histogram of this data.

We can see that this data cannot be properly described using a single distribution like a Gaussian, but we can do it if we use many as we already showed in Figure 7.1; maybe three or four would do the trick. There are good theoretical reasons, which we will ignore and not discuss here, indicating this chemical shifts data comes from a mixture of 40 sub-populations. But just by looking at the data, it seems impossible to recover the true

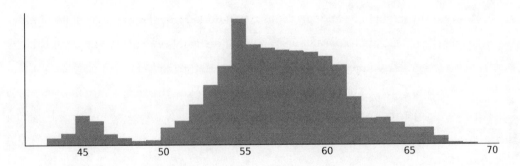

Figure 7.5: Histogram for the chemical shifts data

groups as there is a lot of overlap between them.

The following code block shows the implementation of a Gaussian mixture model of two components in PyMC:

Code 7.1:

```
1  K = 2
2  with pm.Model() as model_kg:
3      p = pm.Dirichlet('p', a=np.ones(K))
4      z = pm.Categorical('z', p=p, shape=len(cs_exp))
5      means = pm.Normal('means', mu=cs_exp.mean(), sigma=10, shape=K)
6      sd = pm.HalfNormal('sd', sigma=10)
7
8      y = pm.Normal('y', mu=means[z], sigma=sd, observed=cs_exp)
9      idata_kg = pm.sample()
```

If you run this code, you will find that it is very slow and the trace looks very bad (refer to Chapter 10 to learn more about diagnostics). Can we make this model run faster? Yes, let's see how.

In `model_kg`, we have explicitly included the latent variable z in the model. Sampling this discrete variable usually leads to poor posterior sampling. One way to solve this issue is to reparametrize the model so z is no longer explicitly a part of the model. This type of reparametrization is called marginalization . Marginalizing out discrete variables usually provides speed-up and better sampling. Unfortunately, it requires some mathematical skills that not everyone has. Luckily for us, we don't need to do this ourselves as PyMC includes a `NormalMixture` distribution. So, we can write the mixture model as follows:

Code 7.2:

```
1  with pm.Model() as model_mg:
2      p = pm.Dirichlet('p', a=np.ones(K))
3      means = pm.Normal('means', mu=cs_exp.mean(), sigma=10, shape=K)
4      sd = pm.HalfNormal('sd', sigma=5)
5      y = pm.NormalMixture('y', w=p, mu=means, sigma=sd, observed=cs_exp)
6      idata_mg = pm.sample()
```

Let's check the results with a forest plot. Figure 7.6 shows something really funny going on. Before moving on to the next section, take some time to think about it. Can you spot it? We will discuss it in the next section.

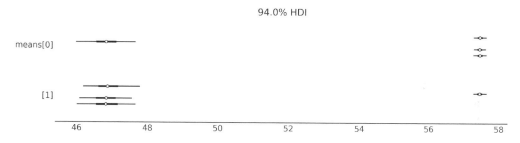

Figure 7.6: Forest plot of the means from `model_mg`

The non-identifiability of mixture models

The `means` parameter has shape 2, and from Figure 7.6 we can see that one of its values is around 47 and the other is close to 57.5. The funny thing is that we have one chain saying that `means[0]` is 47 and the other 3 saying it is 57.5, and the opposite for `mmeans[1]`. Thus, if we compute the mean of `mmeans[0]`, we will get some value close to 55 ($57.5 \times 3 + 47 \times 1$), which is not the correct value. What we are seeing is an example of a phenomenon known as parameter non-identifiability. This happens because, from the perspective of the model, there is no difference if component 1 has a mean of 47 and component 2 has a mean of 57.5 or vice versa; both scenarios are equivalent. In the context of mixture models, this is also known as the label-switching problem.

> **Non-Identifiability**
>
> A statistical model is non-identifiable if one or more of its parameters cannot be uniquely determined. Parameters in a model are not identified if the same likelihood function is obtained for more than one choice of the model parameters. It could happen that the data does not contain enough information to estimate the parameters. In other cases, parameters may not be identifiable because the model is not structurally identifiable, meaning that the parameters cannot be uniquely determined even if all the necessary data is available.

With mixture models, there are at least two ways of parameterizing a model to remove the non-identifiability issue. We can force the components to be ordered; for example, arrange the means of the components in strictly increasing order and/or use informative priors.

Using PyMC, we can implement the first option with a transformation as in the next code block. Notice that we also provide initial values for the means; anything to ensure that the first mean is smaller than the second one will work.

Code 7.3:

```
1  with pm.Model() as model_mgo:
2      p = pm.Dirichlet('p', a=np.ones(K))
3      means = pm.Normal('means', mu=cs_exp.mean(), sigma=10, shape=K,
4                        transform=pm.distributions.transforms.ordered,
5                        initval=np.array([cs_exp.mean()-1, cs_exp.mean()+1]))
6      sd = pm.HalfNormal('sd', sigma=10)
7      y = pm.NormalMixture('y', w=p, mu=means, sigma=sd, observed=cs_exp)
8
9      idata_mgo = pm.sample()
```

Let's check the new results with a forest plot. Figure 7.7 confirms that we have removed the non-identifiability issue:

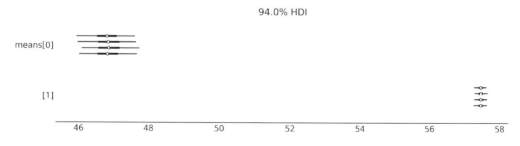

Figure 7.7: Forest plot of the means from model_mgo

How to choose K

One of the main concerns with finite mixture models is how to decide on the number of components. A rule of thumb is to begin with a relatively small number of components and then increase it to improve the model-fit evaluation. As we already know from Chapter 5, model fit can be evaluated using posterior-predictive checks, metrics such as the ELPD, and the expertise of the modeler(s).

Let us compare the model for $K = \{2, 3, 4, 5\}$. To do this, we are going to fit the model four times and then save the data and model objects for later use:

Code 7.4:

```
1 Ks = [2, 3, 4, 5]
2
3 models = []
4 idatas = []
5 for k in Ks:
6     with pm.Model() as model:
7         p = pm.Dirichlet('p', a=np.ones(k))
8         means = pm.Normal('means',
9                     mu=np.linspace(cs_exp.min(), cs_exp.max(), k),
10                    sigma=cs_exp.var() / k, shape=k,
```

```
11                        transform=pm.distributions.transforms.ordered,
12                        )
13       sd = pm.HalfNormal('sd', sigma=5)
14       y = pm.NormalMixture('y', w=p, mu=means, sigma=sd, observed=cs_exp)
15       idata = pm.sample(random_seed=123,
16                         idata_kwargs={"log_likelihood":True}
17                         )
18
19       idatas.append(idata)
20       models.append(model)
```

Figure 7.8 shows the mixture models for K number of Gaussians. The black solid lines are the posterior means, and the gray lines are samples from the posterior. The mean-Gaussian components are represented using a black dashed line.

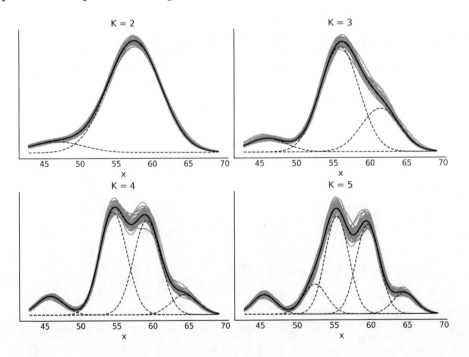

Figure 7.8: Gaussian mixture models for different numbers of Gaussians (K)

Visually, it seems $K = 2$ is too low, but how do we choose a better value? As we have already discussed in Chapter 5, we can use posterior predictive checks of test quantities of interest and compute Bayesian p-values. Figure 7.9 shows an example of such a calculation and visualization. $K = 5$ is the best solution and $K = 4$ comes closes.

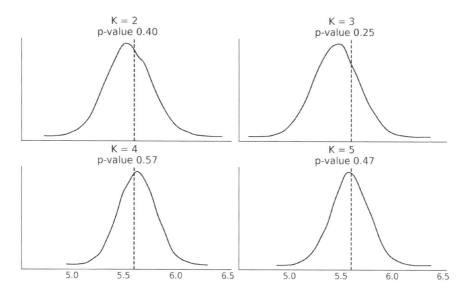

Figure 7.9: Posterior predictive check to choose K

To complement posterior predictive checks, we can compute the ELPD as approximated with the LOO method. This is shown in Figure 7.10. We are comparing the same model but with different values of K. We can see that $K = 5$ is the best solution and $K = 4$ comes close. This is in agreement with the Bayesian p-values shown in Figure 7.9.

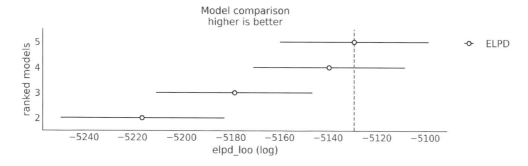

Figure 7.10: Model selection with LOO to choose K

The chemical shifts example, while simple, shows the main ideas about finite mixture models. For this example, we used Gaussians as they provide a good approximation to model the data. However, we are free to use non-Gaussian components if needed. For example, we could use a:

- **Poisson mixture model**: Suppose you are monitoring the number of customers entering a store every hour. A Poisson mixture model can help to identify different patterns of customer traffic, such as peak hours or days, by assuming that the data follows a mixture of Poisson distributions.

- **Exponential mixture model**: Imagine you are studying the lifetimes of a certain type of light bulb. An Exponential mixture model can assist in identifying different groups of light bulbs with varying lifetimes, suggesting potential differences in manufacturing quality or environmental factors.

In the next section, we will explore a very particular type of mixture model, one that involves two processes: one generating zeros and the other generating zeros or non-zeros.

Zero-Inflated and hurdle models

When counting things, like cars on a road, stars in the sky, moles on your skin, or virtually anything else, one option is to not count a thing, that is, to get zero. The number zero can generally occur for many reasons; we get a zero because we were counting red cars and a red car did not go down the street or because we missed it. If we use a Poisson or NegativeBinomial distribution to model such data, we will notice that the model generates fewer zeros compared to the data. How do we fix that? We may try to address the exact cause of our model predicting fewer zeros than the observed and include that factor in the model. But, as is often the case, it may be enough, and simpler, to assume that we have a mixture of two processes:

- One modeled by a discrete distribution with probability ψ

- One giving extra zeros with probability $1 - \psi$

In some texts, you will find that ψ represents the extra zeros instead of $1 - \psi$. This is not a big deal; just pay attention to which is which for a concrete example.

The family of distributions allowing for "extra" zeros is known as a Zero-Inflated distribution. The most common members of that family are:

- Zero-Inflated Poisson

- Zero-Inflated NegativeBinomial

- Zero-Inflated Binomial

In the next section, we are going to use Zero-Inflated Poisson to solve a regression problem. Once you understand how to work with this distribution, working with the Zero-Inflated NegativeBinomial or Zero-Inflated Binomial will become very easy.

Zero-Inflated Poisson regression

To exemplify a Zero-Inflated Poisson regression model, we are going to work with a dataset taken from the Institute for Digital Research and Education (`http://www.ats.ucla.edu/stat/data`). We have 250 groups of visitors to a park. Here are some parts of the data per group: the number of fish they caught (`count`), how many children were in the group (`child`), and whether they brought a camper to the park (`camper`). Using this data, we are going to build a model that predicts the number of caught fish as a function of the child and camper variables.

Using PyMC we can write a model for this data like:

Code 7.5:

```
1  with pm.Model() as ZIP_reg:
2      ψ = pm.Beta('ψ', 1, 1)
3      α = pm.Normal('α', 0, 1)
4      β = pm.Normal('β', 0, 1, shape=2)
5      θ = pm.math.exp(α + β[0] * fish_data['child'] + β[1] * fish_data['camper'])
6      yl = pm.ZeroInflatedPoisson('yl', ψ, θ, observed=fish_data['count'])
7      trace_ZIP_reg = pm.sample()
```

`camper` is a binary variable with 0 for not-camper and 1 for camper. A variable indicating the absence/presence of an attribute is usually denoted as a dummy variable or indicator variable. Note that when `camper` takes the value of 0, the term involving β_1 will also be 0 and the model reduces to a regression with a single independent variable. We already discussed this in Chapter 6 when talking about Categorical predictors.

The results are shown in Figure 7.11. We can see that the higher the number of children, the lower the number of fish caught. Also, people who travel with a camper generally catch more fish. If you check the coefficients for `child` and `camper`, you will see that we can say the following:

- For each additional child, the expected count of the fish caught decreases by ≈ 0.4

- Camping with a camper increases the expected count of the fish caught by ≈ 2

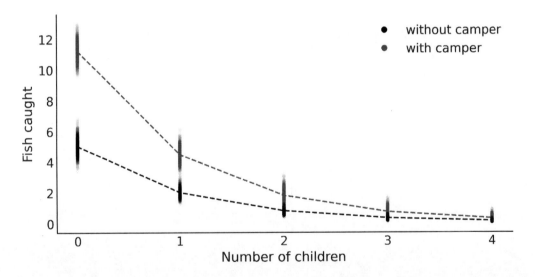

Figure 7.11: Fish caught as a function of the number of children and use of a camper

Zero-Inflated models are closely associated with hurdle models, making it beneficial to learn about hurdle models while the concept of Zero-Inflated models is still fresh in our minds.

Hurdle models

In hurdle models, the Bernoulli probability determines whether a count variable has a value of zero or something greater. If it's greater than zero, we consider the *hurdle* crossed, and the distribution of these positive values is determined using a distribution truncated at zero.

In terms of mixture models, we can think of a Zero-Inflated model as a mixture of zeros and something else, which can be zero or non-zero. Instead, a hurdle model is a mixture of zeros and non-zeros. As a consequence, a Zero-Inflated model can only increase the probability of $P(x = 0)$, but for hurdle models, the probability can be smaller or larger.

The available distributions in PyMC and Bambi for hurdle models are:

- Hurdle Poisson
- Hurdle NegativeBinomial
- Hurdle Gamma
- Hurdle LogNormal

To illustrate hurdle models, we are going to use the horseshoe crab dataset [Brockmann, 1996]. Horseshoe crabs arrive at the beach in pairs for their spawning ritual. Additionally, solitary males also make their way to the shoreline, gathering around the nesting couples and vying for the opportunity to fertilize the eggs. These individuals, known as satellite males, often congregate in sizable groups near certain nesting pairs while disregarding others. We want to model the number of male `satellites`. We suspect this number is related to the properties of the female crabs. As predictors, we are going to use the carapace `width` and `color`. The carapace is the hard upper shell of crabs. The color is encoded using the integers 1 to 4, from lighter to darker tones.

We are going to use Bambi to encode and fit four models. The main difference between the four models is that we are going to use four different likelihoods, or families, namely Poisson, Hurdle Poisson, NegativeBinomial, and Hurdle NegativeBinomial. The models are shown in the next code block:

Code 7.6:

```
1  model_crab_p = bmb.Model("satellite ~ width + C(color)",
2                            family="poisson", data=crab)
3  model_crab_hp = bmb.Model("satellite ~ width + C(color)",
4                             family="hurdle_poisson", data=crab)
5  model_crab_nb = bmb.Model("satellite ~ width + C(color)",
6                             family="negativebinomial", data=crab)
7  model_crab_hnb = bmb.Model("satellite ~ width + C(color)",
8                              family="hurdle_negativebinomial", data=crab)
```

Notice that we have encoded color as C(color) to indicate to Bambi that it should treat it as a Categorical variable, and not a numeric one.

Figure 7.12 shows a posterior predictive check for the four models we fitted to the horseshoe data. The gray bars represent the frequency of the observed data. The dots are the expected values, according to the model. The dashed line is just a visual aid. We can see that the NegativeBinomial is an improvement on the Poisson and the hurdle model is an improvement on the non-inflated models.

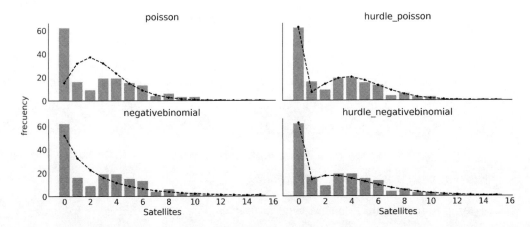

Figure 7.12: Posterior predictive check for 4 models for the horseshoe data

Figure 7.13 shows a model comparison in terms of the ELPD as computed with LOO. The Hurdle NegativeBinomial is the best model and the Poisson one is the worst.

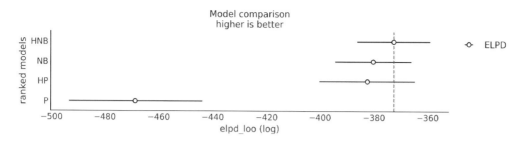

Figure 7.13: Model comparison using LOO for 4 models for the horseshoe data

Figure 7.12 is nice, but there is an alternative representation called hanging rootograms [Kleiber and Zeileis, 2016], which is particularly useful for diagnosing and treating issues such as overdispersion and/or excess zeros in count data models. See Figure 7.14 for an example of the horseshoe data and our four models.

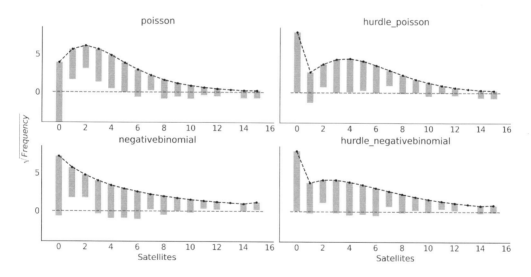

Figure 7.14: Posterior predictive check, with rootograms, for 4 models for the horseshoe data

In hanging rootograms, we plot the square roots of the observed and predicted values. This is a quick way of approximately adjusting for the scale differences across the different counts. In other words, it makes it easier to compare observed and expected frequencies even for low frequencies. Second, the bars for the observed data are *hanging* from the expected values, instead of *growing* from zero, as in Figure 7.12. Because the bars are hanging, if a bar doesn't reach zero (dashed gray line), then the model is overpredicting a count, and if the bar goes below zero, then the model is underpredicting that count.

Let's summarize each of the subplots from Figure 7.12:

- Poisson: The zeros are underpredicted, and counts 1 to 4 are overpredicted. Most counts from 6 onward are also underpredicted. This pattern is an indication of overdispersion in the data, and the huge difference for 0 indicates an excess of zeros.

- NegativeBinomial: We see that overdispersion is much better handled compared to the Poisson model. We still see that the zeros are underpredicted and counts 1 and 2 are overpredicted, probably indicating an excess of zeros.

- Hurdle Poisson: As expected for a hurdle model, we get a perfect fit for the zeros. For the positive values, we still get some deviations.

- Hurdle NegativeBinomial: We see that the model can fit the data very well, with the deviations being very small for most of the counts.

Mixture models and clustering

Clustering or cluster analysis is the data analysis task of grouping objects in such a way that objects in a given group are closer to each other than to those in the other groups. The groups are called clusters and the degree of closeness can be computed in many different ways, for example, by using metrics, such as the Euclidean distance. If instead we take the probabilistic route, then a mixture model arises as a natural candidate to solve clustering tasks.

Performing clustering using probabilistic models is usually known as model-based clustering. Using a probabilistic model allows us to compute the probability of each data point belonging to each one of the clusters. This is known as soft clustering instead of hard clustering, where each data point belongs to a cluster with a probability of 0 or 1. We can turn soft clustering into hard clustering by introducing some rule or boundary. In fact, you may remember that this is exactly what we do to turn logistic regression into a classification method, where we use as the default boundary the value of 0.5. For clustering, a reasonable choice is to assign a data point to the cluster with the highest probability.

In summary, when people talk about clustering, they are generally talking about grouping objects, and when people talk about mixture models, they are talking about using a mix of simple distributions to model a more complex distribution, either to identify subgroups or just to have a more flexible model to describe the data.

Non-finite mixture model

For some problems, such as trying to cluster handwritten digits, it is easy to justify the number of groups we expect to find in the data. For other problems, we can have good guesses; for example, we may know that our sample of Iris flowers was taken from a region where only three species of Iris grow, thus using three components is a reasonable starting point. When we are not that sure about the number of components, we can use model selection to help us choose the number of groups. Nevertheless, for other problems, choosing the number of groups a priori can be a shortcoming, or we may instead be interested in estimating this number directly from the data. A Bayesian solution for this type of problem is related to the Dirichlet process.

Dirichlet process

All the models that we have seen so far have been parametric models, meaning models with a fixed number of parameters that we are interested in estimating, like a fixed number of clusters. We can also have non-parametric models. A better name for these models would probably be non-fixed-parametric models or models with a variable number of parameters, but someone already decided the name for us. We can think of non-parametric models as models with a theoretically infinite number of parameters. In practice, we somehow let the data reduce the theoretically infinite number of parameters to some finite number. As the data *decides* on the actual number of parameters, non-parametric models are very flexible and potentially robust against underfitting and overfitting. In this book, we are going to see three examples of such models: the Gaussian process (GP), Bayesian Additive Regression Trees (BART), and the Dirichlet process (DPs). While the upcoming chapters will focus on GPs and BART individually, our immediate attention will be directed toward exploring DPs.

As the Dirichlet distribution is the n-dimensional generalization of the beta distribution, the Dirichlet process is the infinite-dimensional generalization of the Dirichlet distribution. I know this can be puzzling at first, so let's take the time to re-read the previous sentence before continuing.

The Dirichlet distribution is a probability distribution on the space of probabilities, while the DP is a probability distribution on the space of distributions. This means that a single draw from a DP is actually a distribution. For finite mixture models, we used the Dirichlet distribution to assign a prior for the fixed number of clusters or groups. A DP is a way to assign a prior distribution to a non-fixed number of clusters. We can think of a DP as a way to sample from a prior distribution of distributions.

Before we move on to the actual non-parametric mixture model, let us take a moment to discuss some of the details of the DP. The formal definition of a DP is somewhat obscure unless you know probability theory very well, so instead let me describe some of the properties of a DP that are relevant to understanding its role in non-finite mixture models:

- A DP is a distribution whose realizations are probability distributions. For instance, from a Gaussian distribution, you sample numbers, while from a DP, you sample distributions.
- A DP is specified by a base distribution $\mathcal{H}$ and α, a positive real number, called the concentration parameter. α is analog to the concentration parameter in the Dirichlet distribution.
- $\mathcal{H}$ is the expected value of the DP. This means that a DP will generate distributions around the base distribution. This is somehow equivalent to the mean of a Gaussian distribution.
- As α increases, the realizations become less and less concentrated.
- In practice, a DP always generates discrete distributions.
- In the limit $\alpha \to \infty$, the realizations from a DP will be equal to the base distribution,

thus if the base distribution is continuous, the DP will generate a continuous distribution. For this reason, mathematicians say that the distributions generated from a DP are almost surely discrete. In practice, α is a finite number, thus we always work with discrete distributions.

Priors Over Distributions

We can think of a DP as the prior on a random distribution f, where the base distribution $\mathcal{H}$ is what we expected f to be and the concentration parameter α represents how confident we are about our prior guess.

To make these properties more concrete, let us take a look again at the Categorical distribution in Figure 7.3. We can completely specify this distribution by indicating the position on the x-axis and the height on the y-axis. For the Categorical distribution, the positions on the x-axis are restricted to be integers and the sum of the heights has to be 1. Let's keep the last restriction but relax the former one. To generate the positions on the x-axis, we are going to sample from a base distribution $\mathcal{H}$. In principle, it can be any distribution we want; thus if we choose a Gaussian, the locations would be any value from the real line. Instead, if we choose a Beta, the locations will be restricted to the interval $[0, 1]$, and if we choose a Poisson as the base distribution, the locations will be restricted to be non-negative integers 0, 1, 2, ...

So far so good, but how do we choose the values on the y-axis? We follow a *Gedanken experiment* known as the stick-breaking process. Imagine we have a stick of length 1, then we break it into two parts (not necessarily equal). We set one part aside and break the other part into two, and then we just keep doing this forever and ever. In practice, as we cannot really repeat the process infinitely, we truncate it at some predefined value K, but the general idea holds, at least in practice. To control the stick-breaking process, we use a parameter α. As we increase the value of α, we will break the stick into smaller and smaller portions. Thus, for $\alpha = 0$, we don't break the stick, and for $\alpha = \infty$, we break it into infinite pieces. Figure 7.15 shows four draws from a DP, for four different values of α.

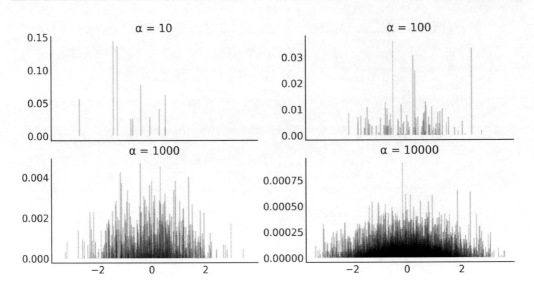

Figure 7.15: Stick-breaking process with a Gaussian as the base distribution

We can see from Figure 7.15 that the DP is a discrete distribution. When α increases, we obtain smaller pieces from the initial unit-length stick; notice the change on the scale of the y-axis. The base distribution, a Normal(0, 1) in this figure, controls the locations. With increasing α, the sticks progressively resemble the base distribution more. In the accompanying notebook for this chapter, you will find the code to generate Figure 7.15. I highly recommend you play with this code to gain a better intuition of DPs.

Figure 7.1 shows that if you place a Gaussian on top of each data point and then sum all the Gaussians, you can approximate the distribution of the data. We can use a DP to do something similar, but instead of placing a Gaussian on top of each data point, we can place a Gaussian at the location of each piece of the original unit-length stick. We then weigh each Gaussian by the length of each piece. This procedure provides a general recipe for a non-finite Gaussian-mixture model.

Alternatively, we can replace the Gaussian for any other distribution and we will have a general recipe for a non-finite mixture model. Figure 7.16 shows an example of such a model. I used a mixture of Laplace distributions, just to reinforce the idea that you are by no means restricted to just using Gaussian mixture models:

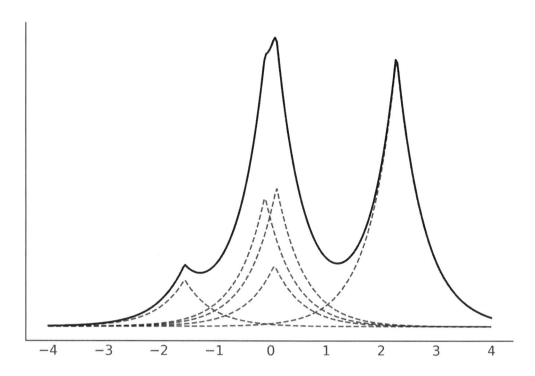

Figure 7.16: Laplace mixture model using a DP

Now we are more than ready to try to implement a DP in PyMC. Let's first define a `stick_breaking` function that works with PyMC:

Code 7.7:

```
1  K = 10
2
3  def stick_breaking(α, K):
4      β = pm.Beta('β', 1., α, shape=K)
5      w = β * pt.concatenate([[1.], pt.extra_ops.cumprod(1. - β)[:-1]]) + 1E-6
6      return w/w.sum()
```

Instead of fixing the value of α, the concentration parameter, we are going to define a prior for it. A common choice for this is a Gamma distribution, as shown in the following code block:

Code 7.8:

```python
with pm.Model() as model_DP:
    α = pm.Gamma('α', 2, 1)
    w = pm.Deterministic('w', stick_breaking(α, K))
    means = pm.Normal('means',
                      mu=np.linspace(cs_exp.min(), cs_exp.max(), K),
                      sigma=5, shape=K,
                      transform=pm.distributions.transforms.ordered,
                      )

    sd = pm.HalfNormal('sd', sigma=10, shape=K)
    obs = pm.NormalMixture('obs', w, means, sigma=sd, observed=cs_exp.values)
    idata = pm.sample()
```

Because we are approximating the infinite DP with a truncated stick-breaking procedure, it is important to check that the truncation value ($K = 10$ in this example) is not introducing any bias. A simple way to do this is to compute the average weight of each component, sort them, and then plot their cumulative sum. To be on the safe side, we should have at least a few components with negligible weight; otherwise, we must increase the truncation value. An example of this type of plot is Figure 7.17.

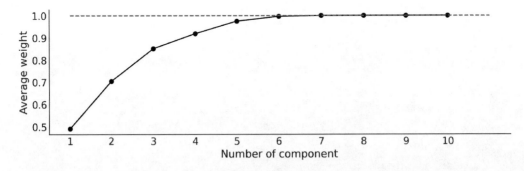

Figure 7.17: Ordered cumulative distribution of average weights of the DP components

We can see that only the first 7 components are somewhat important. The first 7 components represent more than 99.9% of the total weight (gray dashed line in Figure 7.17) and thus we can be confident that the chosen upper value ($K = 10$) is large enough for this data.

Figure 7.18 shows the mean density estimated using the DP model (black line) together with samples from the posterior (gray lines) to reflect the uncertainty in the estimation.

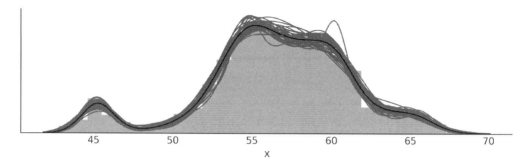

Figure 7.18: DP mixture model for the chemical shifts data

Continuous mixtures

The focus of this chapter was on discrete mixture models, but we can also have continuous mixture models. And indeed we already know some of them. For instance, hierarchical models can also be interpreted as continuous mixture models where the parameters in each group come from a continuous distribution in the upper level. To make it more concrete, think about performing linear regression for several groups. We can assume that each group has its own slope or that all the groups share the same slope. Alternatively, instead of framing our problem as two extreme discrete options, a hierarchical model allows us to effectively model a continuous mixture of these two options.

Some common distributions are mixtures

The BetaBinomial is a discrete distribution generally used to describe the number of successes y for n Bernoulli trials when the probability of success p at each trial is unknown and assumed to follow a beta distribution with parameters α and β:

$$\text{BetaBinomial}(y \mid n, \alpha, \beta) = \int_0^1 \text{Bin}(y \mid p, n) \, \text{Beta}(p \mid \alpha, \beta) dp$$

That is, to find the probability of observing the outcome y, we average over all the possible (and continuous) values of p. Thus, the BetaBinomial can be considered as a continuous mixture model. If the BetaBinomial model sounds familiar to you, it is because you were paying attention in the first two chapters of the book! This is the model we used for the coin-flipping problem, although we explicitly used a Beta and Binomial distribution, instead of using the already *mixed* Beta-Binomial distribution.

In a similar fashion, we have the NegativeBinomial distribution, which can be understood as a Gamma-Poisson mixture. That is, a mixture of Poisson distributions where the rate parameter is Gamma distributed. The Negative-Binomial distribution is often used to circumvent a common problem encountered when dealing with count data. This problem is known as over-dispersion. Suppose you are using a Poisson distribution to model count data, and then you realize that the variance in your data exceeds that of the model; the problem with using a Poisson distribution is that mean and variance are described by the same parameter. One way to account for over-dispersion is to model the data as a (continuous) mixture of Poisson distributions. By considering a mixture of distributions, our model has more flexibility and can better accommodate the mean and variance of the data.

Another example of a mixture of distributions is the Student's t-distribution. We introduced this distribution as a robust alternative to the Gaussian distribution. In this case, the t-distribution results from a mixture of Gaussian distributions with mean μ and unknown variance distributed as an InverseGamma distribution.

Summary

Many problems can be described as an overall population composed of distinct sub-populations. When we know to which sub-population each observation belongs, we can specifically model each sub-population as a separate group. However, many times we do not have direct access to this information, thus it may be appropriate to model that data using mixture models. We can use mixture models to try to capture true sub-populations in the data or as a general statistical trick to model complex distributions by combining simpler distributions.

In this chapter, we divided mixture models into three classes: finite mixture models, non-finite mixture models, and continuous mixture models. A finite mixture model is a finite weighted mixture of two or more distributions, each distribution or component representing a subgroup of the data. In principle, the components can be virtually anything we may consider useful from simple distributions, such as a Gaussian or a Poisson, to more complex objects, such as hierarchical models or neural networks. Conceptually, to solve a mixture model, all we need to do is to properly assign each data point to one of the components. We can do this by introducing a latent variable z. We use a Categorical distribution for z, which is the most general discrete distribution, with a Dirichlet prior, which is the n-dimensional generalization of the Beta distribution. Sampling the discrete variable z can be problematic, thus it may be convenient to marginalize it. PyMC includes a normal mixture distribution and a mixture distribution that performs this marginalization for us, making it easier to build mixture models with PyMC.

One common problem we looked at in this chapter when working with mixture models is that this model can lead to the label-switching problem, a form of non-identifiability. One way to remove non-identifiability is to force the components to be ordered. One challenge with finite mixture models is how to decide on the number of components. One solution is to perform a model comparison for a set of models around an estimated number of components. That estimation should be guided, when possible, by our knowledge of the problem at hand. Another option is to try to automatically estimate the number of components from the data. For this reason, we introduced the concept of the Dirichlet process as an infinite-dimensional version of the Dirichlet distribution that we can use to build a non-parametric mixture model.

Finally, to close the chapter, we briefly discussed how many models, such as the BetaBinomial (the one used for the coin-flipping problem), the NegativeBinomial, the Student's t-distribution, and even hierarchical models, can be interpreted as continuous mixture models.

Exercises

1. Generate synthetic data from a mixture of 3 Gaussians. Check the accompanying Jupyter notebook for this chapter for an example of how to do this. Fit a finite Gaussian mixture model with 2, 3, or 4 components.

2. Use LOO to compare the results from exercise 1.

3. Read and run through the following examples about mixture models from the PyMC documentation:

   - Marginalized Gaussian mixture model: `https://www.pymc.io/projects/exa mples/en/latest/mixture_models/marginalized_gaussian_mixture_mod el.html`

   - Dependent density regression: `https://www.pymc.io/projects/examples/ en/latest/mixture_models/dependent_density_regression.html`

4. Refit `fish_data` using a NegativeBinomial and a Hurdle NegativeBinomial model. Use rootograms to compare these two models with the Zero-Inflated Poisson model shown in this chapter.

5. Repeat exercise 1 using a Dirichlet process.

6. Assuming for a moment that you do not know the correct species/labels for the iris dataset, use a mixture model to cluster the three Iris species, using one feature of your choice (like the length of the sepal).

7. Repeat exercise 6 but this time use two features.

Join our community Discord space

Join our Discord community to meet like-minded people and learn alongside more than 5000 members at:

https://packt.link/bayesian

8

Gaussian Processes

Lonely? You have yourself. Your infinite selves.

\- Rick Sanchez (at least the one from dimension C-137)

In the last chapter, we learned about the Dirichlet process, an infinite-dimensional generalization of the Dirichlet distribution that can be used to set a prior on an unknown continuous distribution. In this chapter, we will learn about the Gaussian process, an infinite-dimensional generalization of the Gaussian distribution that can be used to set a prior on unknown functions. Both the Dirichlet process and the Gaussian process are used in Bayesian statistics to build flexible models where the number of parameters is allowed to increase with the size of the data.

We will cover the following topics:

- Functions as probabilistic objects
- Kernels
- Gaussian processes with Gaussian likelihoods
- Gaussian processes with non-Gaussian likelihoods

- Hilbert space Gaussian process

Linear models and non-linear data

In Chapter 4 and Chapter 6 we learned how to build models of the general form:

$$\theta = \psi(\phi(X)\beta)$$

Here, θ is a parameter for some probability distribution, for example, the mean of a Gaussian, the p parameter of the binomial, the rate of a Poisson, and so on. We call ϕ the inverse link function and ϕ is some other function we use to potentially transform the data, like a square root, a polynomial function, or something else.

Fitting, or learning, a Bayesian model can be seen as finding the posterior distribution of the weights β, and thus this is known as the weight view of approximating functions. As we already saw with polynomial and splines regression, by letting ϕ be a non-linear function, we can map the inputs onto a *feature space*. We also saw that by using a polynomial of the proper degree, we can perfectly fit any function. But unless we apply some form of regularization, for example, using prior distributions, this will lead to models that memorize the data, or in other words models with very poor generalizing properties. We also mention that splines can be as flexible as polynomials but with better statistical properties. We will now discuss Gaussian processes, which provide a principled solution to modeling arbitrary functions by effectively letting the data decide on the complexity of the function, while avoiding, or at least minimizing, the chance of overfitting.

The following sections discuss Gaussian processes from a very practical point of view; we have avoided covering almost all the mathematics surrounding them. For a more formal explanation, you may read *Gaussian Processes for Machine Learning* by Rasmussen and Williams [2005].

Modeling functions

We will begin our discussion of Gaussian processes by first describing a way to represent functions as probabilistic objects. We may think of a function f as a mapping from a set of inputs X to a set of outputs Y. Thus, we can write:

$$Y = f(X)$$

One very crude way to represent functions is by listing for each x_i value its corresponding y_i value as in Table 8.1. You may remember this way of representing functions from elementary school.

x	y
0.00	0.46
0.33	2.60
0.67	5.90
1.00	7.91

Table 8.1: A tabular representation of a function (sort of)

As a general case, the values of X and Y will live on the real line; thus, we can see a function as a (potentially) infinite and ordered list of paired values (x_i, y_i). The order is important because, if we shuffle the values, we will get different functions.

Following this description, we can represent, numerically, any specific function we want. But what if we want to represent functions probabilistically? Well, we then need to encode a probabilitics mapping. Let me explain this; we can let each value be a random variable with some associated distribution. As working with Gaussians is usually convenient, let's say that they are distributed as a Gaussian with a given mean and variance. In this way, we no longer have the description of a single specific function, but the description of a family of distributions.

To make this discussion concrete, let's use some Python code to build and plot two examples of such functions:

Code 8.1:

```
1  np.random.seed(42)
2  x = np.linspace(0, 1, 10)
3  y = np.random.normal(0, 1, len(x))
4  plt.plot(x, y, 'o-', label='the first one')
5  y = np.zeros_like(x)
6
7  for i in range(len(x)):
8      y[i] = np.random.normal(y[i-1], 1)
9  plt.plot(x, y, 'o-', label='the second one')
10 plt.legend()
```

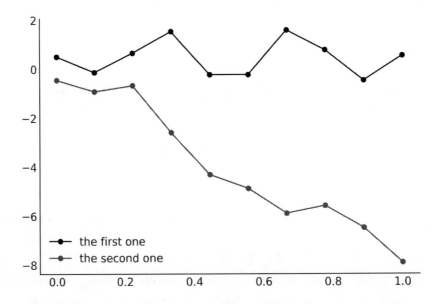

Figure 8.1: Two dummy functions sampled from Gaussian distributions

Figure 8.1 shows that encoding functions using samples from Gaussian distributions is not that crazy or foolish, so we may be on the right track. Nevertheless, the approach used to generate Figure 8.1 is limited and not sufficiently flexible.

While we expect real functions to have some structure or pattern, the way we express the first one function does not let us encode any relation between data points. In fact, each point is completely independent of the others, as we just get them as 10 independent samples from a common one-dimensional Gaussian distribution. For the second one function, we introduce some dependency. The mean of the point y_{i+1} is the value y_i, thus we have some structure here. Nevertheless, we will see next that there is a more general approach to capturing dependencies, and not only between consecutive points.

Before continuing, let me stop for a moment and consider why we're using Gaussians and not any other probability distribution. First, by restricting ourselves to working with Gaussians, we do not lose any flexibility in specifying functions of different shapes, as each point has potentially its own mean and variance. Second, working with Gaussians is nice from a mathematical point of view.

Multivariate Gaussians and functions

In Figure 8.1, we represented a function as a collection of samples from 1-dimensional Gaussian distributions. One alternative is to use an n-dimensional multivariate Gaussian distribution to get a sample vector of length n. Actually, you may want to try to reproduce Figure 8.1 but replacing `np.random.normal(0, 1, len(x))` with `np.random.multivariate_normal`, with a mean of `np.zeros_like(x)` and a standard deviation of `np.eye(len(x)`. The advantage of working with a Multivariate Normal is that we can use the covariance matrix to encode information about the function. For instance, by setting the covariance matrix to `np.eye(len(x))`, we are saying that each of the 10 points, where we are evaluating the function, has a variance of 1. We are also saying that the variance between them, that is, their covariances, is 0. In other words, they are independent. If we replace those zeros with other numbers, we could get covariances telling a different story.

I hope you are starting to get convinced that it is possible to use a multivariate Gaussian in order to represent functions. If that's the case, then we just need to find a suitable covariance matrix. And that's the topic of the next section.

Covariance functions and kernels

In practice, covariance matrices are specified using functions known as kernels. Unfortunately, the term kernel is a very polysemic one, even in the statistical literature. An easy way to define a kernel is any function that returns a valid covariance matrix. But this is a tautological and not very intuitive definition. A more conceptual and useful definition is that a kernel defines a measure of similarity between data points in the input space, and this similarity determines how much influence one data point should have on predicting the value of another data point.

There are many useful kernels, a popular one being the exponentiated quadratic kernel:

$$\kappa(\mathbf{X}, \mathbf{X}') = \exp\left(-\frac{\|\mathbf{X} - \mathbf{X}'\|^2}{2\ell^2}\right)$$

Here, $\|\mathbf{X} - \mathbf{X}'\|^2$ is the squared Euclidean distance:

$$\|\mathbf{X} - \mathbf{X}'\|^2 = (X_1 - X_1')^2 + (X_2 - X_2')^2 + \cdots + (X_n - X_n')^2$$

For this kernel, we can see that we have a symmetric function that takes two inputs and returns a value of 0 if the inputs are the same, or positive otherwise. And thus we can interpret the output of the exponentiated quadratic kernel as a measure of similarity between the two inputs.

It may not be obvious at first sight, but the exponentiated quadratic kernel has a similar formula to the Gaussian distribution. For this reason, this kernel is also called the Gaussian kernel. The term ℓ is known as the length scale (or bandwidth or variance) and controls the width of the kernel. In other words, it controls at what scale the X values are considered similar.

To better understand the role of kernels, I recommend you play with them. For instance, let's define a Python function to compute the exponentiated quadratic kernel:

Code 8.2:

```
1  def exp_quad_kernel(x, knots, ℓ=1):
2      """exponentiated quadratic kernel"""
3      return np.array([np.exp(-(x-k)**2 / (2*ℓ**2)) for k in knots])
```

Figure 8.2 shows how a 4×4 covariance matrix looks for different inputs. The input I chose is rather simple and consists of the values $[-1, 0, 1, 2]$.

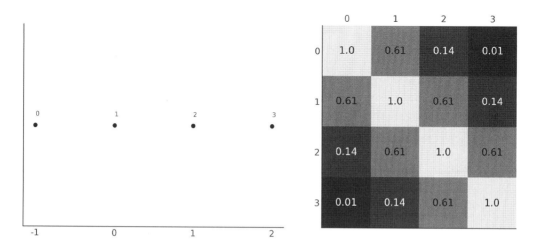

Figure 8.2: Input values (left), covariance matrix (right)

On the left panel of Figure 8.2, we have the input values. These are the values on the x-axis, and we have labeled the points from 0 to 3. Thus, point 0 takes the value -1, point 1 takes 0, and so on. On the right panel, we have a heatmap representing the covariance matrix that we computed using the exponentiated quadratic kernel. The lighter the color, the larger the value of the covariance. As you can see, the heatmap is symmetric, with the diagonal taking the largest values. This makes sense when we realize that the value of each element in the covariance matrix is inversely proportional to the distance between the points, and the diagonal is the result of comparing each data point with itself. The smallest value is the one for the points 0 and 3, as they are the most distant points.

Once you understand this example, you should try it with other inputs. See exercise 1 at the end of this chapter and the accompanying notebook (https://github.com/aloctavod

ia/BAP3) for further practice.

Now that we have a better grasp of how to use a kernel to generate a covariance matrix, let's move one step further and use the covariance matrix to sample functions. As you can see in Figure 8.3, a Gaussian kernel implies a wide variety of functions with the parameter ℓ controlling the smoothness of the functions. The larger the value of ℓ, the smoother the function.

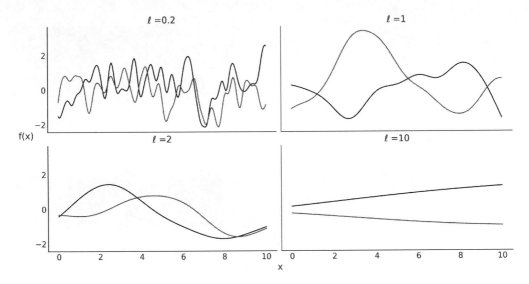

Figure 8.3: *Realizations of a Gaussian kernel for four values of ℓ (two realization per value of ℓ)*

Show me Your Friends and I'll Show you your Future

The kernel translates the distance of the data points along the x axis to values of covariances for values of the expected function (on the y axis). Thus, the closest two points are on the x axis; the most similar we expect their values to be on the y axis.

Gaussian processes

Now we are ready to understand what Gaussian processes (GPs) are and how they are used in practice. A somewhat formal definition of GPs, taken from Wikipedia, is as follows:

"The collection of random variables indexed by time or space, such that every finite collection of those random variables has a MultivariateNormal distribution, i.e. every finite linear combination of them is normally distributed."

This is probably not a very useful definition, at least not at this stage of your learning path. The trick to understanding Gaussian processes is to realize that the concept of GP is a mental (and mathematical) scaffold, since, in practice, we do not need to directly work with this infinite mathematical object. Instead, we only evaluate the GPs at the points where we have data. By doing this, we collapse the infinite-dimensional GP into a finite multivariate Gaussian distribution with as many dimensions as data points. Mathematically, this collapse is achieved by marginalization over the infinitely unobserved dimensions. The theory assures us that it is OK to omit (actually marginalize over) all points, except the ones we are observing. It also guarantees that we will always get a multivariate Gaussian distribution. Thus, we can rigorously interpret Figure 8.3 as actual samples from a Gaussian process!

So far we have focused on the covariance matrix of the MultivariateNormal and we have not discussed the mean. Setting the mean of a multivariate Gaussian at 0 is common practice when working with GPs, since they are flexible enough to model the mean arbitrarily well. But notice that there is no restriction in doing so. Actually, for some problems, you may want to model the mean parametrically and leave the GP to model the residuals.

> GPs are Prior Over Functions
>
> Gaussian processes are prior distributions over functions in such a way that at each point that you evaluate a function, it places a Gaussian distribution with a given mean and variance. In practice, GPs are usually built using kernels, which turn distance on an x axis into similarities on the y axis.

Gaussian process regression

Let's assume we can model a variable Y as a function f of X plus some Gaussian noise:

$$Y \sim \mathcal{N}(\mu = f(X), \sigma = \epsilon)$$

If f is a linear function of X, then this assumption is essentially the same one we used in Chapter 4 when we discussed simple linear regression. In this chapter, instead, we are going to use a more general expression for f by setting a prior over it. In that way, we will be able to get more complex functions than linear. If we decided to use Gaussian processes as this prior, then we can write:

$$f(X) = \mathcal{GP}(\mu_X, \kappa(X, X'))$$

Here, $\mathcal{GP}$ represents a Gaussian process with the mean function μ_X and covariance function $\kappa(X, X')$. Even though in practice, we always work with finite objects, we used the word **function** to indicate that mathematically, the mean and covariance are infinite objects.

I mentioned before that working with Gaussians is nice. For instance, if the prior distribution is a GP and the likelihood is a Gaussian distribution, then the posterior is also a GP and we can compute it analytically. Additionally, its nice to have a Gaussian likelihood because we can marginalize out the GP, which hugely reduces the size of the parameter space we need to sample from. The GP module in PyMC takes advantage of this and then it has different implementations for Gaussian and non-Gaussian likelihoods. In the next sections, we will explore both.

Gaussian process regression with PyMC

The gray line in Figure 8.4 is a sin function. We are going to assume we don't know this function and instead, all we have is a set of data points (dots). Then we use a Gaussian process to approximate the function that generated those data points.

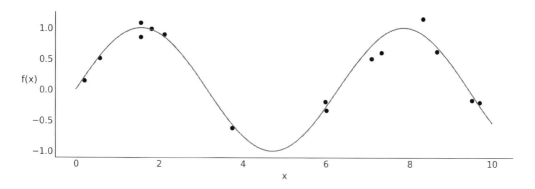

Figure 8.4: Synthetic data (dots) generated from a known function (line)

GPs are implemented in PyMC as a series of Python classes that deviate a little bit from what we have seen in previous models; nevertheless, the code is still very *PyMConic*. I have added a few comments in the following code to guide you through the key steps of defining a GP with PyMC.

Code 8.3:

```
1  # A one-dimensional column vector of inputs.
2  X = x[:, None]
3
4  with pm.Model() as model_reg:
5      # hyperprior for lengthscale kernel parameter
6      ℓ = pm.InverseGamma("ℓ", 7, 17)
7      # instanciate a covariance function
8      cov = pm.gp.cov.ExpQuad(1, ls=ℓ)
9      # instanciate a GP prior
10     gp = pm.gp.Marginal(cov_func=cov)
11     σ = pm.HalfNormal('σ', 25)
12     # Class representing that the observed data is a GP plus Gaussian noise
13     y_pred = gp.marginal_likelihood('y_pred', X=X, y=y, sigma=σ)
14
15     idata_reg = pm.sample()
```

Notice that instead of a Gaussian likelihood, we have used the `gp.marginal_likelihood` method. This method takes advantage of the fact that the posterior has a closed form, as explained in the previous section.

OK, now that we have computed the posterior, let's see how to get predictions of the mean fitted function. We can do this by computing the conditional distribution evaluated over new input locations using `gp.conditional`.

Code 8.4:

```
1  X_new = np.linspace(np.floor(x.min()), np.ceil(x.max()), 100)[:,None]
2  with model_reg:
3      f_pred = gp.conditional('f_pred', X_new)
```

As a result, we get a new PyMC random variable, f_pred, which we can use to get samples from the posterior predictive distribution:

Code 8.5:

```
1  with model_reg:
2      idata_subset = idata_reg.sel(draw=slice(0, None, 100))
3      pred_samples = pm.sample_posterior_predictive(idata_subset,
4                                                    var_names=["f_pred"])
5
6  f_pred = (pred_samples.
7           posterior_predictive.stack(samples=("chain", "draw"))['f_pred'].
8           values)
```

Now we can plot the fitted functions over the original data, to visually inspect how well they fit the data and the associated uncertainty in our predictions. As we did with linear models in Chapter 4, we are going to show different ways to plot the same results. Figure 8.5 shows lines from the fitted function.

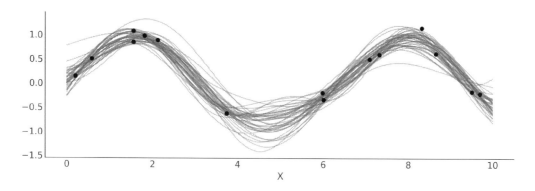

Figure 8.5: Lines represent samples from the posterior mean of `model_reg`

Alternatively, we can use the auxiliary function `pm.gp.util.plot_gp_dist` to get some nice plots as in Figure 8.6. In this plot, each band represents a different percentile, ranging from percentile 99 (lighter gray) to percentile 51 (darker gray).

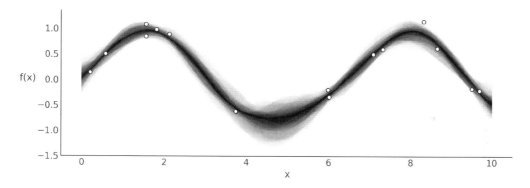

Figure 8.6: Samples from the posterior of `model_reg` *plotted using* `plot_gp_dist` *function*

Yet another alternative is to compute the mean vector and standard deviation of the conditional distribution evaluated at a given point in the parameter space. In Figure 8.7, we use the mean (over the samples in the trace) for ℓ and ϵ. We can compute the mean and variance using the `gp.predict` method.

As we saw in Chapter 4, we can use a linear model with a non-Gaussian likelihood and a proper inverse link function to extend the range of useful linear models. We can do the same for GPs. We can, for example, use a Poisson likelihood with an exponential inverse

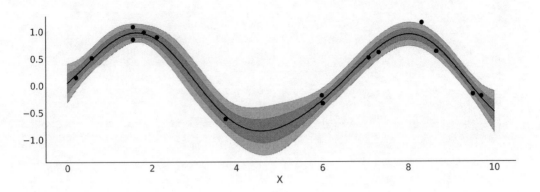

Figure 8.7: Posterior mean of `model_reg` *with bands for 1 and 2 standard deviations*

link function. For a model like this, the posterior is no longer analytically tractable, but, nevertheless, we can use numerical methods to approximate it. In the following sections, we will discuss these types of models.

Setting priors for the length scale

For length-scale parameters, priors avoiding zero usually work better. As we already saw, ℓ controls the smoothness of the function, thus a value of 0 for ℓ implies a non-smooth function; we will get a function like "the first one" from Figure 8.1. But a far more important reason is that for values of ℓ that are larger than 0 but still below the minimum spacing of the covariates, we can get some nasty effects. Essentially, below that point, the likelihood has no way to distinguish between different length scales, so all of them are equally good. This is a type of non-identifiability issue. As a result, we will have a GP that will tend to overfit and exactly interpolate between the input data. Additionally, the MCMC sampler will have a harder time, and we could get longer sampling times or simple unreliable samples. Something similar happens for values beyond the range of the data. If the range of your data is 10 and the value of $\ell >= 10$, this implies a flat function. And again beyond that point, you (and the likelihood) have no way of distinguishing between different values of the parameter. Thus even if you have no idea how smooth or wiggly your function is, you can still set a prior that avoids very low and very high values of ℓ. For instance, to get the prior `pm.InverseGamma("`ℓ`", 7, 17)` we ask PreliZ for the maximum entropy prior that has 0.95 of the mass between 1 and 5:

Code 8.6:

```
pz.maxent(pz.InverseGamma(), 1, 5, 0.95)
```

The InverseGamma is a common choice. Like the Gamma, it allows us to set a prior that avoids 0, but unlike the Gamma, the InverseGamma has a lighter tail toward 0, or in other words, it allocates less mass for small values.

For the rest of this chapter, we will use the function `get_ig_params` to obtain weakly informative priors from the scale of the covariates. You will find the details in the accompanying code (`https://github.com/aloctavodia/BAP3`), but essentially we are using the `maxent` function from PreliZ to set most of the prior mass in a range compatible with the range of the covariates.

Gaussian process classification

In Chapter 4, we saw how a linear model can be used to classify data. We used a Bernoulli likelihood with a logistic inverse link function. Then, we applied a boundary decision rule. In this section, we are going to do the same, but this time using a GP instead of a linear model. As we did with `model_lrs` from Chapter 4, we are going to use the iris dataset with two classes, `setosa` and `versicolor`, and one predictor variable, the `sepal length`.

For this model, we cannot use the `pm.gp.Marginal` class, because that class is restricted to Gaussian likelihoods as it takes advantage of the mathematical tractability of the combination of a GP prior with a Gaussian likelihood. Instead, we need to use the more general class `pm.gp.Latent`.

Code 8.7:

```
1  with pm.Model() as model_iris:
2      ℓ = pm.InverseGamma('ℓ', *get_ig_params(x_1))
3      cov = pm.gp.cov.ExpQuad(1, ℓ)
4      gp = pm.gp.Latent(cov_func=cov)
```

```
5    f = gp.prior("f", X=X_1)
6    # logistic inverse link function and Bernoulli likelihood
7    y_ = pm.Bernoulli("y", p=pm.math.sigmoid(f), observed=y)
8    idata_iris = pm.sample()
```

As we can see, Figure 8.8 looks pretty similar to Figure 4.11. Please take some time to compare these figures.

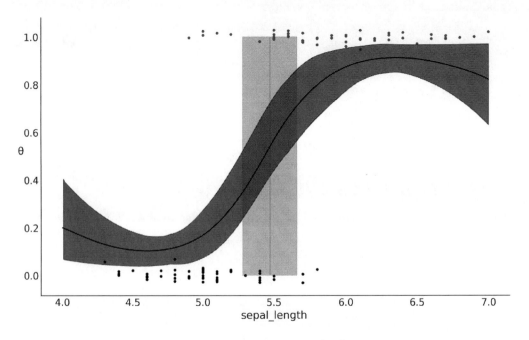

Figure 8.8: Logistic regression, result of `model_lrs`

You probably have already noticed that the inferred function looks similar to a sigmoid curve, except for the tails that go up at lower values of `sepal_length`, and down at higher values of `sepal_length`. Why are we seeing this? Because when there is little or no data available, a GP posterior tends to revert to the GP prior. This makes sense if we think that in the absence of data, your posterior essentially becomes the prior.

If our only concern is the decision boundary, then the behavior at the tails may be irrelevant. But if we want to model the probabilities of belonging to setosa or versicolor at different values of sepal_length, we should do something to improve the model at the tails. One way to achieve this is to add more structure to the Gaussian process. One very nice feature of GP is that we can combine covariance functions. Hence, for the next model, we are going to combine three kernels: the exponential quadratic kernel, a linear kernel, and a white noise kernel.

The linear kernel will have the effect of making the tails go to 0 or 1 at the boundaries of the data. Additionally, we use the white noise kernel just as a trick to stabilize the computation of the covariance matrix. Kernels for Gaussian processes are restricted to guarantee the resulting covariance matrix is positive definite. Nevertheless, numerical errors can lead to violating this condition. One manifestation of this problem is that we get NaNs when computing posterior predictive samples of the fitted function. One way to mitigate this error is to stabilize the computation by adding some noise. As a matter of fact, PyMC already does something similar to this under the hood, but sometimes a little bit more noise is needed, as shown in the following code:

Code 8.8:

```
1  with pm.Model() as model_iris2:
2      ℓ = pm.InverseGamma('ℓ', *get_ig_params(x_1))
3      c = pm.Normal('c', x_1.min())
4      τ = pm.HalfNormal('τ', 5)
5      cov = (pm.gp.cov.ExpQuad(1, ℓ) +
6             τ * pm.gp.cov.Linear(1, c) +
7             pm.gp.cov.WhiteNoise(1E-5))
8      gp = pm.gp.Latent(cov_func=cov)
9      f = gp.prior("f", X=X_1)
10     # logistic inverse link function and Bernoulli likelihood
11     y_ = pm.Bernoulli("y", p=pm.math.sigmoid(f), observed=y)
12     idata_iris2 = pm.sample()
```

We can see the result of this model in Figure 8.9. Notice how this figure looks much more similar now to Figure 4.11 than Figure 8.8.

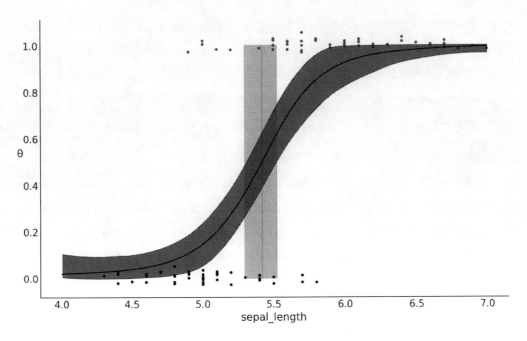

Figure 8.9: Logistic regression, result of `model_lrs`

The example discussed in this section has two main aims:

- Showing how we can easily combine kernels to get a more expressive model
- Showing how we can *recover* a logistic regression using a Gaussian process

Regarding the second point, logistic regression is indeed a special case of Gaussian processes, because a simple linear regression is just a particular case of a Gaussian process. In fact, many known models can be seen as special cases of GPs, or at least they are somehow connected to GPs. If you want to learn more about this, you can read Chapter 15 from Kevin Murphy's Machine Learning: A Probabilistic Perspective (first edition) [Murphy, 2012], and also Chapter 18 from the second edition [Murphy, 2023].

GPs for space flu

In practice, it does not make too much sense to use a GP to model a problem we can just solve with a logistic regression. Instead, we want to use a GP to model more complex data that is not well captured with less flexible models. For instance, suppose we want to model the probability of getting a disease as a function of age. It turns out that very young and very old people have a higher risk than people of middle age. The dataset `space_flu.csv` is a synthetic dataset inspired by the previous description. Figure 8.10 shows a plot of it.

Let's fit the following model and plot the results:

Code 8.9:

```
1  with pm.Model() as model_space_flu:
2      ℓ = pm.InverseGamma('ℓ', *get_ig_params(age))
3      cov = pm.gp.cov.ExpQuad(1, ℓ) + pm.gp.cov.WhiteNoise(1E-5)
4      gp = pm.gp.Latent(cov_func=cov)
5      f = gp.prior('f', X=age)
6      y_ = pm.Bernoulli('y', p=pm.math.sigmoid(f), observed=space_flu)
7      idata_space_flu = pm.sample()
```

Notice, as illustrated in Figure 8.10, that the GP can fit this space flu dataset very well, even when the data demands the function to be more complex than a logistic one. Fitting this data well will be impossible for a simple logistic regression, unless we introduce some ad hoc modifications to help it a little bit (see exercise 6 at the end of the chapter for a discussion of such modifications).

Cox processes

Now we are going to model count data. We will see two examples; one with a time-varying rate and one with a 2D spatially varying rate. To do this, we will use a Poisson likelihood and the rate will be modeled using a Gaussian process. Because the rate of the Poisson distribution is limited to positive values, we will use an exponential as the inverse link function, as we did for the NegativeBinomial regression from Chapter 4.

We can think of a Poisson process as a distribution over collections of points in a given space where every finite collection of those random variables has a Poisson distribution. When the rate of the Poisson process is itself a stochastic process, such as, for example, a Gaussian process, then we have a Cox process.

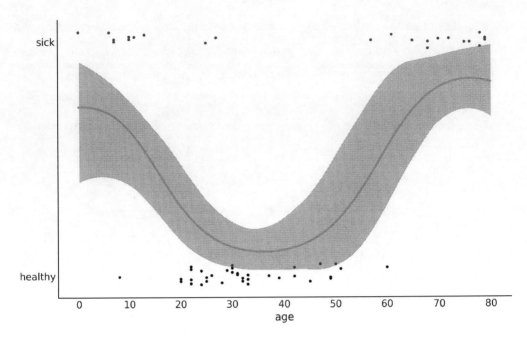

Figure 8.10: Logistic regression, result of `model_space_flu`

Coal mining disasters

The first example is known as the coal mining disasters. This example consists of a record of coal-mining disasters in the UK from 1851 to 1962. The number of disasters is thought to have been affected by changes in safety regulations during this period. We want to model the rate of disasters as a function of time. Our dataset consists of a single column and each entry corresponds to the time a disaster happened. The model we will use to fit the data has the form:

$$f(X) = \mathcal{GP}(\mu_X, \kappa(X, X'))$$

$$y = \text{Pois}(f(X))$$

As you can see, this is a Poisson regression problem. You may be wondering at this point how we're going to perform a regression if we only have a single column with just the date of the disasters. The answer is to discretize the data, just as if we were building a histogram. We are going to use the centers of the bins as the X variable and the counts per bin as the Y variable:

Code 8.10:

```
1  # discretize data
2  years = int((coal_df.max() - coal_df.min()).iloc[0])
3  bins = years // 4
4  hist, x_edges = np.histogram(coal_df, bins=bins)
5  # Compute the location of the centers of the discretized data
6  x_centers = x_edges[:-1] + (x_edges[1] - x_edges[0]) / 2
7  # xdata needs to be 2D for BART
8  x_data = x_centers[:, None]
9  # express data as the rate number of disasters per year
10 y_data = hist
```

Now we define and solve the model with PyMC:

Code 8.11:

```
1  with pm.Model() as model_coal:
2      ℓ = pm.InverseGamma('ℓ', *get_ig_params(x_edges))
3      cov = pm.gp.cov.ExpQuad(1, ls=ℓ) + pm.gp.cov.WhiteNoise(1E-5)
4      gp = pm.gp.Latent(cov_func=cov)
5      f = gp.prior('f', X=x_data)
6      y_pred = pm.Poisson('y_pred', mu=pm.math.exp(f), observed=y_data)
7      idata_coal = pm.sample()
```

Figure 8.11 shows the median disaster rate as a function of time (white line). The bands describe the 50% HDI (darker) and the 94% HDI (lighter). At the bottom, the black markers indicate the moment of each disaster. As we can see, the rate of accidents decreases with time, except for a brief initial increase. The PyMC documentation includes the coal mining disaster but is modeled from a different perspective. I strongly recommend that you check that example as it is very useful on its own and is also useful to compare it with the approach we just implemented here.

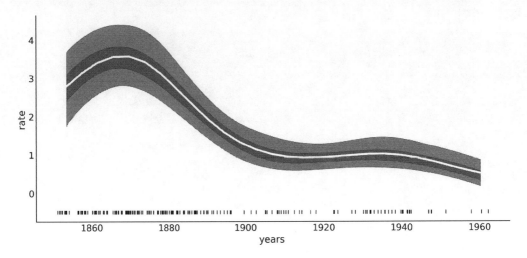

Figure 8.11: Logistic regression, result of `model_coal`

Notice that even when we binned the data, we obtained, as a result, a smooth curve. In this sense, we can see `model_coal` (and, in general, this type of model) as building a histogram and then smoothing it.

Red wood

Let's apply the same approach we just did to a 2D spatial problem. We are going to use the redwood data as shown in Figure 8.12. This dataset (distributed with a GPL license) is from the GPstuff package. The dataset consists of the location of redwood trees over a given area. The motivation of the inference is to obtain a map of a rate, the number of trees in a given area.

As with the coal-mining disaster example, we need to discretize the data:

Code 8.12:

```
1  # discretize spatial data
2  bins = 20
3  hist, x1_edges, x2_edges = np.histogram2d(
```

```
4       rw_df[1].values, rw_df[0].values, bins=bins)
5 # compute the location of the centers of the discretized data
6 x1_centers = x1_edges[:-1] + (x1_edges[1] - x1_edges[0]) / 2
7 x2_centers = x2_edges[:-1] + (x2_edges[1] - x2_edges[0]) / 2
8 # arrange xdata into proper shape for GP
9 x_data = [x1_centers[:, None], x2_centers[:, None]]
10 # arrange ydata into proper shape for GP
11 y_data = hist.flatten().astype(int)
```

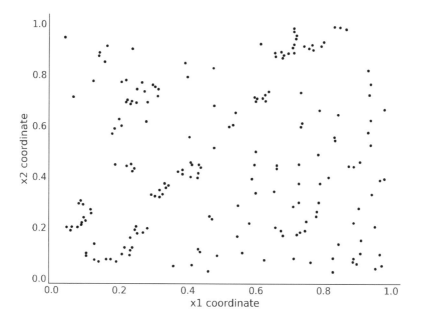

Figure 8.12: Redwood data

Notice that instead of doing a mesh grid, we treat x1 and x2 data as being distinct arrays. This allows us to build a covariance matrix independently for each coordinate, effectively reducing the size of the matrix needed to compute the GP. We then combine both matrices using the LatentKron class. It is important to note that this is not a numerical trick, but a mathematical property of the structure of this type of matrix, so we are not introducing any approximation or error in our model. We are just expressing it in a way that allows faster computations:

Code 8.13:

```
1  with pm.Model() as model_rw:
2      ℓ = pm.InverseGamma('ℓ', *get_ig_params(x_data), shape=2)
3      cov_func1 = pm.gp.cov.ExpQuad(1, ls=ℓ[0])
4      cov_func2 = pm.gp.cov.ExpQuad(1, ls=ℓ[1])
5
6      gp = pm.gp.LatentKron(cov_funcs=[cov_func1, cov_func2])
7      f = gp.prior('f', Xs=x_data)
8
9      y = pm.Poisson('y', mu=pm.math.exp(f), observed=y_data)
10     idata_rw = pm.sample()
```

In Figure 8.13, the darker the shade of gray, the higher the rate of trees. We may imagine that we are interested in finding high-growing rate zones, because we may be interested in how a wood is recovering from a fire, or maybe we are interested in some properties of the soil and we use the trees as a proxy.

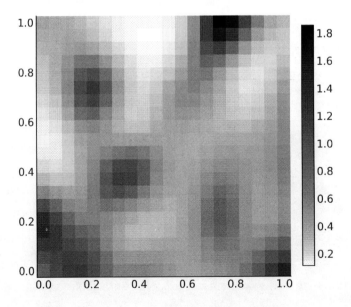

Figure 8.13: Logistic regression, result of `model_rw`

Regression with spatial autocorrelation

The following example is taken from *Statistical Rethinking: A Bayesian Course with Examples in R and STAN, Second Edition by Richard McElreath, Copyright (2020) by Chapman and Hall/CRC. Reproduced by permission of Taylor & Francis Group.* I strongly recommend reading this book, as you will find many good examples like this and very good explanations. The only *caveat* is that the book examples are in R/Stan, but don't worry and keep sampling; you will find the Python/PyMC version of those examples in the `https://github.com/pymc-devs/pymc-resources` resources.

For this example we have 10 different island societies; for each one of them, we have the number of tools they use. Some theories predict that larger populations develop and sustain more tools than smaller populations. Thus, we have a regression problem where the dependent variable is the number of tools and the independent variable is the population. Because the number of tools is a count variable, we can use a Poisson distribution. Additionally, we have good theoretical reasons to think the logarithm of the population is a better variable than absolute size because what really matters (according to the theory) is the order of magnitude of the population.

So far, the model we have in mind is a Poisson regression, but here comes the interesting part. Another important factor affecting the number of tools is the contact rates among the island societies. One way to include the contact rate in our model is to gather information on how frequent these societies were in contact throughout history and to create a categorical variable such as low/high rate. Yet another way is to use the distance between societies as a proxy of the contact rate, since it is reasonable to assume that geographically close societies come into contact more often than distant ones.

The number of tools, the population size, and the coordinates are stored in the file `islands.csv` in the GitHub repo of this book (`https://github.com/aloctavodia/BAP3`).

Omitting the priors, the model we are going to build is:

$$f \sim \mathcal{GP}([0, \ldots, 0], \kappa(X, X'))$$
$$\mu \sim \exp(\alpha + \beta X + f)$$
$$Y = \text{Pois}(\mu)$$

This model is a linear model plus a GP term. We use the linear part to model the effect of the logarithm of the population and the GP term to model the effect of the distance/contact rate. In this way, we will be effectively incorporating a measure of similarity in technology exposure (estimated from the distance matrix). Thus, instead of assuming the total number is just a consequence of population alone and independent from one society to the next, we will be modeling the number of tools in each society as a function of their spatial distribution.

The information about the spatial distribution is in terms of latitudes and longitudes, but the kernels in PyMC assume the distances are all Euclidean. This can be problematic. Probably the cleanest way to circumvent this issue is to work with a distance that takes into account that the islands are on an approximately spherical planet. For instance, we can use the haversine distance, which determines the great-circle distance between two points on a sphere given their longitudes and latitudes. The great-circle distance is the shortest distance between two points on the surface of a sphere, measured along the surface of the sphere. To use this distance, we need to create a new kernel as shown in the next code block. If you are not very familiar with classes in Python, you just need to know that what I did is copy the code for the ExpQuad from the PyMC code base and tweak it a little bit to create a new class, ExpQuadHaversine. The largest change is the addition of the function/method haversine_distance.

Code 8.14:

```
1  class ExpQuadHaversine(pm.gp.cov.Stationary):
2      def __init__(self, input_dims, ls, ls_inv=None, r=6371, active_dims=None):
3          super().__init__(input_dims, ls=ls, ls_inv=ls_inv, active_dims=active_dims)
```

```
4          self.r = r # earth radius in km

5

6      def haversine_distance(self, X):
7          lat = np.radians(X[:, 0])
8          lon = np.radians(X[:, 1])
9          latd = lat[:,None] - lat
10         lond = lon[:,None] - lon
11         d = pt.cos(lat[:,None]) * pt.cos(lat)
12         a = pt.sin(latd / 2)** 2 + d * pt.sin(lond / 2)** 2
13         c = 2 * pt.arctan2(pt.sqrt(a), pt.sqrt(1 - a))
14         return self.r * c

15

16     def full(self, X, _):
17         return pt.exp(-0.5 * self.haversine_distance(X)**2)
```

Now that we have defined the class ExpQuadHaversine we can use it to define the covariance matrix as we did with the previous models with the built-in kernels. For this model, we are going to introduce another change. We are going to define a parameter η. The role of this parameter is to scale the GP in the y-axis direction. It is pretty common to define GPs with both ℓ and η.

Code 8.15:

```
1  with pm.Model() as model_islands:
2      η = pm.Exponential('η', 2)
3      ℓ = pm.InverseGamma('ℓ', *get_ig_params(islands_dist))

4

5      cov = η * ExpQuadHaversine(2, ls=ℓ)
6      gp = pm.gp.Latent(cov_func=cov)
7      f = gp.prior('f', X=X)

8

9      α = pm.Normal('α', 0, 5)
10     β = pm.Normal('β', 0, 1)
11     μ = pm.math.exp(α + β * log_pop + f)
```

```
12      _ = pm.Poisson('tt_pred', μ, observed=total_tools)

13

14      idata_islands = pm.sample()
```

To understand the posterior distribution of covariance functions in terms of distances, we can plot a few samples from the posterior distribution as in Figure 8.14. The black curve represents the posterior median covariance at each distance and the gray curves sample functions from the joint posterior distribution of ℓ and η.

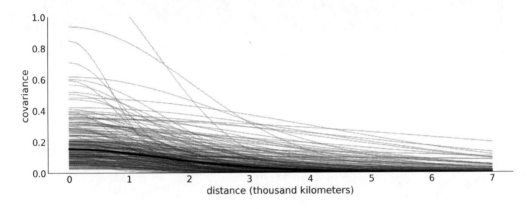

Figure 8.14: Posterior distribution of the spatial covariance

The thick black line in Figure 8.14 is the posterior median of the covariance between pairs of societies as a function of distance. We use the median because the distributions for ℓ and η are very skewed. We can see that the covariance is, on average, not that high and also drops to almost 0 at about 2,000 kilometers. The thin lines represent the uncertainty, and we can see that there is a lot of uncertainty.

Now let's take a look at how strongly correlated the island societies are according to the model and data. To do this, we have to turn the covariance matrix into a correlation matrix. See the accompanying code for details. Figure 8.15 shows a heatmap of the mean correlation matrix.

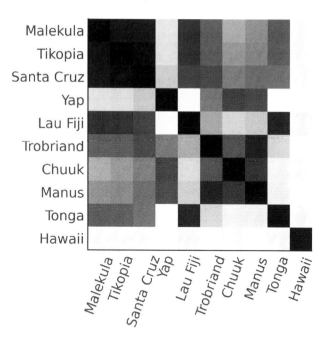

Figure 8.15: Posterior mean correlation matrix

Two observations that stand out from the rest is, first, that Hawaii is very lonely. This makes sense, as Hawaii is very far away from the rest of the island societies. Also, we can see that Malekula (Ml), Tikopia (Ti), and Santa Cruz (SC) are highly correlated with one another. This also makes sense, as these societies are very close together, and they also have a similar number of tools.

The left panel of Figure 8.16 is essentially a map. The island societies are represented in their relative positions. The lines are the posterior median correlations among societies. The opacity of the lines is proportional to the value of the correlations.

On the right panel of Figure 8.16 , we have again the posterior median correlations, but this time plotted in terms of the log population versus the total number of tools. The dashed lines represent the median number of tools and the HDI of 94% as a function of log population. In both panels of Figure 8.16, the size of the dots is proportional to the population of each island society. Notice how the correlations among Malekula, Tikopia,

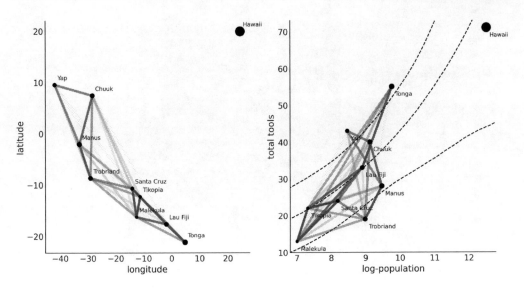

Figure 8.16: Posterior distribution of the spatial covariance

and Santa Cruz describe the fact that they have a rather low number of tools close to the median or lower than the expected number of tools for their populations. Something similar is happening with Trobriand and Manus; they are geographically close and have fewer tools than expected for their population sizes. Tonga has way more tools than expected for its population and a relatively high correlation with Fiji. In a way, the model is telling us that Tonga has a positive effect on Lua Fiji, increasing the total number of tools and counteracting the effect of it on its close neighbors, Malekula, Tikopia, and Santa Cruz.

Hilbert space GPs

Gaussian processes can be slow. The main reason is that their computation requires us to invert a matrix, whose size grows with the number of observations. This operation is computationally costly and does not scale very nicely. For that reason, a large portion of the research around GPs has been to find approximations to compute them faster and allow scaling them to large data.

We are going to discuss only one of those approximations, namely the **Hilbert Space Gaussian Process (HSGP)**, without going into the details of how this approximation is achieved. Conceptually, we can think of it as a basis function expansion similar, in spirit, to how splines are constructed (see Chapter 6). The consequence of this approximation is that it turns the matrix inversion into just matrix multiplication, a much faster operation.

> **But When Will It Work?**
>
> We can only use HSGPs for low dimensions (1 to maybe 3 or 4), and only for some kernels like the exponential quadratic or Matern. The reason is that for the HSGP approximation to work, the kernel has to be written in a special form known as power spectral density, and not all kernels can be written in this form.

Using the HSGP approximation in PyMC is straightforward, as we will demonstrate with the bikes dataset. We want to model the number of rented bikes as a function of the time of the day in hours. The following code block shows the PyMC implementation of such a model.

Code 8.16:

```
1  with pm.Model() as model_hsgp:
2      ℓ = pm.InverseGamma('ℓ', *get_ig_params(X))
3
4      cov = pm.gp.cov.ExpQuad(1, ls=ℓ)
5      gp = pm.gp.HSGP(m=[10], c=1.5, cov_func=cov)
6
7      f = gp.prior('f', X=X)
8      α = pm.HalfNormal('α', 1)
9      _ = pm.NegativeBinomial("obs", np.exp(f), α, observed=y)
10
11     idata_hsgp = pm.sample()
```

The main difference from previous GP models is the use of the pm.gp.HSGP(.) class instead of the pm.gp.Latent(.) class, which we should have used for non-Gaussian likelihoods and standard GPs. The class `pm.gp.HSGP(.)` has two parameters:

- `m` is the number of basic functions we use to approximate the GP. The larger the value of `m`, the better the approximation will be and the more costly the computation.

- `c` is a boundary factor. For a fixed and sufficiently large value of `m`, `c` affects the approximation of the mean function mainly near the boundaries. It should not be smaller than 1.2 (PyMC will give you a warning if you use a value lower than this), and usually 1.5 is a good choice. Changing this parameter does not affect the speed of the computations.

We set `m=10` partially because we are fans of the decimal system and partially based on the recommendations in the paper *Practical Hilbert space approximate Bayesian Gaussian processes for probabilistic programming* written by Riutort-Mayol et al. [2022]. In practice, the results are robust to the exact values of `m` and `c`, as long as they are within a certain range based on what your prior for the length scale is. For details on how HSGP works and some advice on how to use it in practice, you can read Riutort-Mayol et al. [2022].

Now let's see the results. Figure 8.17 shows the mean posterior GP in black and 100 samples (realizations) from the GP posterior (gray lines). You can compare these results to the ones obtained using splines (see Figure 6.8).

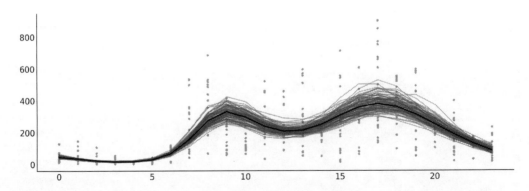

Figure 8.17: Posterior mean for the HSGP model for rented bikes as a function of the time of the day

The HSGP approximation is also implemented in Bambi. Let's see how we can use it.

HSGP with Bambi

To fit the previous model with Bambi, we need to write the following:

Code 8.17:

```
1 bmb.Model("rented ~ 0 + hsgp(hour, m=10, c=1.5)", bikes,
2           family="negativebinomial")
```

This will work, but instead, we will provide priors to Bambi, as we did with PyMC. This will result in a much faster sampling and more reliable samples.

As we saw in Chapter 6, to define priors in Bambi, we just need to pass a dictionary to the `priors` argument of `bmb.Model`. But we must be aware that HSGP terms do not receive priors. Instead, we need to define priors for ℓ (called `ell` in Bambi) and η (called `sigma` in Bambi) and pass those priors to the HSGP terms. One more thing: as in the previous model, we did not use η but since Bambi is expecting it, we use a dirty trick to define a prior that is essentially 1.

Code 8.18:

```
1  prior_gp = {
2      "sigma": bmb.Prior("Gamma", mu=1, sigma=0.01),
3      "ell": bmb.Prior("InverseGamma", **get_ig_params(X))
4  }
5  priors = {
6      "hsgp(hour, m=10, c=1.5)": prior_gp,
7      "alpha": bmb.Prior("HalfNormal", sigma=1)
8  }
9
10 model_hsb = bmb.Model("rented ~ 0 + hsgp(hour, m=10, c=1.5)", bikes,
11                        family="negativebinomial",
12                        priors=priors)
13
14 idata_hsb = model_hsb.fit()
```

I invite you to check that the parameters computed by Bambi are very similar to those we got with PyMC. Figure 8.18 shows the mean posterior GP in black and a band for the HDI of 94%. The figure was generated with `bmb.interpret.plot_predictions`.

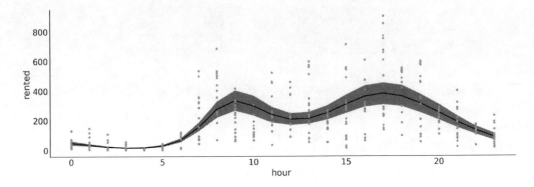

Figure 8.18: Posterior mean for the HSGP model for rented bikes as a function of the time of the day, using Bambi

In this section, we have explored the concept of HSGP as a powerful approximation to scale Gaussian processes to large datasets. By combining the flexibility of PyMC and Bambi with the scalability offered by HSGPs, researchers and practitioners can more effectively tackle complex modeling tasks, paving the way for the application of Gaussian processes on increasingly large and intricate datasets.

Summary

A Gaussian process is a generalization of the multivariate Gaussian distribution to infinitely many dimensions and is fully specified by a mean function and a covariance function. Since we can conceptually think of functions as infinitely long vectors, we can use Gaussian processes as priors over functions. In practice, we do not work with infinite objects but with multivariate Gaussian distributions with as many dimensions as data points. To define their corresponding covariance function, we used properly parameterized kernels; and by learning about those hyperparameters, we ended up learning about arbitrary complex functions.

In this chapter, we have given a short introduction to GPs. We have covered regression, semi-parametric models (the islands example), combining two or more kernels to better describe the unknown function, and how a GP can be used for classification tasks. There are many other topics we could have discussed. Nevertheless, I hope this introduction to GPs has motivated you sufficiently to keep using, reading, and learning about Gaussian processes and Bayesian non-parametric models.

Exercises

1. For the example in the *Covariance functions and kernels* section, make sure you understand the relationship between the input data and the generated covariance matrix. Try using other input such as `data = np.random.normal(size=4)`.

2. Rerun the code generating Figure 8.3 and increase the number of samples obtained from the GP prior to around 200. In the original figure, the number of samples is 2. What is the range of the generated values?

3. For the generated plot in the previous exercise, compute the standard deviation for the values at each point. Do this in the following form:

   - Visually, just observing the plots
   - Directly from the values generated from `pz.MVNormal(.).rvs`
   - By inspecting the covariance matrix (if you have doubts go back to exercise 1)

   Did the values you get from these three methods match?

4. Use test points `np.linspace(np.floor(x.min()), 20, 100)[:,None]` and re-run `model_reg`. Plot the results. What did you observe? How is this related to the specification of the GP prior?

5. Repeat exercise 1, but this time use a linear kernel (see the accompanying code for a linear kernel).

6. Check out `https://www.pymc.io/projects/examples/en/latest/gaussian_pro cesses/GP-MeansAndCovs.html` in PyMC's documentation.

7. Run a logistic regression model for the `space_flu` data. What do you see? Can you

explain the result?

8. Change the logistic regression model in order to fit the data. Tip: Use an order 2 polynomial.

9. Compare the model for the coal mining disaster with the one from the PyMC documentation (`https://www.pymc.io/projects/docs/en/stable/learn/core_notebooks/pymc_overview.html#case-study-2-coal-mining-disasters`). Describe the differences between both models in terms of model specification and results.

Join our community Discord space

Join our Discord community to meet like-minded people and learn alongside more than 5000 members at:

`https://packt.link/bayesian`

9

Bayesian Additive Regression Trees

Individually, we are one drop. Together, we are an ocean.

– Ryunosuke Satoro

In the last chapter, we discussed the **Gaussian process (GPs)**, a non-parametric model for regression. In this chapter, we will learn about another non-parametric model for regression known as Bayesian additive regression trees, or BART to friends. We can consider BART from many different perspectives. It can be an ensemble of decision trees, each with a distinct role and contribution to the overall understanding of the data. These trees, guided by Bayesian priors, work harmoniously to capture the nuances of the data, avoiding the pitfall of individual overfitting. Usually, BART is discussed as a standalone model, and software that implements it is usually limited to one or a few models. In this chapter, we will take a different approach and use PyMC-BART, a Python library that allows the use of BART models within PyMC.

In this chapter, we will cover the following topics:

- Decision trees
- BART models
- Flexible regression with BART
- Partial dependence plots
- Individual conditional expectation plots
- Variable selection

Decision trees

Before jumping into BART models, let's take a moment to discuss what decision trees are. A decision tree is like a flowchart that guides you through different questions until you reach a final choice. For instance, suppose you need to decide what type of shoes to wear every morning. To do so, you may ask yourself a series of questions. "Is it warm?" If yes, you then ask something more specific, like "Do I have to go to the office?" Eventually, you will stop asking questions and reach an output value like flip-flops, sneakers, boots, moccasins, etc.

This flowchart can be conveniently encoded in a tree structure, where at the root of the tree we place more general questions, then proceed along the tree to more and more specific ones, and finally arrive at the leaves of the tree with the output of the different types of shoes. Trees are very common data structures in computer science and data analysis.

More formally, we can say that a tree is a collection of nodes and vertices linking those nodes. The nodes that have questions are called decision nodes, and the nodes with the output of the trees (like the shoes) are called leaf nodes. When the answers are "yes" or "no," then we have a binary tree, because each node can have at most two children. Figure 9.1 shows a decision tree. The rounded squares are leaf nodes. The regular squares are decision nodes.

We can use decision trees to classify, that is, to return discrete categories, like sneakers, flip-flops, slippers, etc. But we can also use them to perform regression, that is, to return

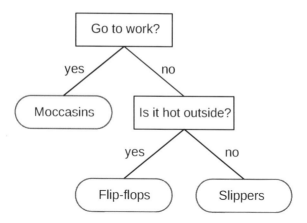

Figure 9.1: A decision tree to choose footwear.

continuous outcomes like 4.24 or 20.9 (and anything in between). Usually, these trees are called regression trees. Figure 9.2 shows a regression tree on the left. We can also see a regression tree as a representation of a piece-wise step-function as shown in the right panel of Figure 9.2. This contrasts with cubic splines or GPs, which represent smooth functions (at least to some degree). Trees can be flexible enough to provide good practical approximations of smooth functions.

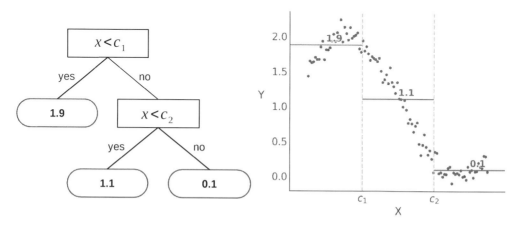

Figure 9.2: On the left, a regression tree; on the right is the corresponding piece-wise step function

Trees can be very flexible; in an extreme case, we could have a tree with as many leaf nodes as observations, and this tree will perfectly fit the data. As we saw in Chapter 5, this may not be a great idea unless we add some regularization. In Bayesian terms, we can achieve such regularization through priors. For instance, we could set a prior that induces shallow trees. In this way, we make it very unlikely that we will end up with a tree with as many nodes as data points.

BART models

A **Bayesian additive regression trees (BART)** model is a sum of m trees that we use to approximate a function [Chipman et al., 2010]. To complete the model, we need to set priors over trees. The main function of such priors is to prevent overfitting while retaining the flexibility that trees provide. Priors are designed to keep the individual trees relatively shallow and the values at the leaf nodes relatively small.

PyMC does not support BART models directly but we can use PyMC-BART, a Python module that extends PyMC functionality to support BART models. PyMC-BART offers:

- A BART random variable that works very similar to other distributions in PyMC like `pm.Normal`, `pm.Poisson`, etc.
- A sampler called PGBART as trees cannot be sampled with PyMC's default step methods such as NUTS or Metropolis.
- The following utility functions to help work with the result of a BART model:
  - `pmb.plot_pdp`: A function to generate partial dependence plots [Friedman, 2001].
  - `pmb.plot_ice`: A function to generate individual conditional expectation plots [Goldstein et al., 2013].
  - `pmb.plot_variable_importance`: A function to estimate the variable importance.
  - `pmb.plot_convergence`: A function that plots the empirical cumulative distribution for the effective sample size and $\hat{R}$ values for the BART random variables.

> **BARTs Are Priors Over Step Functions**
>
> We can think of BART as priors over piece-wise constant functions. Further-more, in the limit of the number of trees $m \to \infty$, BART converges to a nowhere-differentiable Gaussian process.

In the following sections, we will focus on the applied side of BART, specifically examining how to use PyMC-BART. If you are interested in reading more about the details of how BART models work, the implementation details of PyMC-BART, and how changing the hyperparameters of PyMC-BART affects the results, I recommend reading Quiroga et al. [2022].

Bartian penguins

Let's imagine that, for some reason, we are interested in modeling the body mass of penguins as a function of other body measures. The following code block shows a BART model for such a problem. In this example, X = "flipper_length", "bill_depth", "bill_length"] and Y is the body_mass:

Code 9.1:

```
with pm.Model() as model_pen:
    σ = pm.HalfNormal("σ", 1)
    μ = pmb.BART("μ", X, Y)
    y = pm.Normal("y", mu=μ, sigma=σ, observed=Y)
    idata_pen = pm.sample()
    pm.sample_posterior_predictive(idata_pen, extend_inferencedata=True)
```

We can see that using PyMC-BART to define a BART model with PyMC is straightforward. Essentially, we need to define a BART random variable with the arguments X, the covariates, and Y the response variable. Other than that, the rest of the model should look very familiar. As in other regression models, the length of μ will be the same as the observations.

While theoretically, the trees are only a function of X, PyMC-BART asks for Y to obtain an estimate for the initial value for the variance at the leaf nodes of the trees.

Once we have fitted a model with a BART variable, the rest of the workflow is as usual. For instance, we can compute a posterior predictive check simply by calling `az.plot_ppc(.)` and we will get something like Figure 9.3.

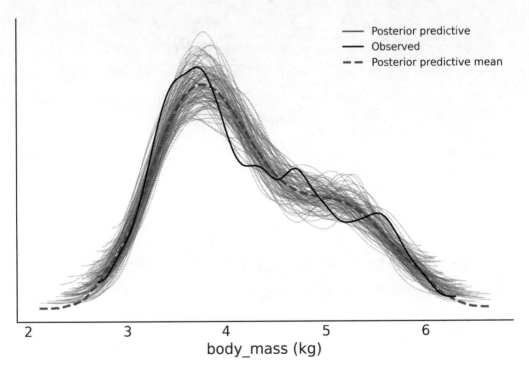

Figure 9.3: Posterior predictive check for `model_pen`

Figure 9.3, shows a reasonable fit. Remarkably, we don't get negative masses even when we use a Normal likelihood. But with PyMC and PyMC-BART, it is super easy to try other likelihoods; just replace the Normal with another distribution like Gamma or a Truncated Normal as you would do in a regular PyMC model and you are good to go. You can then use posterior predictive checks and LOO, as discussed in Chapter 5.

In the next few sections, we are going to discuss how to use and interpret the utility function provided by PyMC-BART (except for `pmb.plot_convergence`, which is discussed in Chapter 10 with other diagnostic methods).

Partial dependence plots

A **partial dependence plot** (**PDP**) is a graphical tool widespread in the BART literature, but it is not exclusive to BART. In principle, it can be used with any method or model. It consists of plotting the predicted response as a function of a given covariate X_i, while averaging over the rest of the covariates X_{-i}. So, essentially, we are plotting how much each covariate contributes to the response variable while keeping all other variables constant. One thing that is particular to BART and other tree-based methods is that the computation of PDPs can be done without refitting the model to synthetic data; instead, it can be efficiently computed from the already fitted trees. This makes BART an attractive choice for model interpretability and understanding the impact of individual features on predictions.

Once a model like model_pen has been fitted, we can compute a PDP with:

Code 9.2:

```
pmb.plot_pdp(μ, X, Y)
```

Notice we passed the BART random variable, the covariates, and the response variable. The response variable is not really needed, but if passed, and if it is a pandas Series, it will use its name for the y-axis label.

Figure 9.4 shows one example of a partial dependence plot from model_pen. We can see that flipper_length shows the largest effect, which is approximately linear, while the other two variables show mostly a flat response, indicating their partial contribution is not very large. For a variable with a null contribution to the response, its expected PDP will be a flat, constant line at a value of the average of the response variable.

In Figure 9.4, we can see that the largest contribution comes from flipper_length, but this does not mean the other two variables are not related to body_mass. We can only say that considering we have flipper_length in the model, the effect of the other two is minimal.

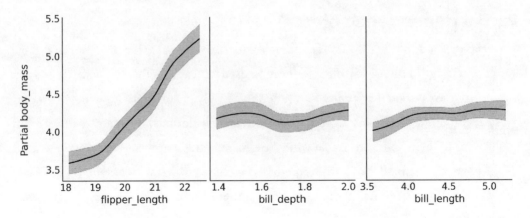

Figure 9.4: Partial dependence plot for `model_pen`

Individual conditional plots

When computing partial dependence plots, we assume that variables X_i and X_{-i} are uncorrelated. In many real-world problems, this is hardly the case, and partial dependence plots can hide relationships in the data. Nevertheless, if the dependence between the subset of chosen variables is not too strong, then partial dependence plots can be useful summaries Friedman [2001].

Individual Conditional Expectation (ICE) plots are closely related to PDPs. The difference is that instead of plotting the target covariates' average partial effect on the predicted response, we plot n conditional expectation curves at given fixed values (10 by default). That is, each curve in an ICE plot reflects the partial predicted response as a function of covariate X_i for a fixed value of X_{-ij}.

Once a model like `model_pen` has been fitted, we can compute an ICE plot with the following command:

Code 9.3:

```
pmb.plot_ice(μ, X, Y)
```

The signature is the same as for PDPs. The result is shown in Figure 9.5. The gray curves are the conditional expectation curves at different values. If we average them, we should get the PDP curve (in black). If the curves in an ICE plot are mostly parallel to each other, it is because the contributions of the covariates to the response variable are mostly independent. This is the case for `flipper_length` and `bill_length`. In this case, the ICE and PDP plots convey the same information. However, if the curve is crossed, it indicates non-independent contributions. In such cases, the PDP would hide the effects. We can see an example of this in Figure 9.5 for `bill_depth`:

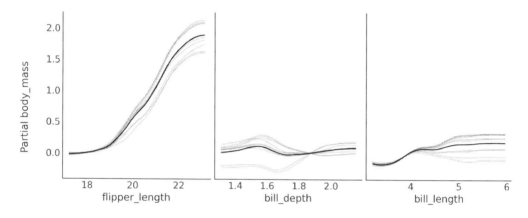

Figure 9.5: Individual conditional expectation plot for `model_pen`

By default, ICE plots are centered, meaning that the gray curves are centered around the partial response evaluated at the lowest value on the x-axis. This helps interpret the plots: for instance, it is easier to see whether the lines cross. This also explains why the scale for the y-axis in Figure 9.5 is different from the scale in Figure 9.4. You can change it with the argument `centered=False`.

Variable selection with BART

In Chapter 6, we already discussed variable selection and explained under which scenarios we may be interested in selecting a subset of variables. PyMC-BART offers a very simple, and almost computational-free, heuristic to estimate variable importance. It keeps track of how many times a covariate is used as a splitting variable. For BART models, the variable importance is computed by averaging over the *m* trees and over all posterior samples. To further ease interpretation, we can report the values normalized so each value is in the interval $[0, 1]$ and the total importance is 1.

In some implementations of BART, the estimation of the variable importance is very sensitive to the number of trees m. The authors of those implementations recommend that you use a relatively low number of trees for variable selection and a higher number of trees for model fitting/predictions. This is not the case with PyMC-BART, for which the estimates of variable importance are robust to the number of trees.

Once we have fitted a model like model_pen to perform variable selection with PyMC-BART, we need to do something like:

Code 9.4:

```
pmb.plot_variable_importance(idata_pen, μ, X)
```

Notice we passed the inference data, the BART random variable, and the covariates. The result is shown in Figure 9.6:

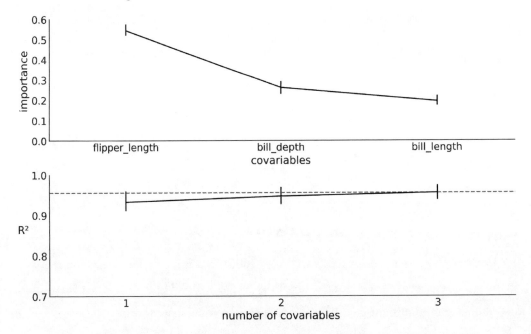

Figure 9.6: Variable importance plot for model_pen

From the top panel, we can see that flipper_length has the largest value of variable importance, followed by `bill_depth` and `fill_length`. Notice that this qualitatively agrees with the partial dependence plots and individual conditional expectation plots.

The simple heuristic of counting how many times a variable enters a tree has some issues. One concerns interpretability, as the lack of a clear threshold separating the *important* variables from the *unimportant* ones is problematic. PyMC-BART offers some help. The bottom panel of Figure 9.6 shows the square of the Pearson correlation coefficient between the predictions generated with the reference model, that is, the model with all covariates, and the predictions generated with the submodels, with fewer covariates. We can use this plot to find the minimal model capable of making predictions that are as close as possible to the reference model. Figure 9.6 tells us that a model with just `flipper_length` will have almost the same predictive performance as the model with all three variables. Notice we may add some small gain by adding `bill_depth`, but it would probably be too small.

Now, let me briefly explain what `pmb.plot_variable_importance` is doing under the hood. Primarily, two approximations are taking place:

- It does not evaluate all possible combinations of covariates. Instead, it adds one variable at a time, following their relative importance (the top subplot in Figure 9.6).

- It does not refit all models from 1 to n covariates. Instead, it approximates the effect of removing a variable by traversing the trees from the posterior distribution for the reference model and it prunes the branches without the variable of interest. This is similar to the procedure to compute the partial dependence plots, with the difference that for the plots, we excluded all but one variable, while for the variable importance we start by excluding all but the most important one, then all but the two most important ones, and so on until we include all variables.

If this procedure for variable selection sounds familiar to you, it is highly likely that you have been paying attention to this chapter and also Chapter 6. The procedure is conceptually similar to what Kulprit does. Here, we also make use of the concept of a reference model, and we evaluate a model in terms of its predictive distribution. But the similarities stop there. PyMC-BART does not use the ELPD, instead using the square of the

Pearson correlation coefficient, and estimating the submodels by pruning the trees fitted with the reference model, not via a Kullback-Liebler divergence projection.

Before moving on to another topic, let me just add some words of caution. As we discussed in Chapter 6, with the output of Kulprit, we should not over-interpret the order of the variables. The sample applies to figures generated with `pmb.plot_variable_importance` like Figure 9.6. If the importance of two variables is very similar, it can easily happen that the order changes if we refit the model with a different random seed or if the data slightly changes, such as after adding or removing a data point. The error bars for the variable importance could help, but it is likely that they underestimate the true variability. Thus, take the order with a pinch of salt, and use it as a guide in the context of your problems.

Distributional BART models

As we saw in Chapter 6, for generalized linear models, we are not restricted to creating linear models for the mean or location parameter; we can also model other parameters, for example, the standard deviation of a Gaussian or even both the mean and standard deviation. The same applies to BART models.

To exemplify this, let's model the bike dataset. We will use `rented` as the response variable and `hour`, `temperature`, `humidity`, and `workday` as predictor variables. As we did previously, we are going to use a NegativeBinomial distribution as likelihood. This distribution has two parameters μ and α. We are going to use a sum of trees for both parameters. The following code block shows the model:

Code 9.5:

```
1  with pm.Model() as model_bb:
2      μ = pmb.BART("μ", X, np.log(Y), shape=(2, 348), separate_trees=True)
3      pm.NegativeBinomial('yl', np.exp(μ[0]), np.exp(μ[1]), observed=Y)
4      idata_bb = pm.sample(2000,
5                           random_seed=123,
6                           pgbart={"batch":(0.05, 0.15)})
```

Let's take a moment to be sure we understand this model. First, notice that we passed a `shape` argument to `pmb.BART()`. When `separate_trees = True`, this instructs PyMC-BART to fit two separate sets of sum-of-trees. Then we index μ in order to use the first dimension for the μ parameter of the NegativeBinomial and the second dimension for the α parameter. If, instead, `separate_trees = False`, then we tell PyMC-BART to fit a single sum-of-trees but each tree will return 2 values at each leaf node, instead of 1. The advantage of this is that the algorithm will run faster and use less memory, as we are only fitting one set of trees. The disadvantage is that we get a less flexible model. In practice, both options can be useful, so which one you should use is another modeling decision.

Another important aspect of `model_bb` is that we take the exponential of μ. We do this to ensure that the NegativeBinomial distribution gets only positive values, both for μ and α. This is the same type of transformation we discussed in the context of generalized linear models. What is particular about PyMC-BART is that we applied its inverse to the value of Y we passed to `pmb.BART()`. In my experience, this helps PyMC-BART to find better solutions. For a model with a Binomial or Categorical likelihood, it is not necessary to apply the inverse of the logistic or softmax, respectively. PyMC-BART handles the Binomial as a particular case and for the Categorical, we have empirically seen good results without the inverse. It is important to remark that the value of Y we passed to `pmb.BART()` is only used to initialize the sampling of the BART variables. The initialization seems to be robust to the values we pass and passing Y or some transformation of it works well in most cases.

The third aspect I want you to pay attention to is that we are passing a new argument to `pm.sample`, namely `pgbart`. The value for this argument is the dictionary `"batch":(0.05, 0.15)`. Why are we doing this? Occasionally, to obtain good-quality samples, it becomes necessary to tweak the hyperparameters of the sampler. In previous examples, we opted to omit this aspect to maintain simplicity and focus. However, as we later discuss in more depth in Chapter 10, paying attention to these adjustments can become important. For the particular case of the PGBART sampler, there are two hyperparameters we can change. One is `num_particles` (defaults to 10), where the larger the number of particles, the more accurate the sampling of BART, but also the more expensive it is. The other is `batch`; by default, this is a tuple (0.1, 0.1), meaning that at each step, the sampler fits 10% of the m trees during the tuning phase and the same for the sampling phase. For the model_bb model, we used (0.05, 0.15), meaning 5% during tuning (2 trees) and 15% (7 trees) during the actual sampling.

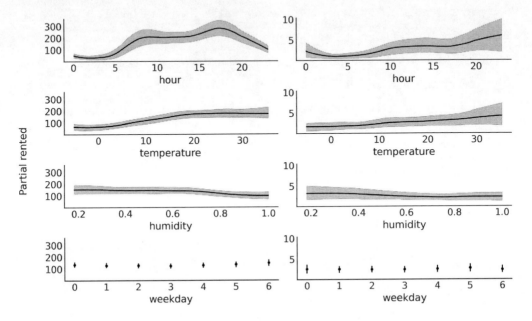

Figure 9.7: Partial dependence plot for model_bb

We can explore the relationship of the covariates to the response for both parameters as in Figure 9.7. Notice that variables appear twice: the first column corresponds to parameter μ and the second column to parameter α. We can see that hour has the largest effect on the response variable for both parameters of the NegativeBinomial.

Constant and linear response

By default, PyMC-BART will fit trees that return a single value at each leaf node. This is a simple approach that usually works just fine. However, it is important to understand its implications. For instance, this means that predictions for any value outside the range of the observed data used to fit the model will be constants. To see this, go back and check Figure 9.2. This tree will return 1.9 for any value below c1. Notice that this will still be the case if we, instead, sum a bunch of trees, because summing a bunch of constant values results in yet another constant value.

Whether this is a problem or not is up to you and the context in which you apply the BART model. Nevertheless, PyMC-BART offers a `response` argument that you pass to the BART random variable. Its default value is `"constant"`. You can change it to `"linear"`, in which case PyMC-BART will return a linear fit at each leaf node or `"mix"`, which will propose (during sampling) trees with either constant or linear values.

To exemplify the difference, let us fit a very simple example: the number of rented bikes versus the temperature. The observed temperature values go from ≈ -5 to ≈ 35. After fitting this model, we will ask for out-of-sample posterior predictive values in the range [-20, 45]. For that reason, we will set up a model with a mutable variable as introduced in Chapter 4.

Code 9.6:

```
1  with pm.Model() as model_tmp1:
2      X_mut1 = pm.MutableData("X_mut1", X)
3      α = pm.HalfNormal('α', 1)
4      μ = pmb.BART("μ", X_mut1, np.log(Y), m=100, response="linear")
5      _ = pm.NegativeBinomial('yl', np.exp(μ), α, observed=Y, shape=μ.shape)
6      idata_tmp1 = pm.sample(random_seed=123)
```

Notice that we passed `shape=μ.shape` to the likelihood. This is something we need to do to be able to change the shape of `X_mut1`, which is also a requirement of PyMC, so this is something you should also do for non-BART models like linear regression.

OK, to continue with the example, in the accompanying code, you will find the code for the `model_tmp0` model, which is exactly the same as **model_tmp1**, except that it has the default constant response. The results from both models are shown in Figure 9.8.

Notice how outside of the range of the data (dashed gray lines), the predictions for the model with constant response are indeed constant. Which one is providing better predictions? I

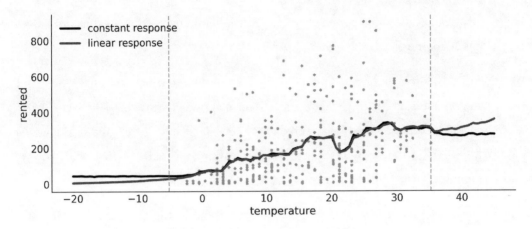

Figure 9.8: Mean predictions with constant and linear responses

am not sure. I will argue that for predictions on the lower end of temperatures, the linear response is better as it predicts that the number of rented bikes will keep decreasing until eventually reaching 0. But on the higher end of temperatures, a plateau or even a decrease should be more likely than an increase. I mean, I have tried riding my bike at 40 or maybe even 42 degrees, and it is not a super nice experience. What do you think?

Choosing the number of trees

The number of trees (m) controls the flexibility of the BART function. As a rule of thumb, the default value of 50 should be enough to get a good approximation. And larger values, like 100 or 200, should provide a more refined answer. Usually, it is hard to overfit by increasing the number of trees, because the larger the number of trees, the smaller the values at the leaf nodes.

In practice, you may be worried about overshooting m because the computational cost of BART, both in terms of time and memory, will increase. One way to tune m is to perform K-fold cross-validation, as recommended by Chipman et al. [2010]. Another option is to approximate cross-validation by using LOO as discussed in Chapter 5. We have observed that LOO can indeed be of help to provide a reasonable value of m [Quiroga et al., 2022].

Summary

BART is a flexible non-parametric model where a sum of trees is used to approximate an unknown function from the data. Priors are used to regularize inference, mainly by restricting trees' learning capacity so that no individual tree is able to explain the data, but rather the sum of trees. PyMC-BART is a Python library that extends PyMC to work with BART models.

We built a few BART models in this chapter, and learned how to perform variable selection and use partial dependence plots and individual conditional plots to interpret the output of BART models.

Exercises

1. Explain each of the following:

    - How is BART different from linear regression and splines?
    - When might you want to use linear regression over BART?
    - When might you want to use Gaussian processes over BART?

2. In your own words, explain why it can be the case that multiple small trees can fit patterns better than one single large tree. What is the difference in the two approaches? What are the trade-offs?

3. Below, we provide two simple synthetic datasets. Fit a BART model with m=50 to each of them. Plot the data and the mean fitted function. Describe the fit.

    - x = np.linspace(-1, 1., 200) and y = np.random.normal(2*x, 0.25)
    - x = np.linspace(-1, 1., 200) and y = np.random.normal(x**2, 0.25)
    - Create your own synthetic dataset.

4. Create the following dataset $Y = 10\sin(\pi X_0 X_1) + 20(X_2 - 0.5)^2 + 10X_3 + 5X_4 + \epsilon$, where $\epsilon \sim \mathcal{N}(0, 1)$ and $X_{0:9} \sim \mathcal{U}(0, 1)$. This is called Friedman's five-dimensional function. Notice that we actually have 10 dimensions, but the last 5 are pure noise.

    - Fit a BART model to this data.
    - Compute a PDP and the variable importance (VI).
    - Do the PDP and VI qualitatively agree? How?

5. Use BART with the penguins dataset. Use `bill_length`, `flipper_length`, `bill_depth`, `bill_length`, and `body_mass` as covariates and the species `Adelie` and `Chistrap` as the response. Try different values of `m`; 10, 20, 50, and 100. Use LOO to pick a suitable value.

6. Check the variable importance for the model in the previous question. Compare the result with one obtained with Kulprit for a generalized linear model with the same covariates and response, built with Bambi.

Join our community Discord space

Join our Discord community to meet like-minded people and learn alongside more than 5000 members at:

`https://packt.link/bayesian`

10

Inference Engines

> The first principle is that you must not fool yourself—and you are the easiest
> person to fool.
>
> – Richard Feynman

So far, we have focused on model building, interpretation of results, and criticism of models. We have relied on the magic of the `pm.sample` function to compute posterior distributions for us. Now we will focus on learning some of the details of the inference engines behind this function.

The whole purpose of probabilistic programming tools, such as PyMC, is that the user should not care about how sampling is carried out, but understanding how we get samples from the posterior is important for a full understanding of the inference process, and could also help us to get an idea of when and how these methods fail and what to do about it. If you are not interested in understanding how these methods work, you can skip most of this chapter, but I strongly recommend you at least read the *Diagnosing samples* section, as this section provides a few guidelines that will help you to check whether your posterior samples are reliable. There are many methods for computing the posterior distribution. In this chapter, we will discuss some general ideas and will focus on the most important methods implemented in PyMC. We will learn about:

- Inference engines
- Metropolis-Hastings
- Hamiltonian Monte Carlo
- Sequential Monte Carlo
- Diagnosing samples

Inference engines

While conceptually simple, Bayesian methods can be mathematically and numerically challenging. The main reason is that the marginal likelihood, the denominator in Bayes' theorem, usually takes the form of an intractable or computationally expensive integral to solve. For this reason, the posterior is usually estimated numerically using algorithms from the **Markov Chain Monte Carlo (MCMC)** family. These methods are sometimes called inference engines, because, at least in principle, they are capable of approximating the posterior distribution for any probabilistic model. Even though inference does not always work that well in practice, the existence of such methods has motivated the development of probabilistic programming languages such as PyMC.

The goal of probabilistic programming languages is to separate the model-building process from the inference process to facilitate the iterative steps of model-building, evaluation, and model modification/expansion. By treating the inference process (but not the model-building process) as a black box, users of probabilistic programming languages such as PyMC are free to focus on their specific problems, leaving PyMC to handle the computational details for them. This is exactly what we have been doing up to this point. So, you may be biased toward thinking that this is the obvious or natural approach. But it is important to notice that before probabilistic programming languages, people working with probabilistic models were also used to writing their own sampling methods, generally tailored to their models, or they were used to simplifying their models to make them suitable for certain mathematical approximations. In fact, this is still true in some academic circles. This tailored approach can be more elegant and can even provide a more efficient way of computing a posterior (for a very specific model), but it is also error-prone and time-consuming, even for experts. Furthermore, the tailored approach is not suitable for most practitioners interested in solving problems with probabilistic models. Software such as PyMC invites people from a very broad background to work with probabilistic models, lowering the mathematical and computational entry barrier. I personally think this is fantastic and also an invitation to learn more about good practices in statistical modeling so we try to avoid fooling ourselves.

The previous chapters have been mostly about learning the basics of Bayesian modeling; now we are going to learn, at a conceptual level, how automatic inference is achieved, when and why it fails, and what to do when it fails.

Before discussing MCMC methods, however, let me explain two other methods that can be useful sometimes, and also provide an intuition of why we usually use MCMC as general methods.

The grid method

The grid method is a simple brute-force approach. Even if you are not able to compute the whole posterior, you may be able to compute the prior and the likelihood point-wise; this is a pretty common scenario, if not the most common one.

Let's assume we want to compute the posterior for a model with a single parameter. The grid approximation is as follows:

1. Define a reasonable interval for the parameter (the prior should give you a hint).
2. Place a grid of points (generally equidistant) on that interval.
3. For each point in the grid, multiply the likelihood and the prior.

Optionally, we may normalize the computed values, that is, we divide each value in the posterior array by the total area under the curve, ensuring that the total area equals 1.

The following code block implements the grid method for the coin-flipping model:

Code 10.1:

```python
1  def posterior_grid(grid_points=50, heads=6, tails=9):
2      """
3      A grid implementation for the coin-flipping problem
4      """
5      grid = np.linspace(0, 1, grid_points)
6      prior = np.repeat(1/grid_points, grid_points)  # uniform prior
7      likelihood = pz.Binomial(n=heads+tails, p=grid).pdf(heads)
8      posterior = likelihood * prior
9      posterior /= posterior.sum() * (1/grid_points)
10     return grid, posterior
```

Figure 10.1 shows the posterior we get for flipping a coin 13 times and observing 3 heads under a Uniform prior. The curve is very rugged, as we used a grid of only 10 points. If you increase the number of points, the curve will look smoother, the computation will be more accurate, and the cost will be higher.

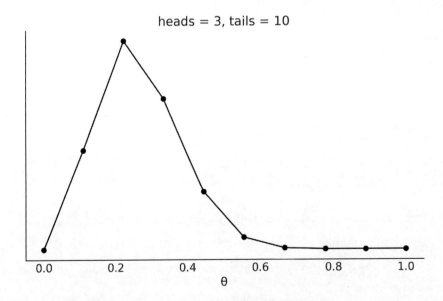

Figure 10.1: Posterior computed using the grid method

The biggest caveat of the grid approach is that this method scales poorly with the number of parameters, also referred to as dimensions. We can see this with a simple example. Suppose we want to sample a unit interval (see Figure 10.2) like in the coin-flipping problem, and we use four equidistant points; this would mean a resolution of 0.25 units. Now, suppose we have a 2D problem (the square in Figure 10.2) and we want to use a grid with the same resolution; we will need 16 points. And lastly, for a 3D problem, we will need 64 (see the cube in Figure 10.2). In this example, we need 16 times as many resources to sample from a cube of side 1 than for a line of length 1 with a resolution of 0.25. If we decide instead to have a resolution of 0.1 units, we will have to sample 10 points for the line and 1,000 for the cube.

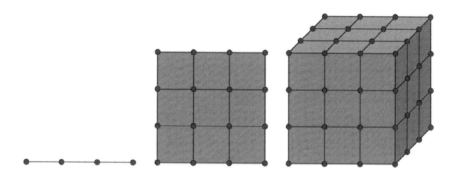

Figure 10.2: A grid with the same resolution in 1, 2, and 3 dimensions

Besides how fast the number of points increases, there is another phenomenon that is not a property of the grid method, or any other method for that matter. It is a property of high-dimensional spaces. As you increase the number of parameters, the region of the parameter space where most of the posterior is concentrated gets smaller and smaller compared to the sampled volume. This is a pervasive phenomenon and is usually known as the curse of dimensionality, or as mathematicians prefer to call it, the concentration of measure.

The curse of dimensionality is the term used to refer to various related phenomena that are absent in low-dimensional spaces but present in high-dimensional spaces. Here are some examples of these phenomena:

- As the number of dimensions increases, the Euclidean distance between any pair of samples tends to resemble the distance between other pairs. That is, in high-dimensional spaces, most points are basically at the same distance from one another.
- For a hypercube, most of the volume is at its corners, not in the middle. For a hypersphere, most of the volume is at its surface and not in the middle.
- In high dimensions, most of the mass of a multivariate Gaussian distribution is not close to the mean (or mode), but in a shell around it that moves away from the mean to the tails as the dimensionality increases. This shell is referred to as the typical set.

For code examples illustrating these concepts, please check out the repository for this book at `https://github.com/aloctavodia/BAP3`.

For our current discussion, all these facts mean that if we do not choose wisely where to evaluate the posterior, we will spend most of our time computing values with an almost null contribution to the posterior, and thus we will be wasting valuable resources. The grid method is not a very smart method to choose to evaluate the posterior distribution, thus making it not very useful as a general method for high-dimensional problems.

Quadratic method

The quadratic approximation, also known as the Laplace method or the normal approximation, consists of approximating the posterior with a Gaussian distribution. To do this, we first find the model of the posterior distribution; numerically, we can do this with an optimization method. Then we compute the Hessian matrix, from which we can then estimate the standard deviation. If you are wondering, the Hessian matrix is a square matrix of second-order partial derivatives. For what we care we can use it to obtain the standard deviation of in general a covariance matrix.

Bambi can solve Bayesian models using the quadratic method for us. In the following code block, we first define a model for the coin-flipping problem, the same one we already defined for the grid method, and then we fit it using the quadratic method, called `laplace` in Bambi:

Code 10.2:

```
1  data = pd.DataFrame(data, columns=["w"])
2  priors = {"Intercept": bmb.Prior("Uniform", lower=0, upper=1)}
3  model = bmb.Model("w ~ 1", data=data, family="bernoulli", priors=priors,
4                    link="identity")
5  results = model.fit(draws=4000, inference_method="laplace")
```

Figure 10.3 shows the computed posterior and the exact posterior. Notice that Bambi also returns samples when using this method. It first approximates the posterior as a Gaussian (or multivariate Gaussian) and then takes samples from it.

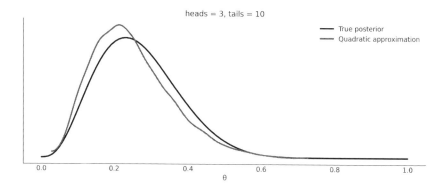

Figure 10.3: A quadratic approximation to the posterior

The quadratic/Laplace method is included in Bambi mostly for pedagogical purposes. One nice feature, though, is that Bambi takes into account the boundaries. For example, for the coin-flipping problem, we know the solution must be in the interval [0, 1]. Bambi ensures this is true, even when we use a Gaussian under the hood. Bambi achieves this by fitting a Gaussian in an unbounded parameter space, and then transforming to the proper bounded space.

The quadratic/Laplace method, while very limited in itself, can be used as the building block of more advanced methods. For instance, the **Integrated Nested Laplace Approximation (INLA)** can be used to fit a wide variety of models very efficiently.

Markovian methods

There is a family of related methods, collectively known as the **Markov chain Monte Carlo** or **MCMC** methods. These are stochastic methods that allow us to get samples from the true posterior distribution as long as we can compute the likelihood and the prior pointwise. You may remember that this is the same condition we needed for the grid method, but contrary to them, MCMC methods can efficiently sample from higher-probability regions in very high dimensions.

MCMC methods visit each region of the parameter space following their relative probabilities. If the probability of region A is twice that of region B, we will obtain twice as many samples from A as we will from B. Hence, even if we are not capable of computing the whole posterior analytically, we could use MCMC methods to take samples from it. In theory, MCMC will give us samples from the correct distribution – the catch is that this theoretical guarantee only holds asymptotically, that is, for an infinite number of samples! In practice, we always have a finite number of samples, thus we need to check that the samples are trustworthy. We are going to learn about that, but let's not get ahead of ourselves; first, let's get some intuition for how MCMC methods work. This will help us understand the diagnostic later. To understand what MCMC methods are, we are going to split the method into the "two MC parts": the Monte Carlo part and the Markov chain part.

Monte Carlo

The use of random numbers explains the Monte Carlo part of the name. Monte Carlo methods are a very broad family of algorithms that use random sampling to compute or simulate a given process. Monte Carlo is a very famous casino located in the Principality of Monaco. One of the developers of the Monte Carlo method, Stanislaw Ulam, had an uncle who used to gamble there. The key idea Stan had was that while many problems are difficult to solve or even formulate in an exact way, they can be effectively studied by taking samples from them. In fact, as the story goes, the motivation was to answer questions about the probability of getting a particular hand in a game of Solitaire.

One way to solve this problem is to follow the analytical combinatorial problem. Another way, Stanislaw argued, is to play several games of Solitaire and count how many of the hands that we play match the particular hand we are interested in! Maybe this sounds obvious to you, or at least pretty reasonable; you may even have used resampling methods to solve statistical problems. But, remember this mental experiment was performed about 70 years ago, a time when the first practical computers were beginning to be developed!

The first application of the Monte Carlo method was to solve a problem of nuclear physics, a hard-to-tackle problem using the tools at the time. Nowadays, even personal computers are powerful enough to solve many interesting problems using the Monte Carlo approach; hence, these methods are applied to a wide variety of problems in science, engineering, industry, and the arts. A classic pedagogical example of using a Monte Carlo method to compute a quantity of interest is the numerical estimation of the number π. In practice, there are better methods for this particular computation, but its pedagogical value remains.

We can estimate the value of π with the following procedure:

1. Throw N points at random into a square of side $2R$.
2. Draw a circle of radius R inscribed in the square and count the number of points M inside the circle.
3. Compute $\hat{\pi}$ as the ratio $4\frac{M}{N}$.

Here are a few notes:

- The area of the circle is proportional to the number of points inside it (M) and the area of the square is proportional to the total points (N).
- We know a point is inside a circle if the following relation holds: $\sqrt{(x^2 + y^2)} \leq R$.
- The area of the square is $(2R)^2$ and the area of the circle is πR^2. Thus, we know that the ratio of the area of the square to the area of the circle is π.

Using a few lines of Python, we can run this simple Monte Carlo simulation and compute π, and also the relative error of our estimate compared to the true value of π. The result of a run is shown in Figure 10.4.

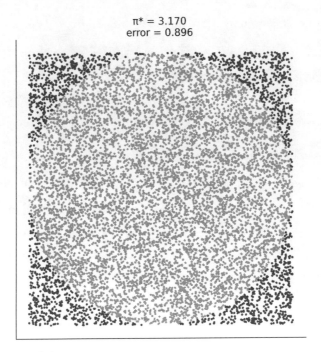

Figure 10.4: A Monte Carlo approximation of π

Markov chain

A Markov chain is a mathematical object that consists of a sequence of states and a set of transition probabilities that describe how to move among the states. You can create a Markov chain yourself; flip a coin and if you get heads take a step to the right, otherwise step to the left. That is a simple 1-dimensional Markov chain. A chain is Markovian if the probability of moving to any other state depends only on the current state.

As a practitioner, you just need to know that Markov chains provide a framework to study the properties of MCMC samplers (among other useful applications). They are not that hard to understand, at least not the most basic properties. But going into the details is not that useful for you as a modeler and thus we will not discuss them any further. You can check Blitzstein [2019] for a nice intro if you want.

The most popular MCMC method is probably the Metropolis-Hasting algorithm, and we will discuss it in the following section.

Metropolis-Hastings

For some distributions, such as the Gaussian, we have very efficient algorithms to get samples from, but for other distributions, this is not the case. Metropolis-Hastings enables us to obtain samples from any probability distribution given that we can compute at least a value proportional to it, thus ignoring the normalization factor. This is very useful since many times the harder part is precisely to compute the normalization factor. This is the case with Bayesian statistics, where the computation of the marginal likelihood can be a deal-breaker.

To conceptually understand this method, we are going to use the following analogy. Suppose we are interested in finding the volume of water in a lake and which part of the lake has the deepest point. The water is really muddy so we can't estimate the depth just by looking through the water to the bottom, and the lake is really big, so a grid approximation does not seem like a very good idea. To develop a sampling strategy, we seek help from two of our best friends: Markovia and Monty. After a fruitful discussion, they came up with the following algorithm, which requires a boat—nothing fancy, we can even use a wooden raft and a very long stick. This is cheaper than sonar and we have already spent all our money on the boat, anyway! Check out these steps:

1. Choose a random place in the lake, and move the boat there.
2. Use the stick to measure the depth of the lake.
3. Move the boat to another point and take a new measurement.
4. Compare the two measures in the following way:
   (a) If the new spot is deeper than the first one, write down in your notebook the depth of the new spot and repeat from step 3.
   (b) If the spot is shallower than the first one, we have two options: to accept or reject. Accepting means we write down the depth of the new spot and repeat from step 3. Rejecting means we go back to the first spot and write down (yes, again!) the value for the depth of the first spot.

The rule for deciding whether to accept or reject is known as the Metropolis-Hastings criteria, and it basically says that we must accept the new spot with a probability that is proportional to the ratio of the depth of the new and old spots.

If we follow this iterative procedure, we will get not only the total volume of the lake and the deepest point, but also an approximation of the entire curvature of the bottom of the lake. As you may have guessed, in this analogy, the curvature of the bottom of the lake is the posterior distribution and the deepest point is the mode. According to our friend Markovia, the larger the number of iterations, the better the approximation. Indeed, the theory guarantees that under certain general circumstances, we are going to get the exact answer if we get an infinite number of samples. Luckily for us, in practice, and for many, many problems, we can get a very accurate approximation using a finite and relatively small number of samples.

The preceding explanation is enough to get a conceptual-level understanding of Metropolis-Hastings. The next few pages contain a more detailed and formal explanation in case you want to dig deeper.

The Metropolis-Hastings algorithm has the following steps:

1. Choose an initial value for a parameter x_i. This can be done randomly or by making an educated guess.
2. Choose a new parameter value x_{i+1}, by sampling from $Q(x_{i+1} \mid x_i)$. We can think of this step as perturbing the state x_i somehow.
3. Compute the probability of accepting a new parameter value by using the Metropolis-Hastings criteria:

$$p_a(x_{i+1} \mid x_i) = \min\left(1, \frac{p(x_{i+1})\, q(x_i \mid x_{i+1})}{p(x_i)\, q(x_{i+1} \mid x_i)}\right)$$

4. If the probability computed in step 3 is larger than the value taken from a Uniform distribution on the [0, 1] interval, we accept the new state; otherwise, we stay in the old state.
5. We iterate from step 2 until we have enough samples.

Here are a couple of notes to take into account:

- Q is called the proposal distribution. It can be anything we want, but it makes sense that we choose a distribution that we find simple to sample from, such as a Gaussian or Uniform distribution.

- Note that Q is not the prior or likelihood or any part of the model. It is a component of the MCMC method, not of the model.

- If Q is symmetric, the terms $q(x_i \mid x_{i+1})$ and $q(x_{i+1} \mid x_i)$ will cancel out. Hence we will just need to evaluate the ratio $\frac{p(x_{i+1})}{p(x_i)}$.

- Step 3 and step 4 imply that we will always accept moving to a more probable state. Less probable parameter values are accepted probabilistically, given the ratio between the probability of the new parameter value x_{i+1} and the old parameter value x_i. This criteria for accepting proposed steps gives us a more efficient sampling approach compared to the grid method while ensuring a correct sampling.

- The target distribution (the posterior distribution in Bayesian statistics) is approximated by a list of sampled parameter values. If we accept, we add x_{i+1} to the list of the new sampled values. If we reject, we add x_i to the list, even if the value is repeated.

At the end of the process, we will have a list of values. If everything was done the right way, these samples would be an approximation of the posterior. The most frequent values in our trace will be the most probable values according to the posterior. An advantage of this procedure is that analyzing the posterior is as simple as manipulating an array of values, as you have already experimented with in all the previous chapters.

The following code illustrates a very basic implementation of the Metropolis algorithm. It is not meant to solve a real problem, only to show it is possible to sample from a probability distribution if we know how to compute its density point-wise. Notice that the following implementation has nothing Bayesian in it; there is no prior and we do not even have data! Remember that MCMC methods are very general algorithms that can be applied to a broad array of problems.

The first argument of the metropolis function is a PreliZ distribution; we are assuming we do not know how to directly get samples from this distribution:

Code 10.3:

```python
1  def metropolis(dist, draws=1000):
2      """A very simple Metropolis implementation"""
3      trace = np.zeros(draws)
4      old_x = 0.5
5      old_prob = dist.pdf(old_x)
6
7      delta = np.random.normal(0, 0.5, draws)
8      for i in range(draws):
9          new_x = old_x + delta[i]
10         new_prob = dist.pdf(new_x)
11         acceptance = new_prob / old_prob
12         if acceptance >= np.random.random():
13             trace[i] = new_x
14             old_x = new_x
15             old_prob = new_prob
16         else:
17             trace[i] = old_x
18     return trace
```

The result of our simple metropolis algorithm is shown in Figure 10.5. The black line shows the true distribution while the bars show the samples we computed.

The efficiency of the algorithm depends heavily on the proposal distribution; if the proposed state is very far away from the current state, the chance of rejection is very high, and if the proposed state is very close, we explore the parameter space very slowly. In both scenarios, we will need many more samples than for a less extreme situation. Usually, the proposal is a multivariate Gaussian distribution whose covariance matrix is determined during the tuning phase. PyMC tunes the covariance adaptively by following the rule of thumb that the ideal acceptance is around 50% for a unidimensional Gaussian and around 23% for an

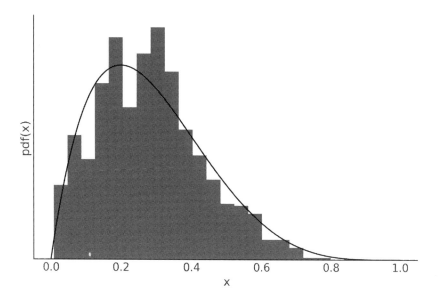

Figure 10.5: Samples from a simple metropolis algorithm

n-dimensional Gaussian target distribution.

MCMC methods often take some time before they start getting samples from the target distribution. So, in practice, people perform a burn-in step, which consists of eliminating the first portion of the samples. Doing a burn-in is a practical trick and not part of the Markovian theory; in fact, it will not be necessary for an infinite sample. Thus, removing the first portion of the samples is just an *ad hoc* trick to get better results, given that we can only compute a finite sample. Having theoretical guarantees or guidance is better than not having them, but for any practical problem, it is important to understand the difference between theory and practice. Remember, we should not get confused by mixing mathematical objects with the approximation of those objects. Spheres, Gaussians, Markov chains, and all the mathematical objects live only in the Platonic world of ideas, not in our imperfect, real world.

At this point, I hope you have a good conceptual grasp of the Metropolis-Hastings method. You may need to go back and read this section a couple of times; that's totally fine. The main ideas are simple but also subtle.

Hamiltonian Monte Carlo

MCMC methods, including Metropolis-Hastings, come with the theoretical guarantee that if we take enough samples, we will get an accurate approximation of the correct distribution. However, in practice, it could take more time than we have to get enough samples. For that reason, alternatives to the Metropolis-Hastings algorithm have been proposed.

Many of those alternative methods, such as the Metropolis-Hastings algorithm itself, were developed originally to solve problems in statistical mechanics, a branch of physics that studies properties of atomic and molecular systems, and thus can be interpreted in a very natural way using analogies of physical systems. One such modification is known as **Hamiltonian Monte Carlo**, or **Hybrid Monte Carlo (HMC)**. In simple terms, a Hamiltonian is a description of the total energy of a physical system. The term *hybrid* is also used because it was originally conceived as a hybridization of Metropolis-Hastings and molecular mechanics, a widely used simulation technique for molecular systems.

Conceptually, we can think of the HMC method as a Metropolis-Hastings but with a proposal distribution that is not random. To get a general conceptual understanding of HMC without going into the mathematical details, let's use the lake and boat analogy again. Instead of moving the boat randomly, we do so by following the curvature of the bottom of the lake. To decide where to move the boat, we let a ball roll onto the bottom of the lake starting from our current position. Our ball is a very special one: not only is it perfectly spherical, it also has no friction and thus is not slowed down by the water or mud. We throw the ball and let it roll for a short moment until we suddenly stop it. Then we accept or reject this proposed step using the Metropolis criteria, just as we did in the vanilla Metropolis-Hastings method. Then the whole procedure is repeated many times. Nicely, this modified procedure results in a higher chance of accepting new positions, even if they are far away relative to the previous position.

Moving according to the curvature of the parameter space turns out to be a smarter way of moving because it avoids one of the main drawbacks of Metropolis-Hastings: an efficient exploration of the sample space requires rejecting most of the proposed steps. Instead, using HMC, it is possible to get a high acceptance rate even for faraway points in the parameter space, thus resulting in a very efficient sampling method.

Let's get out of our Gedankenexperiment and back to the real world. We have to pay a price for this very clever Hamiltonian-based proposal. We need to compute the gradients of our function. A gradient is the generalization of the concept of the derivative to more than one dimension; computing the derivative of a function at one point tells us in which direction the function increases and in which direction it decreases. We can use gradient information to simulate the ball moving in a curved space; in fact, we use the same laws of motion and mathematical machinery used in classical physics to simulate classical mechanical systems, such as balls rolling, the orbits in planetary systems, and the jiggling of molecules.

Computing gradients make us face a trade-off; each HMC step is more expensive to compute than a Metropolis-Hastings step, but the probability of accepting that step is much higher with HMC than with Metropolis. To balance this trade-off in favor of HMC, we need to tune a few parameters of the HMC model (in a similar fashion to how we need to tune the width of the proposal distribution for an efficient Metropolis-Hastings sampler). When this tuning is done by hand, it takes some trial and error and also requires an experienced user, making this procedure a less universal inference engine than we may want. Luckily for us, modern probabilistic programming languages come equipped with efficient adaptive Hamiltonian Monte Carlo methods, such as the NUTS sampler in PyMC. This method has proven remarkably useful and efficient for solving Bayesian models without requiring human intervention (or at least minimizing it).

One caveat of Hamiltonian Monte Carlo methods is that they only work for continuous distribution; the reason is that we cannot compute gradients for discrete distribution. PyMC solves this problem by assigning NUTS to continuous parameters and other samplers to other parameters, such as PGBART for BART random variables or Metropolis to discrete ones.

> ### JAX-Based Sampling
>
> JAX is a library designed to provide high-performance numerical computing
> and automatic differentiation for complex mathematical operations. PyMC use
> a Python version of NUTS. But you can also use JAX-based implementations
> of this sampler. Depending on your model, these samplers can be much faster
> than the default NUTS sampler from PyMC. To used them we need to specify
> the argument `nuts_sampler` for `pm.sample()`. The currently supported options
> are "`nutpie`", "`blackjax`", and "`numpyro`". None of these three samples comes in-
> stalled with PyMC by default, so you will need to install them. For CPUs, nutpie
> is probably the faster option available: `https://github.com/pymc-devs/nutpie`.
> In this book, we used nutpie to sample from GPs – see the Jupyter notebooks for
> Chapter 8.

I strongly recommend you complement this section with this very cool application by Chi
Feng: `https://chi-feng.github.io/mcmc-demo`.

Sequential Monte Carlo

One of the caveats of Metropolis-Hastings and NUTS (and other Hamiltonian Monte Carlo
variants) is that if the posterior has multiple peaks and these peaks are separated by regions
of very low probability, these methods can get stuck in a single mode and miss the others!

Many of the methods developed to overcome this multiple minima problem are based on
the idea of tempering. This idea, once again, is borrowed from statistical mechanics. The
number of states a physical system can populate depends on the temperature of the system;
at 0 Kelvin (the lowest possible temperature), every system is stuck in a single state. On the
other extreme, for an infinite temperature, all possible states are equally likely. Generally,
we are interested in systems at some intermediate temperature. For Bayesian models, there
is a very intuitive way to adapt this tempering idea by writing Bayes' theorem with a twist.

$$p(\theta \mid y)_\beta = p(y \mid \theta)^\beta p(\theta)$$

The parameter β is known as the inverse temperature or tempering parameter. Notice that for $\beta = 0$ we get $p(y \mid \theta)^{\beta} = 1$ and thus the tempered posterior $p(\theta \mid y)_{\beta}$ is just the prior $p(\theta)$, and when $\beta = 1$ the *tempered* posterior is the actual full posterior. As sampling from the prior is generally easier than sampling from the posterior (by increasing the value of β), we start sampling from an easier distribution and slowly morph it into the more complex distribution we really care about.

There are many methods that exploit this idea; one of them is known as **Sequential Monte Carlo (SMC)**. The SMC method, as implemented in PyMC, can be summarized as follows (also see Figure 10.6):

1. Initialize β at 0.
2. Generate N samples S_{β} from the tempered posterior.
3. Increase β a *little bit*.
4. Compute a set of N weights W. The weights are computed according to the new tempered posterior.
5. Obtain S_w by resampling S_b according to W.
6. Run N Metropolis chains, starting each one from a different sample in S_w.
7. Repeat from step 3 until $\beta \geq 1$.

The resampling step works by removing samples with a low probability and replacing them with samples with a higher probability. The Metropolis step perturbs these samples, helping to explore the parameter space.

The efficiency of the tempered method depends heavily on the intermediate values of β, which is usually referred to as the cooling schedule. The smaller the difference between two successive values of β, the closer the two successive tempered posteriors will be, and thus the easier the transition from one stage to the next. But if the steps are too small, we will need many intermediate stages, and beyond some point, this will translate into wasting a lot of computational resources without really improving the accuracy of the results.

Fortunately, SMC can automatically compute the intermediate values of β. The exact cooling schedule will be adapted to the difficulty of the problem; distributions that are

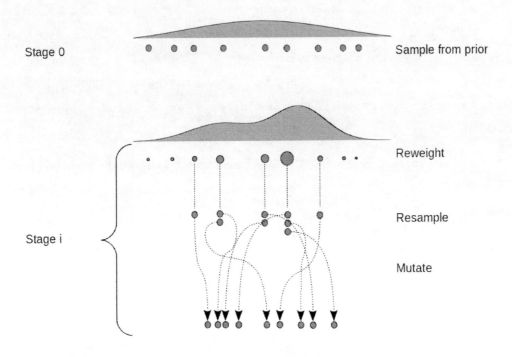

Figure 10.6: Schematic representation of SMC

more difficult to sample will require more stages than simpler ones.

At the top of Figure 10.6, we have nine samples or particles (gray dots) that we obtained from the prior, represented as the very wide distribution on top of everything (stage 0). For the rest of the stages, we re-weight the samples from the previous stage according to their tempered posterior density. And then we resample proportional to those weights. As a result, some particles are lost and replaced by other samples, so the total number is fixed. We then mutate the sample, that is, we apply one or more MCMC steps to the particles. We then increase β and repeat. When we reach $\beta = 1$, the particles (or samples) will be distributed as the posterior.

Besides the intermediate values of β, two more parameters are dynamically computed based on the acceptance rate of the previous stage: the number of steps of each Markov chain and the width of the proposal distribution.

Diagnosing the samples

In this book, we have used numerical methods to compute the posterior for virtually all models. That will most likely be the case for you, too, when using Bayesian methods for your own problems. Since we are approximating the posterior with a finite number of samples, it is important to check whether we have a valid sample; otherwise, any analysis from it will be totally flawed. There are several tests we can perform, some of which are visual and others quantitative. These tests are designed to spot problems with our samples, but they are unable to prove we have the correct distribution; they can only provide evidence that the sample seems reasonable. If we find problems with the sample, there are many solutions to try. We will discuss them along with the diagnostics.

To make the explanations concrete, we are going to use minimalist models, with two parameters: a global parameter a and a group parameter b. And that's it, we do not even have likelihood/data in these models!

Code 10.4:

```
1  with pm.Model() as model_c:
2      a = pm.HalfNormal('a', 10)
3      b = pm.Normal('b', 0, a, shape=10)
4      idata_cm = pm.sample(tune=2000)
5
6  with pm.Model() as model_nc:
7      a = pm.HalfNormal('a', 10)
8
9      b_offset = pm.Normal('b_offset', mu=0, sigma=1, shape=10)
10     b = pm.Deterministic('b', 0 + b_offset * a)
11     idata_ncm = pm.sample(tune=2000)
```

The difference between model_c and model_nc models is that for the former, we fit the group-level parameter directly, and for the latter, we model the group-level parameter as a shifted and scaled Gaussian.

These two models may look too artificial to you, or just weird. However, it is important to notice that these two models have essentially the same structure as the centered and non-centered parametrization we already discussed in Chapter 4.

From the discussion in that chapter, we should expect better samples from `model_nc` than from `model_c`. Let's check if our expectations hold.

Convergence

Theoretically, MCMC methods are guaranteed to converge once we take infinite samples. In practice, we need to check that we have reasonable finite samples. Usually, we say the sampler has converged once we have collected evidence showing that samples are *stable* in some sense. A simple test to do is to run the same MCMC simulation multiple times and check whether we get the same result every time. This is the reason why PyMC runs more by default than on chain. For modern computers, this is virtually free as we have multiple cores. Also, they do not create any waste, as we can combine samples from different chains to compute summaries, plots, etc.

There are many ways to check that different chains are practically equivalent, both visually and with formal tests. We are not going to get too technical here; we are just going to show a few examples and hope they are enough for you to develop an intuition for interpreting diagnostics.

Trace plot

One way to check for convergence is to visually check whether chains look similar. For instance, we can use ArviZ's `plot_trace` function. To better understand what we should look for when inspecting these plots, let's compare the results for the two previously defined models.

The variable b is 10-dimensional. For clarity and brevity we are only going to show one of its dimensions. Feel free to visualize all of them on your own computer. Figure 10.7 shows many issues. In the left column, we have four KDEs, one per chain. We can see that they look different. This is an indication that each chain is sampling slightly different regions of the posterior. In the right column, we have the trace itself. We also have four lines, one per chain, which can be messy, but still we see that one chain is stuck in the neighborhood of 0 from the first step until almost step 400. We see something similar at step ≈800.

The issues become even more clear when we compare Figure 10.7 with Figure 10.8. For the latter, we see that the KDEs for the four chains look much more similar to each other, and the trace looks much more fuzzy, more like *noise*, and very difficult to see a pattern. We want a curve freely meandering around. When this happens, we say we have **good mixing**. We express it like this because it will be difficult to distinguish one chain from the other; they are mixed. This is good because it means that even when we run four (or more) separated chains starting from different points, they all describe the same distribution. This is not proof of convergence but at least we don't see evidence of non-convergence or poor mixing.

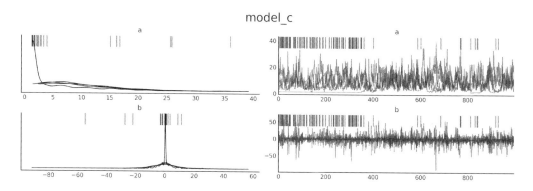

Figure 10.7: Trace plot for model_c

Figure 10.7 also has a few black vertical bars at the top that are absent from Figure 10.8. These are divergences; there is a section dedicated to them later in this chapter.

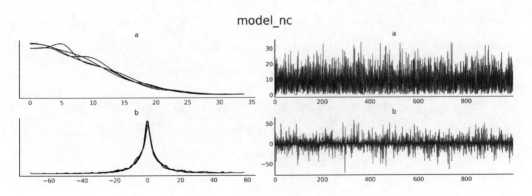

Figure 10.8: Trace plot for model_nc

Rank plot

Trace plots can be difficult to read, especially when we have multiple chains as it is easy to miss some details. An alternative is rank plots [Vehtari et al., 2021]. To build a rank plot for a given parameter we first take all the samples from all the chains, order them, and assign an integer: this is sample 0, this is 1, this is 2, etc. We then group all the ranks according to the original chains. Finally, we plot as many histograms as chains. If all chains are sampled from the same distribution, we can expect that all chains have the same number of low ranks, high ranks, medium ranks, etc. In other words, a histogram of the rank should be uniform.

To get a rank plot we can call ArviZ's plot_trace with the kind="rank_bars" argument. Figures 10.9 and 10.10 are examples of such plots.

On the left, we have the same KDEs we have already shown. On the right, we have the rank plots. Again the result for model_nc looks much better; the deviations from uniformity are very small. On the other hand, we can see a few issues from Figure 10.9; for instance, the histograms for rank 500 or lower look very bad for parameter a and also very bad for parameter b around the rank 2000. There are issues in other regions as well.

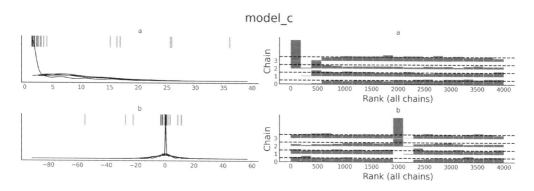

Figure 10.9: Rank plot for `model_c`

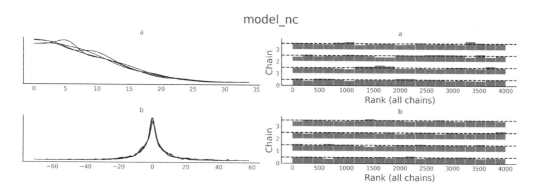

Figure 10.10: Rank plot for `model_nc`

$\hat{R}$ (R hat)

A quantitative way of comparing independent chains is by using the $\hat{R}$ statistic. The idea of this test is to compute the variance between chains with the variance within chains. Ideally, we should expect a value of 1. As an empirical rule, we will be OK with a value below 1.01; higher values signal a lack of convergence. We can compute it using the `az.r_hat` function (see Table 10.1). The $\hat{R}$ diagnostic is also computed by default with the `az.summary` function and optionally with `az.plot_forest` (using the `r_hat=True` argument).

Values around 1.1 could be OK, at the initial phase of modeling, when you are just checking whether a likelihood makes sense, or just trying to find out which model you really want to build. Also, the threshold 1.01 could be too tight for a model with a lot of parameters. The

	a	b_0	b_1	b_2	b_3	b_4	b_5	b_6	b_7	b_8	b_9
model_c	1.2	1.17	1.05	1.17	1.17	1.15	1.11	1.09	1.17	1.18	1.17
model_nc	1.0	1.0	1.0	1.0	1.0	1.0	1.0	1.0	1.0	1.0	1.0

Table 10.1: $\hat{R}$ values for models model_c *and* model_ncm

reason is that even when you really have convergence, you could still get a few $\hat{R}$ values larger than this threshold by chance. For instance, the PyMC-BART package includes the plot_convergence function. This function is intended to check the convergence of BART random variables. When using a BART model, you will get one $\hat{R}$ per observation, and that could be a lot. Thus, plot_convergence shows the cumulative distribution of $\hat{R}$ values and a threshold that includes a correction for multiple comparisons that is automatically computed by taking into account the number of observations.

Figure 10.11 shows an example of such a plot. On the right, we have a cumulative distribution of $\hat{R}$s and a gray dashed line showing the adjusted threshold. Ideally, the entire cumulative curve should be to the left of the dashed line. On the left subplot of Figure 10.11, we have the **Effective Sample Size (ESS)**. We explain the ESS in the next section.

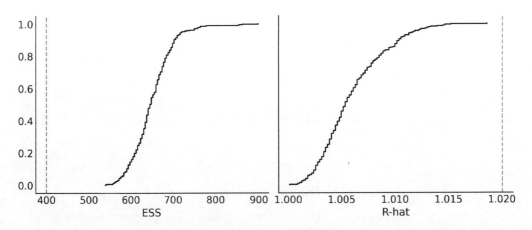

Figure 10.11: Diagnostic plot computed with pmb.plot_convergence(.)

Effective Sample Size (ESS)

MCMC samples can be correlated. The reason is that we use the current position to generate a new position and we accept or reject the next position taking into account the old position. This dependency is usually lower for well-tuned modern methods, such as Hamiltonian Monte Carlo, but it can be high. We can compute and plot the autocorrelation with `az.plot_autocorrelation`. But usually, a more useful metric is to compute the **Effective Sample Size (ESS)**. We can think of this number as the number of useful draws we have in our sample. Due to autocorrelation, this number is usually going to be lower than the actual number of samples. We can compute it using the `az.ess` function (see Table 10.2). The ESS diagnostic is also computed by default with the `az.summary` function and optionally with `az.plot_forest` (using the `ess=True` argument).

	a	b_0	b_1	b_2	b_3	b_4	b_5	b_6	b_7	b_8	b_9
model_cm	14	339	3893	5187	4025	5588	4448	4576	4025	4249	4973
model_ncm	2918	4100	4089	3942	3806	4171	3632	4653	3975	4092	3647

Table 10.2: ESS values for models `model_c` and `model_ncm`

The rule of thumb is that we need, at least, an effective sample size of 400 (100 ESS per chain). If we get values lower than this, not only could our estimates be excessively noisy, but even diagnostics such as $\hat{R}$ might become unreliable.

The quality of the MCMC samples can be different from different regions of the posterior. For instance, at least for some problems, it could be easier to sample the bulk of the distribution than its tails. Thus, we may want to compute ESS for different regions of the posterior. The default value returned by `az.ess()` is the bulk-ESS, which estimates how well the center of the distribution was resolved. This is the ESS you need to check if you are interested in values such as the mean or median of a parameter. If you want to report posterior intervals or you are interested in rare events, you should check the value of the tail-ESS, which is computed as the minimum ESS at the percentiles 5 and 95. If you are interested in specific quantiles, you can ask ArviZ for those specific values using `az.ess(.,` `method='quantile')`. We can even plot the ESS for many quantiles at the same time with the `az.plot_ess(., kind="quantiles"` function, as in Figure 10.12 for parameter a.

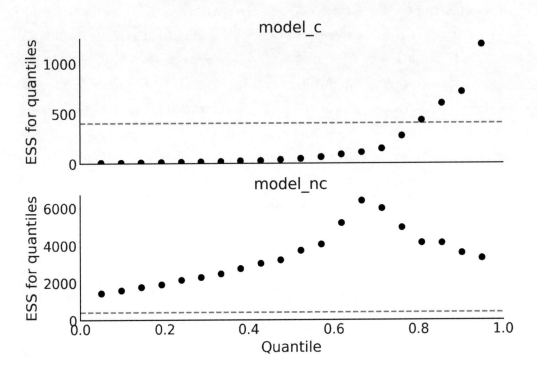

Figure 10.12: ESS for quantiles of parameter a

Finally, when we are running a model and find out that we have a very low ESS, the first reaction may be to increase the number of samples. Sometimes this is enough. But sometimes even a 10-fold increase is not enough. Instead of trial and error, we could use `az.plot_ess(., kind="evolution"`. This will give us a plot of samples versus ESS, as in Figure 10.13. We can use the information to estimate how many samples we need to reach a given value of ESS. For example, in Figure 10.13 we can see that there is not much hope of getting a good ESS value for parameter a in `model_c` just by increasing the number of samples. Compare this with `model_nc`, where the ESS for the bulk is very close to the actual number of samples.

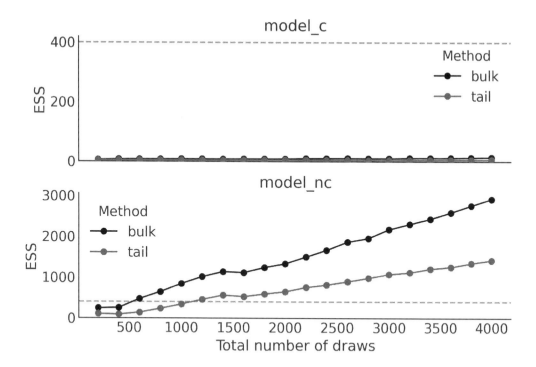

Figure 10.13: Evolution of the ESS for parameter a

Monte Carlo standard error

Even if we have a very low $\hat{R}$ and a very high value of ESS. The samples from MCMC are still finite, and thus we are introducing an error in the estimation of the posterior parameters. Fortunately, we can estimate the error, and it is called the **Monte Carlo Standard Error (MCSE)**. The estimation of the MCSE takes into account that the samples are not truly independent of each other. The precision we want in our results is limited by this value. If the MCSE for a parameter is 0.2, it does not make sense to report a parameter as 2.54. Instead, if we repeat the simulation (with a different random seed), we should expect that for 68% of the results, we obtain values in the range 2.54 ± 0.2. Similarly, for 95% of them, we should get values in the range 2.54 ± 0.4. Here, I am assuming the MCSE distributes normally and then using the fact that $\approx 68\%$ of the value of a Gaussian is within one standard deviation and $\approx 95\%$ is within two standard deviations.

The $\hat{R}$, ESS, and MCSE are related. In practice, we should use the ESS as a scale-free diagnostic to ensure we have enough useful samples. It is scale-free because it does not matter if one parameter goes from 0 to 1 and another from 0 to 100. We can compare their ESSs. With ESS, the larger the better, with a minimum of at least 400. If we have the minimum, we check we have a low enough $\hat{R}$. We can also visually check a rank plot or a trace plot (we should also check for divergences, as we will explain later). If everything looks fine, then we check that we have a low enough MCSE for the parameters and precision we want to report. Hopefully, for most problems, we will have an MCSE that is way below the precision we want.

> ### Too Many Digits can Hurt
>
> When reporting results in text, tables, or plots, it is important to be aware that excessive digits can make the numbers difficult to read and comprehend. It is easier to read a number like 0.9 than 0.909297, and it is also easier to retain in working memory. Also note that when a number is reported with more digits than warranted, a technical audience may assume that you are implying a higher level of significance than actually exists. So you will mislead this audience into trying to find meaning in differences that are actually meaningless. Finally, including too many digits can make your figures, tables, and graphs look cluttered and visually overwhelming. So always remember to be aware of the context of the data interests of your audience.

Divergences

We will now explore divergences, a diagnostic that is exclusive to NUTS, as it is based on the inner workings of the method and not a property of the generated samples. Divergences are a powerful and sensitive method that indicate the sampler has most likely found a region of high curvature in the posterior that cannot be explored properly. A nice feature of divergences is that they usually appear close to the problematic parameter space region, and thus we can use them to identify where the problem may be.

Let's discuss divergences with a visual aid:

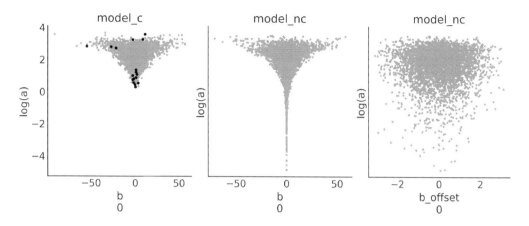

Figure 10.14: Pair plot for selected parameters from models model_c *and* model_nc

As you can see, Figure 10.14 shows the following three subplots:

- The left subplot: We have a scatter plot for two parameters of model model_c; namely, one dimension of the parameter b (we just picked one at random – feel free to pick a different one), and the logarithm of the parameter a. We take the logarithm because a is restricted to be positive (it is a scale parameter). Before sampling, PyMC transforms all bounded parameters into unbounded ones. For parameters such as a, the transformation is a logarithm. We do the same here because we want to understand what the sampler is *seeing*. OK, so we have a scatter plot where the gray dots are the samples. Look at the shape of the parameter. This shape is known as Neal's funnel and it is typical in hierarchical models. The black dots are divergences; they are scattered around, but we can see that many of them are around the tip of the funnel. This geometry is problematic for most MCMC methods because it is difficult to tune the sampler in such a way that we can get both good samples from the tip and the top of a funnel. One is a more "spherical" region, where the sampler can move both up-down and left-right, and the other is "narrower," where the sampler has to move more in the up-down direction and very little in the left-right direction.
- The middle subplot: We basically have the same as before but for model model_nc,

now the funnel shape is even more accentuated. But we don't have divergences. And we already know from previous sections that samples from this model are actually better. What is going on? The key to understanding this is in the model definition. You will notice that for this model, b is not actually sampled: b is a deterministic variable, a combination of b_offset and a, and those two are plotted on the last subplot.

- The right subplot: We have b_offset versus a, and we can see that the geometry is more "spherical". It is this and not the middle subplot that the sampler is "seeing." Because this geometry is easier to sample, we do not get divergences and we get much better diagnostics overall.

Changing the parametrization of a model is a way to remove divergences, but unless you are already aware of an alternative parametrization of your model, it can be very time-consuming to find one. An alternative that is often easy to try is to change the value of target_accept, an argument of pm.sample. Sometimes you may need both a different parametrization and a different value for target_accept. But what is target_accept? It is a parameter that controls the tuning of the NUTS sampler in PyMC. It controls the acceptance rate of the proposed samples, which defaults to 0.8. This means accepting 80% of the proposed samples. The NUTS sampler adaptively adjusts the step size of the Hamiltonian dynamics simulation to achieve the target acceptance rate. 80% is a good default, but for some models, you may want to try larger values like 0.90, 0.95, 0.99, or even 0.999 if you refuse to lose all hope.

Keep calm and keep trying

What should we do when diagnostics show problems? We should try to fix them. Sometimes, PyMC will provide suggestions on what to change. Pay attention to those suggestions, and you will save a lot of debugging time. Here, I have listed a few common actions you could take:

- Check for typos or other silly mistakes. It is super common even for experts to make "silly" mistakes. If you misspell the name of a variable, it is highly likely that the model will not even run. But sometimes the mistake is more subtle, and you still get a syntactically valid model that runs, but with the wrong semantics.

- Increase the number of samples. This might help for very mild problems, like when you're close to the target ESS (or MCSE), or when $\hat{R}$ is slightly higher than 1.01 but not too much.

- Remove some samples from the beginning of the trace. When checking a trace plot, you may observe that a few samples from the first few steps have overall higher or lower values compared to the rest of the trace, which otherwise looks OK. If that's the case, simply removing those first few samples may be enough. This is known as burn-in, and it was a very common practice in the old days. Modern samplers have reduced the need for it. Also, PyMC already discards the samples from the tuning phase, so this tip is not as useful as it used to be.

- Modify sampler parameters, such as increasing the length of the tuning phase, or increasing the `target_accept` parameter for the NUTS sampler.

- Transform the data. For example, for linear regression models, centering the covariates (subtracting their means) usually speeds up the sampler and also reduces sampling issues.

- Spend some time thinking about your priors. You should not tweak the priors to speed up the sampler or get rid of bad diagnostics. You should use your priors to encode prior knowledge. But it is often the case that when you do that, you also make the sampler's life much easier. Use tools such as PreliZ and prior predictive checks to help you encode better priors.

- Re-parametrize the model, that is, express the model in a different but equivalent way. This is not always easy to do, but for some common models such as hierarchical models, you already know of alternative parametrizations.

Summary

In this chapter, we have taken a conceptual walk through some of the most common methods used to compute the posterior distribution. We have put special emphasis on

MCMC methods, which are designed to work on any given model (or at least a broad range of models), and thus are sometimes called universal inference engines. These methods are the core of any probabilistic programming language as they allow for automatic inference, letting users concentrate on iterative model design and interpretations of the results.

We also discussed numerical and visual tests for diagnosing samples. Without good approximations of the posterior distribution, all the advantages and flexibility of the Bayesian framework vanish. Thus, evaluating the quality of the samples is a crucial step before doing any other type of analysis.

Exercises

1. Use the grid method with other priors; for example, try with `prior = (grid <= 0.5).astype(int)` or `prior = abs(grid - 0.5)`, or try defining your own crazy priors. Experiment with other data, such as increasing the total amount of data or making it more or less even in terms of the number of heads you observe.

2. In the code we use to estimate π, keep N fixed and re-run the code a couple of times. Notice that the results are different because we are using random numbers, but also check that the errors are more or less in the same order. Try changing the number of N points and re-run the code. Can you guesstimate how the number of N points and the error are related? For a better estimation, you may want to modify the code to compute the error as a function of N. You can also run the code a few times with the same N and compute the mean error and standard deviation of the error. You can plot these results using the `plt.errorbar()` function from Matplotlib. Try using a set of Ns, such as 100, 1,000, and 10,000; that is, a difference of one order of magnitude or so.

3. Modify the `dist` argument you pass to the metropolis function; try using the values of the prior from Chapter 1. Compare this code to the grid method; which part should be modified to be able to use it to solve a Bayesian inference problem?

4. Compare your answer from the previous exercise to this code by Thomas Wiecki:

```
http://twiecki.github.io/blog/2015/11/10/mcmc-sampling/
```

5. Revisit at least a few of the models from previous chapters and run all the diagnostic tools we saw in this chapter.

6. Revisit the code from all previous chapters, find those with divergences, and try to reduce the number of them.

Join our community Discord space

Join our Discord community to meet like-minded people and learn alongside more than 5000 members at:

```
https://packt.link/bayesian
```

11
Where to Go Next

Statistician is the technical term for a cynical data scientist.

– Jim Savage

I wrote this book to introduce the main concepts and practices of Bayesian statistics to those who are already familiar with Python and the Python data stack, but not very familiar with statistical analysis. Having read the previous ten chapters, you should have a reasonable practical understanding of many of the main topics of Bayesian statistics. Although you will not be an expert-Bayesian-ninja hacker (whatever that could be), you should be able to create your own probabilistic models to solve your own data analysis problems. If you are really into Bayesian statistics, this book will not be enough – no single book will be enough.

To become fluent in Bayesian statistics, you will need practice, time, patience, more practice, enthusiasm, problems, and even more practice. You will also benefit from revisiting ideas and concepts from a different perspective. To gather extra material, you should check the PyMC documentation at `https://www.pymc.io`, the Bambi documentation at `https://bambinos.github.io/bambi/`, the ArviZ documentation at `https://python.arviz.org`, and the PreliZ documentation at `https://preliz.readthedocs.io`. Be sure to check the examples sections, which are full of many examples of models that were covered in this book and many others that were not. With the ArviZ team, we are writing an educational resource titled *Exploratory Analysis of Bayesian Models*. We hope this will be a useful reference, especially for newcomers to Bayesian modeling: `https://arviz-devs.github.io/Exploratory-Analysis-of-Bayesian-Models/`.

If you would like to provide any feedback, either on the text or the code, you can file an issue at `https://github.com/aloctavodia/BAP3`. If you have questions about Bayesian statistics, especially those related to PyMC, ArviZ, or Bambi, you can ask questions at `https://discourse.pymc.io`.

In the following list, I have put together some resources that I think you may find useful to continue learning about Bayesian statistics:

- In the repository at `https://github.com/pymc-devs/pymc-resources`, you can find code in Python/PyMC from books originally written in other programming languages.

- *Bayesian Modeling and Computation in Python* is another book I have co-authored: `https://bayesiancomputationbook.com`. While some of the topics overlap with the ones presented in this book, you may still find it useful as many of them are presented from a different perspective or using different examples. Additionally, some topics complement or extend what we have discussed here.

- There are many good books about Bayesian statistics out there, but some of my favorite introductory/practical ones are *Statistical Rethinking*, *Doing Bayesian Data Analysis*, *Regression and other stories*, and *Bayes rules!* If you want something more on the machine learning side and with more math, *Machine Learning: A Probabilistic Perspective* is a great resource.

- *Learning Bayesian Statistics* is a fortnightly podcast where researchers, developers, and practitioners from many different fields talk about Bayesian statistics: `https:`

`//learnbayesstats.com/`.

- *PyMCon* is an asynchronous-first virtual conference for the Bayesian community: `https://pymcon.com/`. There are many good talks there, and also an opportunity for you to present your own talk!

- *Intuitive Bayes* is a paid series of courses and community-designed to get you from Bayes-curious to practitioner real fast: `https://www.intuitivebayes.com/`.

As a child, I dreamed of flying cars, clean unlimited energy, vacations on Mars or the Moon, and a global government pursuing the well-being of the entire human race... yeah, I know... I used to be a dreamer! For many reasons, we have none of that. Instead, we got something that was completely unimaginable, at least for me, just a couple of decades ago: relatively easy access to very powerful computer methods (at least for some people).

One of the side effects of the computer revolution is that any person with a modest understanding of a programming language like Python now has access to a plethora of computational methods for data analysis, simulations, and other complex tasks. I think this is great, but is also an invitation to be extra careful about these methods. The way I learned about statistics as an undergrad and how I had to memorize the use of canned methods was frustrating, useless, and completely unrelated to all of these advances. On a very personal level, this book is perhaps a response to that frustrating experience. I tried to write a statistical book with an emphasis on a modeling approach and a judicious context-dependent analysis. I am unsure whether I have really succeeded on that front, but if I haven't, one reason for it could be that I still need to learn more about this (maybe, even, we as a community need to learn more about this). Another reason is that a proper statistical analysis should be guided by domain knowledge and context, and providing context is generally difficult in an introductory book with a very broad target audience. Nevertheless, I hope that I have provided a sane, skeptical perspective regarding statistical models, some useful examples, and enough momentum for you to keep learning.

Join our community Discord space

Join our Discord community to meet like-minded people and learn alongside more than 5000 members at:

`https://packt.link/bayesian`

Bibliography

Oriol Abril-Pla, Virgile Andreani, Colin Carroll, Larry Dong, Christopher J. Fonnesbeck, Maxim Kochurov, Ravin Kumar, Jupeng Lao, Christian C. Luhmann, Osvaldo A. Martin, Michael Osthege, Ricardo Vieira, Thomas Wiecki, and Robert Zinkov. Pymc: A modern and comprehensive probabilistic programming framework in python. *PeerJ Computer Science*, 9:e1516, 2023. doi: 10.7717/peerj-cs.1516.

Agustina Arroyuelo, Jorge A. Vila, and Osvaldo A. Martin. Exploring the quality of protein structural models from a bayesian perspective. *Journal of Computational Chemistry*, 42(21):1466–1474, 2021. doi: https://doi.org/10.1002/jcc.26556. URL `https://onlinelibrary.wiley.com/doi/abs/10.1002/jcc.26556`.

Joseph K. Blitzstein. *Introduction to Probability 2ed.* Chapman and Hall/CRC, Boca Raton, 2 edition edition, February 2019. ISBN 978-1-138-36991-7.

Luis Jorge Borges. *Ficciones.* Sur, 1944.

H. Jane Brockmann. Satellite male groups in horseshoe crabs, limulus polyphemus. *Ethology*, 102(1):1–21, 1996. doi: https://doi.org/10.1111/j.1439-0310.1996.tb01099.x. URL `https://onlinelibrary.wiley.com/doi/abs/10.1111/j.1439-0310.1996.tb01099.x`.

Peter G. Bryant and Marlene A. Smith. *Practical data analysis: case studies in business statistics.* Irwin, Chicago, 1995. ISBN 978-0-256-15829-8. OCLC: 726362789.

Tomás Capretto, Camen Piho, Ravin Kumar, Jacob Westfall, Tal Yarkoni, and Osvaldo A Martin. Bambi: A simple interface for fitting bayesian linear models in python. *Journal of Statistical Software*, 103(15):1–29, 2022. doi: 10.18637/jss.v103.i15. URL `https://www.jstatsoft.org/index.php/jss/article/view/v103i15`.

Hugh A. Chipman, Edward I. George, and Robert E. McCulloch. BART: Bayesian Additive Regression Trees. *The Annals of Applied Statistics*, 4(1):266–298, March 2010. ISSN 1932-6157. doi: 10.1214/09-AOAS285.

Aubrey Clayton. *Bernoulli's Fallacy: Statistical Illogic and the Crisis of Modern Science*. Columbia University Press, New York, August 2021. ISBN 978-0-231-19994-0.

Scott Cunningham. *Causal Inference: The Mixtape*. Yale University Press, New Haven ; London, January 2021. ISBN 978-0-300-25168-5.

Jerome H. Friedman. Greedy function approximation: A gradient boosting machine. *The Annals of Statistics*, 29(5):1189 – 1232, 2001. doi: 10.1214/aos/1013203451. URL `https://doi.org/10.1214/aos/1013203451`.

Andrew Gelman. The folk theorem of statistical computing, May 2008. URL `https://statmodeling.stat.columbia.edu/2008/05/13/the_folk_theore/`.

A. Goldstein, Adam Kapelner, Justin Bleich, and Emily Pitkin. Peeking inside the black box: Visualizing statistical learning with plots of individual conditional expectation. *Journal of Computational and Graphical Statistics*, 24:44 – 65, 2013.

Charles R. Harris, K. Jarrod Millman, Stéfan J. van der Walt, Ralf Gommers, Pauli Virtanen, David Cournapeau, Eric Wieser, Julian Taylor, Sebastian Berg, Nathaniel J. Smith, Robert Kern, Matti Picus, Stephan Hoyer, Marten H. van Kerkwijk, Matthew Brett, Allan Haldane, Jaime Fernández del Río, Mark Wiebe, Pearu Peterson, Pierre Gérard-Marchant, Kevin Sheppard, Tyler Reddy, Warren Weckesser, Hameer Abbasi, Christoph Gohlke, and Travis E. Oliphant. Array programming with NumPy. *Nature*, 585(7825):357–362, September 2020. doi: 10.1038/s41586-020-2649-2. URL `https://doi.org/10.1038/s41586-020-2649-2`.

Allison Marie Horst, Alison Presmanes Hill, and Kristen B Gorman. *palmerpenguins:*

Palmer Archipelago (Antarctica) penguin data, 2020. URL `https://allisonhorst.githu b.io/palmerpenguins/`. R package version 0.1.0.

Stephan Hoyer and Joe Hamman. Xarray: N-D Labeled Arrays and Datasets in Python. *Journal of Open Research Software*, 5(1), April 2017. ISSN 2049-9647. doi: 10.5334/jors.1 48.

J. D. Hunter. Matplotlib: A 2d graphics environment. *Computing in Science & Engineering*, 9(3):90–95, 2007. doi: 10.1109/MCSE.2007.55.

Alejandro A. Icazatti, Oriol Abril-Pla, Arto Klami, and Osvaldo A. Martin. Preliz: A tool-box for prior elicitation. *Journal of Open Source Software*, 2023.

Gareth James, Daniela Witten, Trevor Hastie, Robert Tibshirani, and Jonathan Taylor. *An Introduction to Statistical Learning: with Applications in Python*. Springer, September 2023. ISBN 978-3-031-39189-7.

Alex Kale, Francis Nguyen, Matthew Kay, and Jessica Hullman. Hypothetical outcome plots help untrained observers judge trends in ambiguous data. *IEEE Transactions on Visualization and Computer Graphics*, 25(1):892–902, 2019. doi: 10.1109/TVCG.2018.28 64909.

Robert E. Kass and Adrian E. Raftery. Bayes Factors. *Journal of the American Statistical Association*, 90(430):773–795, June 1995. ISSN 0162-1459. doi: 10.1080/ 01621459.1995.10476572. URL `https://www.tandfonline.com/doi/ab s/10.1080/01621459.1995.10476572`. Publisher: Taylor & Francis_eprint: https://www.tandfonline.com/doi/pdf/10.1080/01621459.1995.10476572.

Christian Kleiber and Achim Zeileis. Visualizing Count Data Regressions Using Rootograms. *The American Statistician*, 70(3):296–303, July 2016. ISSN 0003-1305, 1537-2731. doi: 10.1080/00031305.2016.1173590. URL `http://arxiv.org/abs/1605.01311`. arXiv:1605.01311 [stat].

John Kruschke. *Doing Bayesian Data Analysis, Second Edition: A Tutorial with R, JAGS, and*

Stan. Academic Press, Boston, 2 edition edition, November 2014. ISBN 978-0-12-405888-0.

Ravin Kumar, Colin Carroll, Ari Hartikainen, and Osvaldo Martin. Arviz a unified library for exploratory analysis of bayesian models in python. *Journal of Open Source Software*, 4(33):1143, 2019.

David J. C. MacKay. *Information Theory, Inference and Learning Algorithms.* Cambridge University Press, Cambridge, UK ; New York, October 2003. ISBN 978-0-521-64298-9.

Wes McKinney. *Python for Data Analysis: Data Wrangling with pandas, NumPy, and Jupyter.* O'Reilly Media, Beijing Boston Farnham Sebastopol Tokyo, September 2022. ISBN 978-1-09-810403-0.

Yann McLatchie, Sölvi Rögnvaldsson, Frank Weber, and Aki Vehtari. Robust and efficient projection predictive inference, June 2023. URL http://arxiv.org/abs/2306.15581. arXiv:2306.15581 [stat].

Petrus Mikkola, Osvaldo A. Martin, Suyog Chandramouli, Marcelo Hartmann, Oriol Abril Pla, Owen Thomas, Henri Pesonen, Jukka Corander, Aki Vehtari, Samuel Kaski, Paul-Christian Bürkner, and Arto Klami. Prior Knowledge Elicitation: The Past, Present, and Future. *Bayesian Analysis*, pages 1 – 33, 2023. doi: 10.1214/23-BA1381. URL https://doi.org/10.1214/23-BA1381.

Kevin P. Murphy. *Machine Learning: A Probabilistic Perspective.* The MIT Press, Cambridge, MA, 1 edition edition, August 2012. ISBN 978-0-262-01802-9.

Kevin P. Murphy. *Probabilistic Machine Learning: Advanced Topics.* MIT Press, 2023. URL http://probml.github.io/book2.

K. W. Penrose, A. G. Nelson, and A. G. Fisher. GENERALIZED BODY COMPOSITION PREDICTION EQUATION FOR MEN USING SIMPLE MEASUREMENT TECHNIQUES. *Medicine & Science in Sports & Exercise*, 17(2):189, April 1985. ISSN 0195-9131. URL

https://journals.lww.com/acsm-msse/citation/1985/04000/generalized_body_c
omposition_prediction_equation.37.aspx.

Juho Piironen and Aki Vehtari. Sparsity information and regularization in the horseshoe and other shrinkage priors. *Electronic Journal of Statistics*, 11(2):5018 – 5051, 2017. doi: 10.1214/17-EJS1337SI. URL https://doi.org/10.1214/17-EJS1337SI.

Juho Piironen, Markus Paasiniemi, and Aki Vehtari. Projective inference in high-dimensional problems: Prediction and feature selection. *Electronic Journal of Statistics*, 14(1):2155 – 2197, 2020. doi: 10.1214/20-EJS1711. URL https://doi.org/10.1214/20-E JS1711.

Miriana Quiroga, Pablo G Garay, Juan M. Alonso, Juan Martin Loyola, and Osvaldo A Martin. Bayesian additive regression trees for probabilistic programming, 2022.

Sebastian Raschka, Yuxi Liu, Vahid Mirjalili, and Dmytro Dzhulgakov. *Machine Learning with PyTorch and Scikit-Learn: Develop machine learning and deep learning models with Python*. Packt publishing, Birmingham Mumbai, February 2022. ISBN 978-1-80181-931-2.

Carl Edward Rasmussen and Christopher K. I. Williams. *Gaussian Processes for Machine Learning*. The MIT Press, Cambridge, Mass, November 2005. ISBN 978-0-262-18253-9.

Riemann integral. Riemann integral, May 2023. URL https://en.wikipedia.org/w/ind ex.php?title=Riemann_integral&oldid=1152570392. Page Version ID: 1152570392.

Gabriel Riutort-Mayol, Paul-Christian Bürkner, Michael R. Andersen, Arno Solin, and Aki Vehtari. Practical hilbert space approximate bayesian gaussian processes for probabilistic programming, 2022.

Aki Vehtari, Andrew Gelman, Daniel Simpson, Bob Carpenter, and Paul-Christian Bürkner. Rank-Normalization, Folding, and Localization: An Improved $\hat{R}$ for Assessing Convergence of MCMC (with Discussion). *Bayesian Analysis*, 16(2):667 – 718, 2021. doi: 10.1214/20-BA1221. URL https://doi.org/10.1214/20-BA1221.

Wes McKinney. Data Structures for Statistical Computing in Python. In Stéfan van der Walt and Jarrod Millman, editors, *Proceedings of the 9th Python in Science Conference*, pages 56 – 61, 2010. doi: 10.25080/Majora-92bf1922-00a.

Peter H Westfall. Kurtosis as peakedness, 1905–2014. rip. *The American Statistician*, 68(3): 191–195, 2014.

Andrew Gordon Wilson and Pavel Izmailov. Bayesian Deep Learning and a Probabilistic Perspective of Generalization, March 2022. URL http://arxiv.org/abs/2002.08791. arXiv:2002.08791 [cs, stat].

www.packt.com

Subscribe to our online digital library for full access to over 7,000 books and videos, as well as industry leading tools to help you plan your personal development and advance your career. For more information, please visit our website.

Why subscribe?

- Spend less time learning and more time coding with practical eBooks and Videos from over 4,000 industry professionals
- Improve your learning with Skill Plans built especially for you
- Get a free eBook or video every month
- Fully searchable for easy access to vital information
- Copy and paste, print, and bookmark content

Did you know that Packt offers eBook versions of every book published, with PDF and ePub files available? You can upgrade to the eBook version at packt.com and as a print book customer, you are entitled to a discount on the eBook copy. Get in touch with us at customercare@packtpub.com for more details.

At www.packt.com, you can also read a collection of free technical articles, sign up for a range of free

Other Books You May Enjoy

If you enjoyed this book, you may be interested in these other books by Packt:

Machine Learning with PyTorch and Scikit-Learn

Sebastian Raschka , Yuxi (Hayden) Liu, Vahid Mirjalili

ISBN: 978-1-80181-931-2

- Explore frameworks, models, and techniques for machines to learn from data
- Use scikit-learn for machine learning and PyTorch for deep learning
- Train machine learning classifiers on images, text, and more
- Build and train neural networks, transformers, and boosting algorithms
- Discover best practices for evaluating and tuning models
- Predict continuous target outcomes using regression analysis
- Dig deeper into textual and social media data using sentiment analysis

Machine Learning with R - Fourth Edition

Brett Lantz

ISBN: 978-1-80107-132-1

- Learn the end-to-end process of machine learning from raw data to implementation
- Classify important outcomes using nearest neighbor and Bayesian methods
- Predict future events using decision trees, rules, and support vector machines
- Forecast numeric data and estimate financial values using regression methods
- Model complex processes with artificial neural networks
- Prepare, transform, and clean data using the tidyverse
- Evaluate your models and improve their performance
- Connect R to SQL databases and emerging big data technologies such as Spark, Hadoop, H2O, and TensorFlow

Machine Learning for Time-Series with Python

Ben Auffarth

ISBN: 978-1-80181-962-6

- Understand the main classes of time series and learn how to detect outliers and patterns
- Choose the right method to solve time-series problems
- Characterize seasonal and correlation patterns through autocorrelation and statistical techniques
- Get to grips with time-series data visualization
- Understand classical time-series models like ARMA and ARIMA
- Implement deep learning models, like Gaussian processes, transformers, and state-of-the-art machine learning models
- Become familiar with many libraries like Prophet, XGboost, and TensorFlow

Packt is searching for authors like you

If you're interested in becoming an author for Packt, please visit authors.packtpub.com and apply today. We have worked with thousands of developers and tech professionals, just like you, to help them share their insight with the global tech community. You can make a general application, apply for a specific hot topic that we are recruiting an author for, or submit your own idea.

Share your thoughts

Once you've read *Bayesian Analysis with Python, Third Edition*, we'd love to hear your thoughts! Scan the QR code below to go straight to the Amazon review page for this book and share your feedback.

https://packt.link/r/1805127160

Your review is important to us and the tech community and will help us make sure we're delivering excellent quality content.

Index

A

Akaike Information Criterion (AIC)
159, 160

ArviZ

predictive accuracy, calculating
166

predictive accuracy, calculating
with   165

B

Bambi

model, interpreting with
207–209

syntax   186

using with HSGP   285

Bartian penguins   293

Bayes factors   58, 168–170

and inference   178, 179

calculating, analytically   171–173

Savage-Dickey density ratio
175

Sequential Monte Carlo (SMC)
174

Bayesian additive regression trees

(BART) model   292

Bartian penguins   293

constant and linear response
302

individual conditional plots   296

partial dependence plots (PDP)
295

using, for variable selection   297

Bayesian analysis

posterior, summarizing   43, 44

Bayesian modeling   4

Bayesian p-value   152

Bayes' theorem   23–26

BetaBinomial   12

bike linear model   114

posterior mean, interpreting
116–119

posterior predictions, interpreting
119

posterior predictive check   123

bike model   190–192

bikes

counting   121, 122

C

Categorical distribution   226

categorical predictors   200

    categorical penguins   200–202

    relations, to hierarchical models
        203

center hierarchical models

    versus noncentered hierarchical
        models   139, 140

chemical shift   64, 93

clustering

    and mixture models   240

Cohen's d   83

coin-flipping problem

    PyMC way   51

conditional probability   20

continuous mixtures   247

continuous random variables

    distributions   16–18

convergence   328

    R hat   331

    rank plots   330

    trace plots   328

count data   121

covariance functions   258

cox processes   271

    coal mining disasters   272

    red wood   274

cross-validation   158, 161, 162

    approximating   162–164

cumulative distribution function (cdf)
    18

D

decisions trees   290–292

diagnostics issues

    actions   338

Dirichlet distribution   226

Dirichlet process   241

discrete random variables

    distributions   11–13, 15, 16

distributional BART models   300

distributional models   198

divergences   336

E

Effective Sample Size (ESS)   333

expected values   22

F

finite mixture models   224

    Categorical distribution   226

    chemical shifts   227

    Dirichlet distribution   226

Friedman's five-dimensional function
    305

G

Gaussian distribution   16

Gaussian kernel   258

Gaussian processes (GPs)   261

    classification   267

    for space flu   270

Gaussian processes (GPs) regression
    262

    with PyMC   262

Gaussian processes (GPs) regression,
          with PyMC
     length scale   266
Gaussians
     inferences   64
Generalized Linear Model (GLM)   120
grid method   309
group comparison   78
     Cohen's d   83
          posterior analysis of mean
               differences   85
          probability of superiority   84
          tips dataset   80

H

Hamiltonian Monte Carlo   322
heteroskedasticity
     distributional models   198
          variable variance   133
hierarchical linear regression   136,
          138
hierarchical models   92, 93
          applications, in domains   103
hierarchical shifts   93
Highest-Density Interval (HDI)   43
Hilbert Space Gaussian Process (HSGP)
          282
          using, with Bambi   285
hurdle models   237
Hybrid Monte Carlo (HMC)   322
hyperpriors   92

I

independent and identically
               distributed (iid)   30
Individual Conditional Expectation
               (ICE) plots   296
inference engines   308
InferenceData   76
inferential statistics   2
information criteria   157–159
          Akaike Information Criterion
               159, 160
          widely applicable information
               criteria   160
interactions   204
inverse link function   120

J

JAX-based sampling   324

K

K-fold cross-validation   161
kernels   258
Kulprit   212

L

Laplace method   312
latent variable   224
leaf nodes   290
leave-one-out crossvalidation (LOOCV)
               161
length scale   266
likelihood   25
linear model

generalizing   120, 121

linear regression models

usage scenarios   112

log space   175

logistic regression   126

coefficients, interpreting with
131

logistic model   126–129

used, for classification   129

loss function   61

M

marginal distributions   21

marginal likelihood   26, 168

marginalizing   228

Markov chain   316

Markov Chain Monte Carlo (MCMC)
308, 314

maximum a posteriori (MAP)   159

maximum entropy distribution   40

maximum likelihood   37

Metropolis-Hastings   317

mixture models   222

and clustering   240

non-identifiability   229

mixture of distributions   247

model averaging   167

model comparison

parameters, leading to overfitting
155, 156

parameters, leading to overfitting
154

parameters, leading to

underfitting   156, 157

simplicity and accuracy   154

modeling functions   255

moments of distribution   22

Monte Carlo   314

Monte Carlo Standard Error (MCSE)
335

multilevel models   92

multiple linear regression   141–144

multivariate Gaussians   257

N

Neal's funnel   337

non-finite mixture model   241

Dirichlet process   241

non-identifiability   229

non-linear modeling   254, 292

noncentered hierarchical models

versus center hierarchical models
139

Normal distribution   16

Normal model

robust version   72

number of trees

selecting   304

O

observed value   153

Occam's razor   154

out-of-sample accuracy   157

outliers   123

P

parameters   50

Pareto smooth importance sampling leave-one-out cross-validation   162

partial dependence plot (PDP)   295

partially pooled model   92

polynomial regression   193–195

pooled model   92

posterior

summarizing   54

posterior analysis

of mean differences   85

posterior distribution   25

posterior predictive checks   68, 148–154

posterior-based decisions   57

loss functions   61

Region Of Practical Equivalence (ROPE)   59, 60

Savage-Dickey density ratio   58

predictive accuracy

calculating, with ArviZ   165, 166

predictive accuracy measures   157

cross-validation   161, 162

information criteria   158, 159

prior distribution   25

priors

regularizing   179, 180

selecting   38–41

probabilistic programming   50

probabilistic programming languages (PPLs)   50

probabilities   28, 29

interpreting   26–28

probability density function (pdf)   16

probability mass function (pmf)   13, 16

probability of superiority   84

probability theory elements

conditional probability   20, 22, 23

continuous random variables   16–18

cumulative distribution function   18

discrete random variables   11–15

expected values   22

random variables   9

sample space and events   5

projective prediction inference   211

PyMCon

reference link   345

PyTensor   54

Q

quadratic method   312

R

R hat   331

random variables   9

rank plot   55, 330

Region Of Practical Equivalence (ROPE)   59, 60

regression

with spatial autocorrelation   277

regression trees   291

regularization   160, 179

regularizing priors   39

robust inferences

degrees of normality   71

robust inferences   70

robust regression   123

example   123, 124

S

samples

diagnosing   327

Savage-Dickey density ratio   58, 175

Sequential Monte Carlo (SMC)   174, 324–326

shrinkage   100

sigmoid function   126

simple linear regression   112

single-parameter inference

coin-flipping problem   29, 30

influencing, with prior   37, 38

likelihood, selecting   30, 31

posterior, obtaining   33–36

prior, selecting   31

splines   195–198

T

tips dataset   80

trace plot   328

U

uncertainty   28, 29

unpooled model   92

V

variable selection   209, 210

projection predictive inference   211

projection predictive, with Kulprit   212

variable variance (heteroskedasticity)   133

W

water quality

analyzing   97

widely applicable information criteria (WAIC)   160

within-sample accuracy   157

Z

Zero-Inflated model   234

Zero-Inflated Poisson regression   235

Download a free PDF copy of this book

Thanks for purchasing this book!

Do you like to read on the go but are unable to carry your print books everywhere? Is your eBook purchase not compatible with the device of your choice?

Don't worry, now with every Packt book you get a DRM-free PDF version of that book at no cost.

Read anywhere, any place, on any device. Search, copy, and paste code from your favorite technical books directly into your application.

The perks don't stop there, you can get exclusive access to discounts, newsletters, and great free content in your inbox daily

Follow these simple steps to get the benefits:

1. Scan the QR code or visit the link below

https://packt.link/free-ebook/9781805127161

2. Submit your proof of purchase

3. That's it! We'll send your free PDF and other benefits to your email directly